*f*P

THE AMERICAN WAY OF WAR

GUIDED MISSILES, MISGUIDED MEN, AND A REPUBLIC IN PERIL

EUGENE JARECKI

FREE PRESS
New York London Toronto Sydney

Free Press
A Division of Simon & Schuster, Inc.
1230 Avenue of the Americas
New York, NY 10020

First Free Press hardcover edition October 2008

FREE PRESS and colophon are trademarks of Simon & Schuster, Inc.

For information about special discounts for bulk purchases, please contact Simon & Schuster Special Sales at 1-800-456-6798 or business@simonandschuster.com.

Jacket design by Eric Fuentecilla and Joe Posner

Manufactured in the United States of America

1 3 5 7 9 10 8 6 4 2

Library of Congress Cataloging-in-Publication Data

Jarecki, Eugene.
The American way of war : guided missiles, misguided men, and a republic in peril / Eugene Jarecki.
p. cm.
Includes bibliographical references.
1. United States—History, Military. 2. United States—Military policy. 3. United States—Foreign relations—Philosophy. 4. National characteristics, American. 5. Militarism—United States—History. 6. Executive power—United States—History. 7. Bush, George W. (George Walker), 1946– —Political and social views. 8. United States—Foreign relations—2001– 9. Iraq War, 2003– —Causes. 10. Interviews—United States. I. Title.
E181.J27 2008
973.931—dc22 2008029242

ISBN-13: 978-1-4165-4456-2
ISBN-10: 1-4165-4456-9

For Anna and Jonas,
whose early-morning joy
wakes me to see the forest
for the trees

Contents

THE AMERICAN WAY OF WAR

Introduction: Mission Creep

> *What are we fighting for? Why do we bury our sons and brothers in lonely graves far from home? For bigger and better business? You know the answer. We're fighting for liberty—the most expensive luxury known to man. These rights, these privileges, these traditions are precious enough to fight for, precious enough to die for.*
>
> Lieutenant General Brehon Somervell
> Fort Belvoir, Virginia
> March 9, 1944

First, a confession. This book is not written by a policy scholar, nor a soldier, nor an insider to the workings of America's military establishment. I am first and foremost a filmmaker, whose 2006 documentary *Why We Fight* sought to make sense of America's seemingly inexorable path to the tragic quagmire in Iraq. Though I lost friends in the attacks of 9/11 and thus understood the public outrage they produced, I was distressed to see a national tragedy converted by the White House into the pretext for a preemptive war. Still, following the attacks, and prior to being drowned out by war drums from the White House, there was a period of soul-searching among many of the people I knew.

This spirit was briefly magnified by the mainstream media into the inflammatory query, "Why do they hate us?"—a question that exaggerated the issue, equating any effort simply to understand the roots of the crisis with blaming America for the attacks committed against it. "Why do they hate us?" also did more to forge a gulf between "them" and "us" than to address the deeper questions on people's minds: questions about the state of the world and America's role in it, such as "How did we get to this point?", and "where are we going?"

Before long, as war became inevitable, attention to these questions faded, and public discourse turned predictably partisan. As pro- and antiwar camps hardened, I sought to examine the forces that had so quickly plunged the nation into conflict on several fronts—from the unlimited battle space of the so-called war on terror to the front lines of Iraq. During the earliest days of World War II, the legendary Hollywood director Frank Capra had made his *Why We Fight* films for the U.S. military, examining America's reasons for entering that war. At a new time of war, Capra's driving questions take on renewed resonance: "Why are we Americans on the march? What turned our resources, our machines, our whole nation into one vast arsenal, producing more and more weapons of war instead of the old materials of peace?"

A half century since Capra posed these questions, the answers seemed less clear than ever. In order first to research my film and then, upon its release, to show it to audiences, I traveled to the farthest reaches of America's military and civilian landscapes, to military bases and defense plants, to small towns and large towns from the Beltway to the heartland. Among the many things I learned on my travels is that neither supporters nor critics of the Bush administration seemed to understand how its warmaking and sweeping assertions of executive power fit into the long history of the American Republic. Instead, for the most part, critics and supporters were locked in a shallower debate, with one side citing 9/11 as grounds for the administration's radical doctrine of preemption, and the other side vilifying George W. Bush and his team as an overwhelming threat to all that is great and good about America. Lost in this shouting match was any real understanding of what Bush and his wars represent in the larger story of what a thoughtful Air Force colonel described to me as "the American way of war."

Along my journey, I met the characters who appear in these pages. Whether civilian or military, each has been touched by the Iraq War and past American wars in one way or another. And each has a story to tell that sheds light on war's larger political, economic, and spiritual implications for American life. While this book is principally a survey of the evolution of the American system from its birth in a war of revolution to its contemporary reality as the world's sole superpower, it is ultimately a human system—composed of humans and guided by the ideas, aspirations, and contradictions of humans. As such, the characters in this book lend humanity to its analysis, reminding us that the faceless forces examined here have been set in motion by humans and can thus be redirected by them.

Many of the people portrayed in this book are themselves self-acknowledged works-in-progress. What I came to admire about many of them is their courage in having traveled great personal distance in their understanding of the system in which they have operated, and in many cases continue to operate. Their stories not only illuminate their particular areas of expertise but, by demonstrating their personal capacity to change and grow, remind us of that prospect for ourselves, and for the system of which we are all a part.

As America now hopes to leave the traumatic first years of the twenty-first century behind and move into a period of loftier ambitions, the nation remains embroiled in a tragic conflict with no clear objective or foreseeable exit. Given all that has come to light about the errors and misdeeds of the Bush years, there is an understandable temptation to dwell on how George W. Bush and those around him could have so misguided the nation, destabilized the world, and compromised America's position in it. Yet, while accountability for these actions is vital, it must be accompanied by rigorous efforts to understand the historical forces that brought America to a place from which Bush's radicalization of policy was possible. Without such vigilance by what Eisenhower called "an alert and knowledgeable citizenry," the system is prone to repeat and, worse, to build on the regrettable patterns of recent years.

From her birth, America was shaped by a contradiction of impulses among the founders. On the one hand, given their difficult experience as colonists under British rule, these men sought to design a republic that would avoid the errors of past major powers. On the other hand, they saw the nation's vast potential and recognized that, no matter how well intended, its government could one day face the dilemmas encountered by its imperialist precursors. The Roman Republic had been overwhelmed by Caesar's imperial ambitions, and the framers recognized that the American system would need to keep the power of its leaders in check. "If men were angels," James Madison noted, "no government would be necessary."

From this insight followed the brilliant concept of the separation of powers, with checks and balances between them; and among these, none was more important to the framers than the constraints placed on the power of any individual to take the country to war. They thus intentionally entangled the authority to declare and prosecute war in a complex web of interlocking responsibilities between the branches.

Looking back from a contemporary vantage point—at a time of great friction among the branches over the separation of powers—it's remarkable both how prescient the framers were and yet how much, despite their efforts, events have come to fulfill their worst fears.

In his 1796 Farewell Address, George Washington provided several pieces of indispensable guidance for the generations that would follow. Warning against "permanent alliances with any portion of the foreign world," he declared that "overgrown military establishments" were antithetical to republican liberties. Washington's idea was simple. If America stayed clear of the infighting that had historically gone on between European nations, it would much less often face the pressure to go to war and incur its attendant political, economic, and spiritual costs.

Almost two centuries later, on January 17, 1961, another general-turned-president would echo Washington in his own Farewell Address. "We have been compelled to create a permanent armaments industry of vast proportions," declared Dwight D. Eisenhower, warning famously that America must "guard against the acquisition of unwarranted influence . . . by the military-industrial complex." Eisenhower's warning against the "MIC," as it has come to be known, was a milestone in American history. From his firsthand experience, Eisenhower felt compelled to warn the nation that in the wake of World War II and amid its efforts to fight the Cold War, military, industrial, and political interests were forming an "unholy alliance" that was distorting America's national priorities.

As the chapters of this book explore, between Washington's time and Eisenhower's, and in turn between Eisenhower's and today, with each of the wars America has fought, she has drifted ever further from the framers' desired balance between a certain measure of isolationism and the necessity to defend the country. With each war, too, the separation of powers has suffered, with the executive branch coming to far outweigh the others in influence, agency, and power.

Examining the history of how this came to pass is in no way intended to minimize the errors, moral compromises, and outright offenses perpetrated by George W. Bush and his administration. Yet it does offer a deeper explanation of how such a radical chapter in the history of American policy was made possible by what preceded it. Only by getting at these roots of the American way of war can we begin to develop a realistic prescription for the nation's repair.

At the heart of this analysis is a military concept known as "mission creep." This term could have been used to describe any number of American wars from Korea to Vietnam to Iraq. But it first appeared in 1993 in articles on the UN peacekeeping mission in Somalia. Since then, it has swept into the parlance of Pentagon planners and, like so many terms that start in the military, spread into other fields. It means simply "the gradual process by which a campaign or mission's objectives change over time, especially with undesirable consequences."[1]

Not since John F. Kennedy has the relationship between a sitting president and his father been as talked about as that between George W. Bush and George H. W. Like Kennedy, George Junior grew up in the shadow of a powerful patriarch to whom his political ascent was widely attributed. But unlike Kennedy, George Junior's presidency was from the start undermined by rumors of significant ideological difference, distance, and disapproval from his father. George Senior has at times tried to dispel this impression, yet his body language and public statements by key members of his inner circle betray otherwise.

Nowhere does the gulf between father and son reveal itself more vividly than in the first Bush's 1992 memoir, entitled *A World Transformed.* Explaining his decision not to pursue the overthrow of Saddam Hussein after the 1991 Gulf War, the forty-first president could not have imagined that his words might one day challenge his son's decision to do just that:

> We would have been forced to occupy Baghdad and, in effect, rule Iraq. The coalition would instantly have collapsed, the Arabs desert-

> ing it in anger and other allies pulling out as well. Under the circumstances, there was no viable "exit strategy" we could see. . . .

Released during the Clinton years, Bush's memoir was generally perceived as a faint echo of a bygone time. But as George Junior's war in Iraq began slipping into a quagmire he hadn't anticipated, his father's words were brought back by critics to haunt him.

> Had we gone the invasion route, the U.S. could conceivably still be an occupying power in a bitterly hostile land. It would have been a dramatically different—and perhaps barren—outcome.

It's almost painful to read how clearly the elder Bush can foresee the fate that awaits his son. But beyond the battlefield, Bush Senior also predicted the larger danger of drifting policy rationales:

> Trying to eliminate Saddam, extending the ground war into an occupation of Iraq would have violated our guideline about not changing objectives in midstream, engaging in "mission creep," and would have incurred incalculable human and political costs.[2]

As George W. Bush's rational for war in Iraq shifted—from a link between Saddam and 9/11, to Iraq's possession and development of weapons of mass destruction, to the goal of liberating the Iraqi people, to suppressing an insurgency, and now to scrambling to contain the fallout of a tragically misguided conflict—the Iraq War has been a case study in mission creep.

Still, this book is not about the drifting mission of George Junior's misadventure in Iraq. Rather, it sees this drift as a symptom—and a predictable one—of a broader mission creep that has afflicted the country since its very founding. Though the Bush administration has, without question, asserted unprecedented executive powers and done far-reaching damage to the republic, the foreign and domestic policies of George W. Bush were not born overnight. And just as American soldiers now retread paths well worn during past engagements in the Iraqi desert and elsewhere, so too Bush's trespasses at home and abroad have deep roots in the country's history.

1

The Tip of the Spear

The deliberate and deadly attacks which were carried out yesterday against our country were more than acts of terror. They were acts of war.

George W. Bush
September 12, 2001

At 5:10 a.m. an F-117 Stealth Nighthawk banked silently through the first rays of sunrise. Inside the cockpit, the pilot noticed the stars and moon still shining on the Tigris below.

"The sun, the moon, the stars," he now recalls wistfully. "If I'd been anywhere else in the world at that time, flying around on a training mission, I'd have said, 'This is the coolest thing I've ever seen.' But then I realized where I was sitting. Over enemy territory, about to unleash a couple of two-thousand-pound bombs into a city I knew had lots of antiaircraft artillery. So it was that one moment of peace and then back to work."

Major Mark "Fuji" Hoehn and his mission partner Colonel Dave "Tooms" Toomey are members of the elite 379th Air Expeditionary Wing of the U.S. Air Force.[1] On March 19, 2003, they were selected to carry out an order issued directly from the Pentagon—a top-secret assassination attempt on Saddam Hussein, using GPS-guided bunker-busters. Though they did not know it, their mission was to be the opening strike of Operation Iraqi Freedom.

"We really didn't know who was there and who was gonna take the blow of what we were about to do," recalls Tooms.[2]

Gliding silently and alone through Iraqi airspace, there was much that these men knew. They had spent the bulk of their adult lives stationed in the Middle East, and so they knew significant landmarks on their flight plan. They knew their jobs. They knew they needed to penetrate the air defenses of a heavily guarded city, deliver their payloads, and return to base as quietly as they came. They believed in the mission of the United States of America, and they knew that theirs was not to question.

But what they did not know was that they were the tip of a very long spear—one that stretches far back in the country's history. And despite their faith that the spear is straight and narrow, it is a crooked one. It has been pulled, scarred, and disfigured by two centuries of American war. Fuji and Tooms did not know that their mission, which will one day be the stuff of tales for their grandchildren, was the culmination of America's evolution from its birth in a war of independence to this latest war of broken promises, imperial overreach, and shattering loss. In the intervening years, America's mission has drifted—slowly and imperceptibly, but meaningfully. Yet at the rarefied altitude at which they fly, Fuji and Tooms were either too deeply indoctrinated or too far removed from the decision making to notice.

There is a wistful glimmer in Fuji's eyes as he recalls those moments. "I remember thinking to myself, 'If we did our job today, this whole thing might be over tomorrow.' "

Of course, it would not be over the next day or the next. More than three years later, on November 27, 2006, Operation Iraqi Freedom quietly surpassed the length of American involvement in World War II. Rather than joining D-Day, Iwo Jima, or San Juan Hill in the pantheon of glorious American operations, Fuji and Tooms' mission has become just a flameout in the dark, impenetrable fog of another misbegotten war.

But why was their mission so ill-conceived? And more broad, how has the American way of war drifted so far off course?

MAN IN THE LOOP

Today's American military subscribes to a technological principle called "man in the loop." It's a safeguard against overmechanization in an age of high-tech war. As defense systems become more intricate and autonomous, maintaining the "human element" in a command chain has become a design imperative.

As Fuji and Tooms pressed toward their target that night, they were the mission's men in the loop. The plane they flew—the legendary F-117 Stealth Nighthawk—is a technological marvel, its triangular frame scored with origamilike angles that diffract even the most sophisticated radar, making it all but imperceptible to the enemy. Overseeing the plane's highly automated operation, Fuji and Tooms were chiefly responsible for the "lethality" of the mission, meaning the actual deployment of weapons.

"We pretty much let the airplane fly itself," Tooms explains. "That way, I can dedicate a hundred percent of my time to making sure I put my weapons where they belong."

"The 'man in the loop' principle gives you some final control to the last second," Fuji elaborates. "We train to hit our intended target and minimize collateral damage to everything else around that. You can't eliminate the risk a hundred percent of the time, and we realize that. But we can *try* to minimize it one hundred percent of the time."

Consummate professionals, Fuji and Tooms explain in painstaking detail the lengths to which they go to minimize error in the execution of an operation. Yet given the nature of military hierarchy, the human element they are expected to provide is necessarily limited. While the man in the loop is asked to assess and minimize the risk of operational error, he is hierarchically barred from considering the possibility of error in the larger conception of the operation.

"Being a military officer," Tooms explains, "my job is to support my president and the mission that he gave me."

"From a soldier's perspective," Fuji echoes flatly, "it gets old listening to the debates on policy. It's not ours to decide. We do what we're told."

At the time they are speaking, Operation Iraqi Freedom has been under way for six months—much shorter than it will ultimately last but, as was true for so many Americans, longer than either Fuji or Tooms expected. Catchphrases like "cakewalk" and "Mission Accomplished" are already commonly understood to reflect wishful thinking, and there is a hint of defensiveness in their accounts of the mission.

As soldiers, they maintain that their missions are not of their own choosing. By the time an order comes to them, they must trust that it has been well-considered and produced by the processes outlined in the Constitution they've sworn to serve. The individuals along a chain of command are limited in their authority, reduced to a narrow set of functions. Simply put, those who drop the bombs do not give the order and those who give the order do not see the consequences of their decision. Everyone in between has an even more tenuous connection to the operation.

The term "man in the loop" turns out to be catchy but deceptive. For the command chain does not really want a man in the loop, just certain *parts* of the man. Flying the F-117 and operating its bomb-guidance systems, Fuji and Tooms' faculties are fully engaged—eyes on the dials, hands on the joystick, mind on the checklist—but as men they are decidedly *out* of the loop. Of course no military can work properly if every functionary asks probing questions about strategy. Dedicated airmen like Fuji and Tooms may perform their mission flawlessly and yet be left scratching their heads at how their precision-guided strike could have launched such a misguided war.

Unbeknownst to them, Fuji and Tooms' mission to "decapitate the snake" (their words) by eliminating Saddam Hussein launched a pioneering doctrine of preemptive, surgical war. It reflected a radical new vision of America's global role, and yet one that had taken shape over generations. It was the first salvo in a war fueled by post-9/11 national unity, yet one that would bitterly divide the country. Operation Iraqi Freedom, justified by its proponents as necessary to bring democracy to a foreign land, would bring great challenges to democracy at home.

In a broader historical context, Fuji and Tooms' secret sortie represents no less than the culmination of the American way of war over two centuries. Though the "Bush Doctrine" it heralded is widely seen as an aberrant escalation of American militarism, the debate between its advocates and critics reflects a tension between isolationist restraint and expansionist aggression that dates back to the dawn of the Republic. What is new about the Doctrine is that it effectively abandons any regard for the isolationist side of that debate and forecloses on the possibility that the debate itself is necessary for the health of the republic.

REVENGE OF THE NERDS

As Operation Iraqi Freedom exploded into the full tragedy of the Iraq War, leaving the ambitious goals of its planners smoldering in the streets of Baghdad, the mainstream media began to investigate how America became entangled in what even former top U.S. commander in Iraq Ricardo Sanchez has called "a nightmare with no end in sight."[3] Generally, the investigation into who was responsible for shaping this misguided policy amounted to a shifting blame game. From Dick Cheney's Halliburton ties to the Bush family's oil interests to the Israeli lobby to the invisible hand of the military-industrial complex, the mainstream media considered several potential suspects before settling on the so-called neoconservatives. This small but influential cadre of policy planners are suspected of having "cooked the books" to turn 9/11 into a cause for war against Saddam.

Though the neocons certainly bear their share of responsibility for the push for war, it is inaccurate to attribute it entirely to them. Their real impact should rather be assessed in a longer historical context, as the latest episode in an ever-shifting dialogue among policy planners over America's optimal role in the world. This is not to deny that the neocons have had a radical influence on U.S. foreign policy and have exerted powerful, misguided influence. They have. Yet what too many analyses of the war have overlooked is that their ideas, and the appeal of those ideas, have deep roots.

Conventional wisdom on the neoconservatives goes something like this: The Bush Doctrine and Iraq War arose out of a moment when an attack on America returned a group of marginalized misfits from a former time to center stage, where they zealously paved the way to Baghdad. Several of these neocons had made an ill-fated appearance during the tenure of Bush's father. When the collapse of the Soviet Union left America an unrivaled colossus astride the globe, many saw a chance for a peace dividend. Others, like then–defense secretary Cheney, under secretary of defense Paul Wolfowitz, and his deputy I. Lewis Libby, didn't. To these and other members of Bush 41's administration, losing the country's only superpower rival merely underscored the need to prevent any other nation from accruing similar power in the future. As secretary of defense, Cheney instructed Wolfowitz and a group of policy thinkers to draft a new American foreign policy.

Under the innocuous title "Defense Planning Guidance for the 1994–99 Fiscal Years," this new policy was leaked to the press before completion, generating a storm of controversy.[4] In the years since, the document has become one of those unsettling blueprints from the Strangelovian depths of the system that fuels endless blogosphere fantasies. And it was a doozy. Designed to ensure "a world dominated by one superpower" and to "prevent the re-emergence of a new rival,"[5] it would, if adopted, have proved the most radical expansion of American hard power since the Truman Doctrine. Whereas Truman called on America to develop permanent military preparedness in order to protect "free peoples" anywhere from the threat of communism, Wolfowitz's document went further. It recommended that America commit herself "to establish and protect a new order . . . deterring potential competitors from even aspiring to a larger regional or global role." The means to such deterrence would include, when necessary, the use of preemptive force. The memo specifically advocated military intervention in Iraq to assure "access to vital raw material, primarily Persian Gulf Oil" and to prevent the spread of Saddam's suspected weapons of mass destruction.

At the time, though, this doctrine was widely rejected as too radical a departure from the country's practice of using force only when facing a clear threat to its people, allies, or interests. In an embarrassed scramble, Wolfowitz's draft was disavowed by the administration, hastily retracted, and rewritten by Cheney and Colin Powell, then chairman of the Joint Chiefs of Staff. Its tone was softened, but its authors' imperial ambitions had already attracted attention. Then, with Bush 41's loss to Bill Clinton in the 1992 election, the debate became academic. Wolfowitz and other key thinkers were relegated to Washington's policy bullpen, where they whiled away a decade in the shadows of think tanks and private pressure groups.

Several of these groups, such as the American Enterprise Institute, the Center for Security Policy, and the Heritage Foundation, have gained notoriety in recent years, but none more so than the ambitiously conceived Project for the New American Century (PNAC), founded in 1997 by neoconservatives William Kristol and Robert D. Kagan. In 1996, *Foreign Affairs* had published an article in which Kristol and

Kagan took the unpopular view that, in the wake of the Cold War, America should act as a "benevolent hegemon." They wrote of "resisting, and where possible undermining, rising dictators and hostile ideologies . . . providing assistance to those struggling against the more extreme manifestations of human evil." Echoing the earlier Wolfowitz doctrine, they challenged the prevailing post–Cold War wisdom that America should enjoy the benefits of newfound peace and turn away from foreign entanglement.

In 1998, PNAC published an open letter to President Clinton warning of Saddam Hussein's weapons of mass destruction and advocating preemptive action to overthrow him. Clinton rejected the call, emphasizing the next day in a message to Congress that his focus was instead on the rise of "terrorists who threaten to disrupt the Middle East peace process."[6] Clinton's disagreement with the neoconservatives was, though, more one of degree than of principle. Indeed, his decision to involve America in the conflict in Bosnia took a page directly from PNAC's "benevolent hegemon" playbook.

As Kristol himself affirms, "we supported President Clinton when he intervened in Bosnia in December 1995, antagonizing some conservative Republicans who didn't like President Clinton. Then we ended up through most of the late nineties becoming critical of Clinton and what we regarded as his somewhat weak and wishful multilateralism."[7]

In 2000, frustrated by Clinton's unwillingness to pursue regime change in Iraq, PNAC published a broader policy report entitled *Rebuilding America's Defenses*. The document praised the leaked 1992 "Defense Planning Guidance" memorandum and advocated an expanded international role for the United States and, implicitly, a sweeping overhaul of its arsenal to establish a "Pax Americana." A "revolution in military affairs," as PNAC's authors called it, was required "to change today's force into tomorrow's force, replacing the notion of brute force with an ideal of maneuverability, speed, and flexibility."[8] Mentioned eighteen times in the report, precision-guided munitions would be the vanguard of this revolution. The weaponry deployed by Fuji and Tooms in their opening strike—a combined laser- and GPS-guided EGBU-27 bomb launched from a single-seat Stealth fighter—was the apotheosis of the technological "revolution" championed by PNAC.

Though George W. Bush came to embrace these views, before 9/11 he ignored PNAC's call to arms just as Clinton had. During the 2000 presidential campaign, Bush had called for a "humble" foreign policy, arguing that it was not "the role of the United States to go around the world and say this is the way it's got to be."[9] Nonetheless, many neoconservatives, including a number who had been signatories of PNAC's 2000 report and 1998 letter to Clinton, were appointed to key posts in his administration:

- Donald Rumsfeld, Secretary of Defense
- Paul Wolfowitz, Deputy Defense Secretary
- Stephen A. Cambone, Under Secretary of Defense for Intelligence
- Abram Shulsky, director of the Pentagon's Office of Special Plans
- John R. Bolton, Under Secretary of State and later ambassador to the UN
- Peter W. Rodman, Assistant Secretary of Defense for International Security
- Eliot A. Cohen and Devon Cross, members of the Pentagon's Defense Policy Board
- I. Lewis Libby, Chief of Staff to Vice President Dick Cheney
- Dov Zakheim, Defense Department Comptroller
- Zalmay Khalilzad, head of Bush-Cheney DoD transition team and U.S. ambassador to Iraq
- Elliott Abrams, special assistant to the president and later deputy national security adviser for Global Democracy and Strategy
- Francis Fukuyama, member, President's Council on Bioethics
- Bruce Jackson, president, U.S. Committee on NATO
- Richard Armitage, Deputy Secretary of State
- Richard Perle, chairman of the Pentagon's Defense Policy Board
- Robert Zoellick, Deputy Secretary of State
- Paula Dobriansky, Under Secretary of State for Democracy and Global Affairs

That people of one view were being appointed to positions of influence at a time Bush was endorsing an opposing view can be interpreted either as an intentional bait-and-switch or as an accident of the Bush team not yet having settled on a cohesive foreign policy vision.

Richard Perle, who served as an adviser to the administration and chairman of the Pentagon's Defense Policy Board, recalls these formative days firsthand. "The president, as he was preparing to run, knew that there was a great deal he didn't know about global politics," Perle explains. "He also knew that it was important to learn those things, and he was eager to learn them. And he brought people in who he believed could help him comprehend the world."[10]

Bush and the neocons made strange bedfellows. William Kristol confesses to a certain initial ambivalence among neoconservatives toward the new president. "When George Bush was elected in 2000, he wasn't necessarily our favorite candidate," says Kristol. "Just as we regarded Republicans in Congress as neo isolationists in their disdain for getting involved in trouble spots around the world, we were critical of him in the first few months of his administration."

The shock of the 9/11 attacks made the difference. As the policy for war in Iraq took shape after 9/11, the 2000 PNAC report began to read like the administration's foreign policy blueprint. The prevailing wisdom argues that Bush's dramatic conversion was due to the influence of the neocons, though the neocons themselves generally downplay their role in swaying him.

Kristol is one of those who pooh-poohs the neocons' influence. "I wouldn't exaggerate the influence of the Project for the New American Century or any of our particular reports," he says. "Like every think tank, we put out things and most of them were ignored at the time." He also challenges the notion that Bush was somehow duped by them. "You know," he argues, "there are some people in Europe who think that Bush is kind of a dunce, and they were therefore very eager to find a small bunch of thinkers somewhere, preferably acting in a slightly conspiratorial way, who came up with these ideas and somehow bamboozled the administration into embracing them." Yet even Kristol acknowledges that just as 9/11 "changed everything," the 2000 report did have "some influence" after the attacks. "In some respects," he almost gloats, "I suppose you might say we argued for elements of the Bush Doctrine before the Bush Doctrine existed or before George W. Bush became president."

Eliot Cohen, a foreign policy scholar who was one of the signatories of the 2000 PNAC report, shares his colleague's skepticism of the neocons' influence. "It's tremendously flattering to the vanity of intellectuals," Cohen laughs, "to think that you write a paper, people read it, and then they go off and change the foreign policy of the United States. But it doesn't work that way."[11]

When asked about his own influence on the administration, Richard Perle gives a coquettish answer. "I think those of us who have been arguing for this administration's current policies are obviously pleased that there is an administration that has adopted them," he says matter-of-factly. "The people who came in with the president, or many of them anyway, were certainly prepared to shift in a radical direction. I think it's fair to say radical. *Radical* reform of the military establishment, *radical* reassertion of American power. A *radical* unwillingness to suffer attacks that went unrequited."

However influential the neocons may judge themselves, there is no denying that much of what PNAC advocated in its 1998 letter to Clinton and 2000 report became administration policy between 2002 and 2006. For example, the 2000 report:

- Urged the repudiation of the Anti-Ballistic Missile Treaty and a commitment to a global missile defense system. The administration has pursued both courses.
- Recommended that to project the power to enforce a worldwide "Pax Americana," the United States would have to increase defense spending from 3 percent of gross domestic product to as much as 3.8 percent. For the 2002 fiscal year, the Bush administration indeed requested a defense budget of $379 billion, almost exactly 3.8 percent of GDP.
- Advocated the "transformation" of the U.S. military to meet such expanded obligations, including the cancellation of outmoded defense programs like the Crusader artillery system. On May 8, 2002, Secretary Rumsfeld announced his decision to cancel the Crusader program.
- Urged the development of small nuclear warheads "required in targeting the very deep, underground hardened bunkers that are being built by many of our potential adversaries." In 2002, the Pentagon sought funding from Congress to develop such a weapon, called the Robust Nuclear Earth Penetrator. The House approved. The Senate did not.

The impression of PNAC's influence is deepened by haunting parallels between language in the PNAC report and that used by the administration in its September 2002 declaration of policy, entitled the National Security Strategy of the United States of America. "As the 20th century draws to a close, the United States stands as the world's most preeminent power," the PNAC report declared. "For most of the 20th century, the world was divided by a great struggle . . . that great struggle is over," the National Security Strategy echoed. "The United States possesses unprecedented—and unequaled—strength and influence in the world."

In addition to advocating foreign military projection, the PNAC report emphasized the need for domestic security: "Finally, we have argued that we must restore the foundation of American security and the basis for U.S. military operations abroad by improving our homeland defenses." The National Security Strategy concurred: "While we recognize that our best defense is a good offense, we are also strengthening America's homeland security to protect against and deter attack."

The PNAC report expressed in imperative terms a commitment to stop rogue powers from threatening U.S. interests: "We cannot allow," it warned, "North Korea, Iran, Iraq or similar states to undermine American leadership, intimidate American allies or threaten the American homeland itself."

This heightened rhetoric identifying key U.S. adversaries would wind its way with haunting similarity into the president's 2003 State of the Union address, in which he notoriously portrayed Iraq, Iran, and North Korea as "an axis of evil." Officially committing the nation to a longstanding tenet of neoconservative thought, Bush declared that "the United States of America will not permit the world's most dangerous regimes to threaten us with the world's most destructive weapons."

Reinforcing the perception of the neocons' influence was the fact that they seemed almost to revel in a ghoulish public image, even jokingly referring to themselves as "the cabal."[12] Yet while a degree of influence is certainly evident, and while the scenario of a cohort of zealots hijacking the country's foreign policy may provide some explanation for how America ended up in Iraq, it is incomplete. To understand the true roots of the Iraq War, one must recognize that the tension between those who would have America mind her own business and those who would advocate a more international role is as old as the republic. What is new is the extent to which the neoconservatives under Bush managed to skew policy so vigorously toward intervention.

FALSE IDOLS: WHERE ON EARTH DID NEOCONSERVATISM COME FROM?

Neoconservative thought has deep and varied roots. According to noted scholar Francis Fukuyama, a common misperception among critics of neoconservatism is the belief that it represents a single, monolithic worldview. In fact, Fukuyama argues, it is a collection of ideas that coalesced in the minds of academics over decades struggling to reconcile conflicting lessons of the twentieth century—about the rise of the Communist threat and the dangers for democracy, about when to go to war and how to fight, and ultimately about America's place in the world.[13]

Despite the extent to which neoconservatives are credited with instigating the Iraq War, there is much debate on precisely what the definition of a neoconservative is. In a blurb written for the collection of essays *The Neocon Reader*, Henry Kissinger praised its editor, Irwin Stelzer, for "demythologizing the neoconservative 'movement,' clarifying the American traditions from which it arises, and illustrating the broad spectrum of views it embraces."[14] No short summary of neoconservative ideas could suffice to characterize the tangled web of thought it represents. Yet for the purposes of evaluating neocon influence on the Bush administration's foreign policy, and more specifically on the Iraq war plan, this summary of neocon thought, written by one of its key proponents, Robert Kagan, is illuminating: "When employed fairly neutrally to describe a foreign policy worldview," he writes, "neoconservatism usually has a recognizable meaning. It connotes a potent moralism and idealism in world affairs, a belief in America's exceptional role as a promoter of the principles of liberty and democracy, a belief in the preservation of American primacy and in the exercise of power, including military power, as a tool for defending and advancing moralistic and idealistic causes, as well as a suspicion of international institutions and a tendency toward unilateralism."[15]

As the inadequacy of postwar planning in Iraq became apparent, the neocons were widely criticized as zealously ideological and terribly shortsighted. Many traced their misguided vision to the political philosopher Leo Strauss, an influential professor of political science at the University of Chicago from 1949 to 1969. Those who have drawn a connection between Strauss and the neocons stress Strauss' view of the threat totalitarianism poses to democracy and the need for the world's democracies to combat this threat vigorously in their foreign policies and promulgate liberal principles. As Seymour Hersh wrote in his May 12, 2003, *New Yorker* article "Selective Intelligence," "Strauss's influence on foreign-policy decision-making (he never wrote explicitly about the subject himself) is usually discussed in terms of his tendency to view the world as a place where isolated liberal democracies live in constant danger from hostile elements abroad, and face threats that must be confronted vigorously and with strong leadership."

Also highlighted has been the elitism of Strauss' view that good government sometimes requires deceiving the public. One prominent critic of Strauss, Shadia Drury, links this inclination on Strauss' part to his admiration for Plato's concept of the "noble lie."[16] The neocons, Drury asserts, called on this argument to justify to themselves the deceptions about Saddam's possession of weapons of mass destruction. On a related note, Hersh quotes Strauss critic Robert Pippin to say that "Strauss believed that good statesmen have powers of judgment and must rely on an inner circle. The person who whispers in the ear of the King is more important than the King. If you have that talent, what you do or say in public cannot be held accountable in the same way."

During the 1970s at the University of Chicago, Strauss briefly taught future under secretary of defense Paul Wolfowitz and his deputy, Abram Shulsky, and his influence was also traced to Richard Perle, Eliott Abrams, and influential neoconservative pundit William Kristol. Though these last three had never directly studied under Strauss, they had studied under Harvard professor Harvey Mansfield, a noted Straussian. The neocons themselves have, however, tended to minimize Strauss' influence on their arguments for war.

Three days after Hersh's article appeared, Wolfowitz was interviewed by *Vanity Fair* about the "Straussian connection." Though he confirmed having taken a couple of "terrific courses" from Strauss at the University of Chicago, Wolfowitz dismissed the notion that Strauss was the inspirational figure behind the neoconservative movement. Such a connection, Wolfowitz argued, is just "a product of fevered minds who seem incapable of understanding that September 11th changed a lot of things and changed the way we need to approach the world."[17] Neoconservative author Francis Fukuyama, who has worked closely with Wolfowitz over the years and studied with Strauss's protégé Allan Bloom, concurs with Wolfowitiz that the media has overdrawn the "Straussian connection." In *America at the Crossroads*, Fukuyama echoes Hersh in pointing out that "Leo Strauss said virtually nothing about foreign policy, however much students or students of students may have sought to translate his philosophical ideas into policies."

Fukuyama, Wolfowitz, and Perle all trace the foreign policy dimension of neoconservatism instead to Albert Wohlstetter. A mathematician trained in the intricacies of the method of strategic analysis known as game theory who worked at the influential RAND Corporation think tank during the 1950s and 1960s, Wohlstetter was skeptical of the doctrine of massive retaliation—Mutually Assured Destruction (MAD)—that guided U.S. foreign policy during the Cold War. While at RAND, he wrote a number of policy papers outlining new strategic approaches to fighting the Cold War with a specific focus on the nuclear arms race. As Fukuyama argues, Wohlstetter believed that, on both moral and strategic grounds, "the threat to wipe out tens or hundreds of millions of civilians was both immoral and noncredible," so that the MAD doctrine, instituted during the Eisenhower years, should be abandoned. To Wohlstetter, overreliance on the logic behind MAD was dangerous. As he wrote in a highly influential paper in 1958 entitled *The Delicate Balance of Terror*, "Is deterrence a necessary consequence of both sides having a nuclear delivery capability, and is all-out war nearly obsolete? Is mutual extinction the only outcome of a general war?" Wohlstetter thought not. "Deterrence . . . is not automatic," he wrote. "While feasible, it will be much harder to achieve in the 1960s than is generally believed." America's strategic advantage should instead lie, he argued, in developing precision weaponry and engaging in more limited wars, conducting preemptive strikes only if it was deemed strategically advantageous. Wohlstetter was a proponent of the development of both "smart" weapons and smaller-scale nuclear weaponry that could actually be used, and he objected to the constraints on the development of new nuclear weapons imposed by arms limitations treaties.[18]

During the late 1960s, several leading neoconservative figures crossed paths with and were influenced by Wohlstetter, including Wolfowitz and Perle (who once dated Wohlstetter's daughter). "He was probably the greatest strategic thinker this country has produced," Perle recalls. "We became friends and spent many hours talking. And that was just the tip of the iceberg. And under the iceberg was a lengthy and meticulous study of U.S. strategy that led to massive revisions in the way we thought about defense, the way we thought about nuclear deterrence, and how we organized our military forces." Among Wohlstetter's primary arguments was that the United States must avail itself of the best technology available to develop sophisticated tactical weapons that would inflict ever decreasing "collateral damage" on civilian populations.[19]

Wohlstetter's influence is manifestly clear in the Iraq war plan's emphasis on precision weaponry. But again, his vision—like Strauss's—is only one component of neoconservative thought.

Fukuyama sees the true origins of neoconservatism in the 1930s, when a group of New York–based, left-leaning academics, including Irving Kristol (William's father), Daniel Bell, Nathan Glazer, and Daniel Patrick Moynihan, grew disillusioned with communism. This group, according to Fukuyama, "sympathized with the social and economic aims of communism, but in the course of the 1930s and 1940s came to realize that 'existing socialism' had become a monstrosity of unintended consequences," undermining its own idealistic goals.[20] In the way that disillusionment with one view can be converted to intense zeal for another, this group of disappointed lefties came to oppose communism and the Soviet Union as strongly as anyone on the right. The intensity of their views put them at odds through the years both with the American left and with realists on the right, whom they found too accommodating of communism. Years later, the realpolitik of Kissinger's détente policy likewise seemed too great a compromise with a system they saw as immoral and malevolent.

It was the socialist Michael Harrington who coined the term "neoconservative" in an article in *Dissent* magazine in 1973 and attached it to this group as a pejorative stab at what he saw as the dubious origins of their thinking. The prominent latter-day neocon Michael Novak writes:

> In those days (the mid-1970s), it was thought that there was really no genuinely conservative movement in the United States as there always had been in Europe. In America, it was said, there is only one variant or another of liberalism—the old fuddy-duddy liberalism of the 18th and 19th centuries, or some blend of European socialism/social democracy.
>
> Thus, to call a foe who had long been identified with the Left a "conservative" was thought to be a lonely literary ostracism. To prefix *that* with "neo" was to suggest something like "pseudo" or "not even genuine." No historical tradition or cultural movement called by that name could be decried anywhere in sight. Just a tiny band, cast out into the darkness of intellectual isolation.[21]

Eventually they would come in from the cold. Among politicians who took up the anticommunism cause of Kristol and company, the primary champion was a former liberal B-movie actor and the most beloved Republican president since Abraham Lincoln. From as early as the late forties, Ronald Reagan's anticommunism was so rabid that the Screen Actors Guild president—called "Informant T-10" by the FBI—secretly helped to blacklist fellow actors he suspected were Communists. "How do you tell a Communist?" Reagan joked hypothetically. "Well, it's someone who reads Marx and Lenin. And how do you tell an anti-Communist? It's someone who *understands* Marx and Lenin."[22]

Like Kristol, Bell, and their fellow protoneocons, Reagan started out as a liberal Democrat; but as he began to feel that the Democrats had fallen out of step with his values, he evolved into a conservative Republican. Even in the face of the debacle of the Vietnam War, Reagan was unflinching in his conviction that America should assume a more vigorous pursuit of global primacy over the Soviet Union, which he later dubbed the "Evil Empire."

Vietnam produced a period of American soul-searching about the costs—human, economic, and spiritual—the nation had incurred in the fight against communism. Several public scandals in the late seventies—

exposed by the Church and Pike Commissions as well as the House Select Committee on Assassinations—revealed that members of the Nixon administration had prosecuted their anticommunism in defiance of U.S. and international law. The CIA and FBI were accused of spying on Americans, wiretapping their phones, and opening their mail; the CIA was accused of plotting to assassinate Fidel Castro, among other dubious covert activities. These revelations further eroded support for aggressive anticommunist intervention. In this climate, Reagan narrowly lost a bid for the 1976 Republican presidential nomination.

He would return just four years later, however, to defeat Jimmy Carter, and his victory would signal a new day for American hegemony. Reagan advocated a rejection of the restraints America had imposed on her own internationalism after Vietnam. His two-term presidency delivered on his promise to reinvigorate America's global role a crusade that seemed to culminate in the fall of the Soviet Union in 1989. The neoconservatives applauded him, and he was a hero, according to their thinking as it developed in the years following the Cold War. Reagan increasingly became a hero for their cause.

"Neoconservatives sprang up in the 1970s after the Vietnam War," recalls Arizona senator John McCain, "when there was a perception that the liberals were dismantling our intelligence capabilities, destroying our military, soft on communism, etc. And they have gradually evolved—and in some ways I am one, in some ways—in that the United States is the greatest force for good in the world. And we have not an obligation to go out and fight and start wars and conflicts and intervene. But to certainly do everything we can to spread democracy and freedom throughout the world. . . . That was the vision of Ronald Reagan. And he is sort of our icon."[23]

William Kristol echoes McCain's view of Reagan's significance: "Ronald Reagan began reversing the lesson of Vietnam in the 1980s when his policy of military strength and support for freedom fighters around the world did help bring down the Soviet Union." Though scholars debate the extent to which the Soviet collapse should be credited to Reagan's efforts, it was without question an outcome he sought and thus one in which his supporters basked.

"There's a story about George Shultz that's relevant here," concurs Richard Perle, sharing his enthusiasm for Reagan by way of an anecdote about Reagan's secretary of state. "Shultz used to interview all the Foreign Service officers sent abroad as ambassadors. And he would bring them into his small private office and go over to a globe of the world that he had on a table. And he'd say, 'Show me your country.' Invariably they'd point to the country they were accredited to. And Shultz would spin the globe around, and put his finger on the United States and say, '*That's* your country.' " Perle goes on to put an even finer point on Reagan's view of American primacy. "He thought the Soviet Union was a candidate for oblivion," Perle laughs. "And he meant to send it there. And he did."

For Perle, Kristol, and other neoconservatives, the fall of the Soviet Union opened a kind of door, enabling them to conceive of a "New American Century"—one free of the restraints of Vietnam's humiliation.[24] The end of the Cold War marked the dawn of an era in which the neoconservative movement began to coalesce into more than the sum of its parts. Wolfowitz and those who had drafted the 1992 "Defense Planning Guidance" took Reagan's internationalism one step further, forging a new doctrine that outstripped Reagan's simple anticommunism and asserting opposition to any nation becoming, in Wolfowitz's controversial words, "a new rival."

Thus, when Reagan's successor George H. W. Bush launched his war to expel Saddam Hussein from Kuwait in August 1990, the neocons applauded. But when he then refrained from going the full distance of overthrowing Saddam, they saw his constraint as unacceptable appeasement. Less than six months into the Iraq War, PNAC founder William Kristol expressed this view, even citing Bush Senior's failure to depose Saddam as a cause of 9/11: "When the first President Bush committed a half million U.S. troops to the Gulf in 1990–91, the power of Vietnam was still evident in the fact that we pulled them out as quickly as we could," he notes. "That was driven by a kind of false realpolitik calculation among Democrats and Republicans that we could make deals with dictators. We were worried about quagmires and we didn't want to take on the responsibility of nation building. This was a shortsighted miscalculation. And we paid a great price on September 11th."

The neoconservatives saw their views as the natural extension of the longer fight for U.S. hegemony, necessary for shoring up democratic freedoms in a world of hostile adversaries. In this, they rightfully saw themselves as carrying on a long tradition of arguing for a more aggressive role for the United States in foreign affairs. Indeed, one of neoconservatism's leading voices, Robert Kagan, defended the neocons' aggressive foreign policies in his book *Dangerous Nation*, arguing that, since America has from birth been a more aggressive, imperialist country than many want to believe, she should simply continue to do what has made her great.[25]

ONE THING THE NEOCONS GOT RIGHT

Decrying what he calls "the myth of American innocence," Kagan charges that many of the neocons' critics have a naive view of American history. In contrast to the "realism" with which the neocons identify themselves, he sees these naive critics as believing both that the outside world is safer than she is and that America has historically been more isolationist than she has. Only under such illusions, argues Kagan, could anyone see the neoconservative policies that led America into Iraq as an alarming departure.

"Far from the modest republic that history books often portray," Kagan asserts, "the early United States was an expansionist power from the moment the first pilgrim set foot on the continent; and it did not stop expanding—territorially, commercially, culturally, and geopolitically—over the next four centuries."[26] It's provocative comments like these that knock some neocons off people's Christmas lists; but Kagan's view is at least partially true. But only partially—and that's the catch. For Kagan misses the crucial point that the United States has always been conflicted about its militarism. Indeed, this long-standing inner conflict accounted for the neocons' zealous plan for war on the one hand and woeful lack of a plan for reconstruction on the other. In planning for war, Bush and his advisers subscribed to both conflicting arguments for what sort of power the United States should be: aggressive—even preemptive—exerting her will through shock and awe, but at the same time, not an imperialist power that would conduct a protracted occupation. The tension between these competing impulses has long plagued America but was never more crudely manifested than in the wreckage of America's half-baked misadventure in Iraq.

America's founding spirit of isolationism has traditionally been associated with the 1796 Farewell Address of George Washington, in which he cautioned the young country to "steer clear of permanent alliances with any portion of the foreign world." Jefferson put an even finer point on the matter when he cautioned against America becoming "entangled in the affairs of Europe." And yet, it bears remembering that these comments followed on two hundred years of expansionist European history in the Americas. During that time, the region had been a bloody staging ground for the brutal persecution of Native American and Amerindian peoples, as well as for the African slave trade. While Kagan is correct to point out these imperialist roots, there is also no denying that with their Declaration of Independence and the drafting of a Constitution, the framers sought to forge a new identity for the nation. A significant measure of isolationism thus figured into the founding discourse at the Constitutional Convention of 1787 and in *The Federalist Papers* of 1787–88.

In the debates between Hamilton and Jefferson specifically, the tension between a commitment to isolationism on the one hand and strong internationalism on the other is central. The framers agreed that the republic they had established must not become an empire. They were determined not to repeat the tragedy of Rome, a republic that had, through military expansion, become an empire and destroyed itself from within. As Roman soldiers found themselves increasingly stationed at distant battlefields, they grew to support their generals' political ambitions more than the government itself, until ultimately Augustus Caesar declared himself emperor.[27] Through carefully calibrated checks and balances on the power of the presidency, particularly on the power to authorize military force, the framers sought to prevent the kind of domestic tyranny that can result from foreign wars.

As Jefferson wrote to Madison in 1789, "We have already given . . . one effectual check to the Dog of war by transferring the power of letting him loose from the Executive to the Legislative body." In a letter back, Madison went further, arguing that "the Constitution supposes, what the History of all Governments demonstrates, that the Executive is the branch of power most interested in war, and most prone to it."[28]

In 1795, Madison would put an even finer point on the issue. "Of all the enemies to public liberty," he wrote, "war is, perhaps, the most to be dreaded, because it comprises and develops the germ of every other. War is the parent of armies; from these proceed debts and taxes; and armies, and debts, and taxes are the known instruments for bringing the many under the domination of the few."[29]

By assigning the task of deciding whether to go to war to the legislature and assigning that of actually commanding the military to the executive, the Constitution reflected the view that, in Hamilton's words, "those who are to conduct a war cannot in the nature of things, be proper or safe judges, whether a war ought to be commenced, continued or concluded."[30]

Though Madison and Jefferson agreed on the need to harness the nation's temptation to entangle itself in foreign affairs, there was from the start discord between the individual framers (and even within their own minds) over America's prospects as an imperial power. Just as the neoconservatives in advance of the Iraq War were pitted against ideological opponents who saw regime change in Iraq as inconsistent with America's mission, so too there was heated debate between Adams, Madison, and Jefferson on the one side and Hamilton and Franklin on the other as to the nature and scope of America's mission.

"America goes not abroad in search of monsters to destroy," John Quincy Adams said in 1821. "She is the well-wisher to the freedom and independence of all."

Yet alongside this benevolent impulse, an irrepressible sense of destiny pervaded the framers' thinking from the start. Alexander Hamilton betrayed this in 1774 when he prophesied that "in fifty or sixty years, America will be in no need of protection from Great Britain. She will then be able to protect herself, both at home and abroad. She will have a plenty of men and a plenty of materials to provide and equip a formidable navy. As a result, the scale will then begin to turn in her favour, and the obligation, for future services, will be on the side of Great Britain." By 1795, Hamilton would take this further, calling America "the embryo of a great empire."

Hamilton's premonition also appears in Washington's thinking. "However unimportant America may be considered at present," Washington wrote to the marquis de Lafayette in 1786, "there will assuredly come a day when this country will have some weight in the scale of Empires."

Though Washington's farewell warning against foreign alliances was inspired by his fear of the fate of past empires, he would appear to have been resigned to the prospect of America becoming an empire herself.

As Kagan writes in *Dangerous Nation*, "for American statesmen such as Washington, Jefferson, Jay, and Henry Knox, territorial expansion, increasing national power, and the achievement of continental dominance seemed foreordained."[31] Unlike Hamilton, who sought American expansion abroad, Washington, Jefferson, and Franklin sought to grow America westward within the continent. Jefferson's "empire of liberty" is a catchy phrase, yet one that, by his own lights, would seem contradictory. For in order to achieve the kind of "empire" Jefferson sought through westward expansion, military force would be required, and as he of all people knew, this would challenge the very liberties he sought to protect in the Constitution.

When Robert Kagan claims that "the early United States was an expansionist power from the moment the first pilgrim set foot on the continent," he glosses over the strong spirit of isolationism at the founding. Yet Kagan's claim that the country "did not stop expanding—territorially, commercially, culturally, and geopolitically—over the next four centuries" is wholly accurate. As America has grown from a colony to a superpower, her domain and global influence have expanded, first westward across the continent, then outward to the hemisphere and beyond. Over her history, America has formally declared war only eleven times,[32] yet she has deployed her military and used force over a hundred times.[33] This growth has made her more prosperous but has come at a cost.

The nation has indeed experienced a rising curve of just the kind of ever-increasing "foreign entanglement" the framers feared. And these experiences of war have taken a toll not only in blood and national treasure, but on the integrity of the checks and balances between the branches and on the liberties provided for in the Constitution and Bill of Rights. There have been dips in the curve along the way—episodes during which the spirit of isolationism has resurged. Yet the original conflict between isolationism and expansionism has given way, inexorably, to dominance by imperialist impulses.

WIDENING HORIZONS: A ROUGH DOCTRINAL SURVEY OF THE REPUBLIC

From Manifest Destiny to the Monroe Doctrine to the Roosevelt Corollary to Wilson's Fourteen Points to FDR's "arsenal of democracy" to the Truman Doctrine and beyond, the country has transformed over two centuries from a modest republic with remote imperial prospects into a global superpower with remote republican roots. With apologies in advance to historians who will no doubt find fault with it, what follows is a cursory survey of these doctrines through time, divining a pattern by which each has built upon the one before.

- **Manifest Destiny.** Despite Washington's isolationist message at the close of the eighteenth century, the nineteenth would indeed prove one of extensive foreign entanglement. At home, wars of conquest against Native Americans aggravated tensions with colonial European rivals, inspiring the rallying cry, coined by columnist John L. O'Sullivan, that America possessed a "manifest destiny to overspread the continent. . . ."[34]
- **The Monroe Doctrine** expanded the vision of America's Manifest Destiny beyond her borders. In 1823, faced with the prospect of European military action in the Spanish colonies of South America, the fifth U.S. president, James Monroe, declared that America would remain neutral in wars between European powers and between those powers and their colonies. If, though, a European power were to try to expand its influence in the western hemisphere, America would see such action as hostile to herself. While appearing to discourage European colonialism, the Monroe Doctrine thus expanded America's military mandate from continental control to self-appointed stewardship of the western hemisphere. By the end of the nineteenth century, the Monroe Doctrine had guided America into several engagements with European powers. This "New Imperialism" culminated in the Spanish-American War of 1898, which won America—once a colony herself—the former Spanish colonies of the Philippines, Guam, and Puerto Rico, as well as a controlling hand in Cuba.
- **The Roosevelt Corollary (to the Monroe Doctrine)** expanded its precursor to give America greater latitude to act militarily in the

western hemisphere. Though Theodore Roosevelt rejected accusations of imperialism, his Corollary stripped away Monroe's requirement that America respond militarily only to acts of aggression against herself or her neighbors. It could now be based upon America's perception of any circumstance in the western hemisphere requiring police action. Declaring this a moral imperative "in flagrant cases of such wrongdoing or impotence," the Corollary committed America to "the exercise of an international police power" throughout the hemisphere, thus continuing the steady expansion of her perceived military mandate.

- **Wilson's Fourteen Points** exploded the hemispheric constraints of the Roosevelt Corollary to reflect the vastly expanded global role America assumed in World War I. When war broke out in Europe, President Woodrow Wilson was at first reluctant to involve America in European affairs. Though this reluctance was consistent with the isolationism of the framers, the country had already strayed so far from this spirit that the term "isolationist" had become a pejorative. On April 2, 1917, following a series of German attacks on American merchant ships, Wilson requested a declaration of war from Congress. This request did not articulate a new doctrine, yet World War I implicitly expanded America's international footprint beyond anything previously contemplated. As it wound down, Wilson proposed to Congress a fourteen-point plan for a lasting peace, including a "general association of nations," the prospect of international treaties between them, and the need for fair resolution of conflict between nations and their colonies. Though America returned to a period of relative isolationism in the wake of World War I, these Fourteen Points marked the most significant philosophic departure yet from the framers' commitment against foreign entanglements.
- **The Great Arsenal of Democracy,** a concept introduced by thirty-second president Franklin Delano Roosevelt prior to American entry into World War II, did not articulately expand upon Wilson's Fourteen Points, yet it guided American entry into the most expansive single conflict in the nation's history. It's noteworthy that despite presiding over World War II, Roosevelt never issued a foreign policy doctrine per se. Nonetheless, like Monroe, Roosevelt, and Wilson before him, FDR vastly expanded the nation's overseas commit-

ments to meet a perceived threat—in this case the rise of hostilities overseas.[35] But a resurgence of isolationist sentiment in the wake of World War I made it politically infeasible to involve America militarily in the war. He could, though, involve America behind the scenes as a supplier of arms and matériel to her allies, recasting the nation as what he called "the great arsenal of democracy." This was seen by FDR's domestic critics and America's would-be adversaries as a back door tactic to "entangle" the country in foreign affairs. Between 1939 and 1945, America indeed became an arsenal of unprecedented scale, first supplying her allies and later, after the attack at Pearl Harbor, using force herself. The formation and deployment of such a massive military establishment proved decisive for victory yet expanded America's global footprint to the farthest reaches of the earth, rendering the framers' concerns about foreign entanglements virtually obsolete.

- **The Truman Doctrine**, introduced in 1947 as the Cold War was dawning, was the most fundamental change in American foreign policy since the Monroe Doctrine. Though America's signature to the United Nations Charter in 1945 made the multilateral spirit of Wilson's Fourteen Points official U.S. foreign policy, the Truman Doctrine, introduced by President Harry S. Truman to a joint session of Congress on March 12, 1947, committed America to a hegemonic global posture more closely aligned with the Roosevelt Corollary. Suddenly, in contrast to the relative reluctance of Washington and Jefferson, America was committed diplomatically and militarily to a central role not only in "the affairs of Europe" but with respect to the entire world. Just as Monroe had once expanded America's military mandate from self-defense to the defense of all free peoples in the western hemisphere, Truman's doctrine saw a threat to free people anywhere as a threat to America. This expanded definition blurred the line between peacetime and war, effectively calling for permanent military preparedness.

Despite episodic modifications by Truman's successors from Eisenhower to Reagan to Clinton, the Truman Doctrine dominated U.S. foreign policy for the latter half of the twentieth century, until it was displaced by the Bush Doctrine after September 11, 2001. By asserting the right to use preemptive military force against a potential adversary, the Bush Doctrine has expanded the Truman Doctrine's commitment to defend free people anywhere from a clear and present danger to the far more liberal commitment to use force even in the absence of such clarity. As such, it liberates the nation to start wars with far less evidence of danger, and with equally little scrutiny of the potential consequences. Though the Bush Doctrine must be seen as an extension of the doctrines that preceded it, its expanded vision of American primacy and the role of hard power to secure that primacy must not be underestimated.

The almost glib calm with which Kagan mounts his ideologically charged argument for hegemony has become a neoconservative trademark. When asked to explain the doctrine of preemption, Richard Perle shared a similarly flip calculation. "It isn't rocket science," he laughed, "it's common sense. If you saw a missile about to be launched and you could kick it over before it could be launched, you'd do it, of course. If you saw someone about to shoot at you and you thought you could shoot first, you'd do it. I don't know anybody who doesn't agree with that. So what's the big fuss about preemption?"

For a seasoned political thinker like Richard Perle to wonder at the "fuss" caused by a change in American foreign policy as significant as preemption seems too cute by half. Yet in their zealotry, the neoconservatives habitually overplay their hand, painting a political picture that lacks a regard for complexity. That the succession of doctrines described above leads ultimately to the Bush Doctrine of preemption confirms the framers' specific fear that the "Dog of war" would become ever harder to check. Successive wars have created new and entangling alliances, and each doctrine has set forth an expanded precedent for those that followed. While the cursory overview of the doctrines above does not suffice to explain the rise of the neoconservatives, it does illustrate how some of their most controversial ideas—American hegemony, unilateralism, preemptive military force, nation building—have been steadily gaining currency through time.

So too their notion that America could win the Iraq War without a protracted process of nation building also has deeper roots. This reluctance to play the role of occupier would seem to stem from an anti-imperial tradition of isolationism. Whether as a pragmatic concession to public opinion or as an internal contradiction in their thinking, at the core of their strategy was a failure to acknowledge that a large ground force would be required for the war and that a massive social reengineering plan—including occupation—would be necessary for the postwar period. This fatal flaw in the neocons' thinking led even longtime neocon Francis Fukuyama to turn against his former comrades.

For Fukuyama, however defensible the roots of neoconservatism may be, Wolfowitz, Kristol, and other neoconservatives lost their way during the Bush years. "I have concluded that neoconservatism," he writes in his autopsy of neoconservatism, *America at the Crossroads*, "has evolved into something I can no longer support."[36] Beyond the vast errors in judgment, understanding, and planning demonstrated by the neoconservatives in their vision for the Iraq War, Fukuyama sees in their notion of "regime change" an internal contradiction and a troubling departure from the wisdom of their origins.

According to Fukuyama, the neoconservatives inherited from Strauss an emphasis on the notion of a country's "regime"—a set of formal political and social institutions that vitally shape the life of the society. As Strauss scholar Stephen B. Smith describes, Strauss drew on classical political philosophy in conception. "The regime refers to more than the form of government in the relatively narrow sense; it refers to the entire way of life in a society, its habits, customs, and moral beliefs . . ."[37] This definition, facing Islamic fundamentalism, ought to have led the neoconservatives to the conclusion that simply changing Iraq's government would not therefore truly transform the country's regime. Instead, they twisted the logic of Strauss's emphasis on regimes into the idea that "regime change" could be pursued to reshape Iraqi society from the top down. Simply put, one could change Iraq by changing its leadership. By "decapitating the snake," Fuji, Tooms, and the U.S. military could liberate Iraqi society from the grip of Saddam's regime. To defend this misapplication of Strauss's concept of regime, Richard Perle reflects: "I don't believe that we can implement democracy with force. But sometimes, before you can bring about democratic change, you have to remove the obstacle to democratic change. You have to remove a Saddam Hussein, because there's no hope for democracy with Saddam there."

According to Fukuyama, this idea of regime change is contradictory to a basic tenet of neoconservative thought. From their disappointment with communism to their critiques of Lyndon Johnson's Great Society, the New York–based protoneocons and their progeny in Perle, Wolfowitz, and others exhibited what Fukuyama calls "a distrust of ambitious social engineering projects."[38] The ambitious undertaking to pursue regime change in Iraq is directly at odds with such distrust of efforts to engineer society. It can be argued that the shortcomings of the war—from the misconception that without Saddam's regime Iraqi society would neatly transition into democracy, to the lack of preparedness for the task of reengineering Iraqi society by force—derive from this contradiction. While the neocons had convinced themselves that removing Saddam would unmake the old regime, at the same time they shied away from a massive effort to engineer the social, economic, and democratic reforms required to create a new one. "Neither the Bush administration nor its neoconservative supporters," Fukuyama laments, "gave adequate thought before the Iraq War to how this conundrum could be resolved."[39] Fukuyama's willingness to apologize for the error of his adherence to neoconservative views is both admirable and tragic. Recalling his participation in a PNAC letter to Bush on September 20, 2001, advocating a "determined effort to remove Saddam Hussein from power in Iraq,"[40] one cannot help but wish that he and his neoconservative colleagues' political education could have come at a lesser cost than the lives and treasure senselessly wasted in Iraq. Nonetheless, at a time in history when accountability in public life is so rare, Mr. Fukuyama's mea culpa is a welcome exception.

In his farewell to his neocon comrades, Fukuyama, somewhat oddly, makes them more sympathetic than they usually appear. Rather than a "cabal" of political operatives foisting their alien worldview onto an unsuspecting system, he presents them as a misguided group seeking in various ways to grapple with the same questions about American power that have confronted policymakers since the nation's founding. While his characterization may be true, it does not excuse the fact that the neocons' arguments—so forcefully implemented—have proved so tragically wrong.

A NEW PEARL HARBOR: WHERE NEOCONSERVATISM LOST A WHEEL

Following 9/11, as public attention turned to the role of neoconservatives in the administration's campaign for war against Iraq, one element of their thinking went largely overlooked by the mainstream press, yet generated near mass hysteria in the blogosphere. On page 51 of PNAC's now infamous 2000 report *Rebuilding America's Defenses*, having described the "revolution in military affairs" so central to the "New American Century" they seek, the authors added a startling qualifier. "The process of transformation," they wrote, "even if it brings revolutionary change, is likely to be a long one, absent some catastrophic and catalyzing event—like a new Pearl Harbor."

The invocation of Pearl Harbor one year before 9/11 by a group of political actors who would later join the administration and advocate war in Iraq set off an explosion of blogosphere suspicions that members of the administration were somehow implicated in the attacks.

These suspicions are predicated on the idea that certain neocons not only saw that without such an attack their hoped-for transformation of U.S. policy would be long and difficult, but that their mere mention of such an eventuality in a policy paper suggests a role in having made the attacks happen. This accusation is conjecture of a dangerous kind, one whose inevitable controversy outweighs its evidence. Worse still, it allows an inflammatory discussion of the unproven to take the place of a considered discussion of what is truly knowable. It may thus be a less productive pursuit than simply looking at what the PNAC report reveals per se about the zealotry of the neoconservatives.

When the report recognizes how "a new Pearl Harbor" would help avert an otherwise long process of policy transformation, it is enough to note what this recognition reveals at a minimum—that, however tragic such an attack might be, PNAC's leaders see its utility for helping realize their goal to transform U.S. policy. That neoconservatives in the administration were so quick to convert the attacks of 9/11 into a cause for war against Iraq is disconcerting, for it suggests a vision so zealously pursued that its proponents could, without missing a beat, seize upon a massive tragedy to realize their goals.

This is not meant to suggest that neoconservatives were in some way unmoved by the events of 9/11. To the contrary, they clearly see 9/11 as an event of massive and tragic proportions. What it does provide, though, is a window into the ideological fervor with which they grew to perceive the world in the decade before 9/11. Like any movement that has grown ideologically extremist, the neoconservatives came to the ominous belief that their goal of promoting American hegemony could be pursued by any means necessary. When the prospect of "a new Pearl Harbor" is envisioned as a necessary evil in the process of easing public resistance to increased international involvement, the American way of war risks gravely losing its way.

In *Dangerous Nation*, after recognizing that America has long been a voracious player on the world's stage, Kagan's reasoning becomes circular. He argues that since America is a great country and has always acted imperially, it should continue to do so with impunity. This cynical assumption undermines the gloriful rhetoric that infused so much of the promotion of the Iraq War—that America has always acted on the side of the angels, and not for imperial reasons. Despite Kagan's self-reinforcing reasoning that a historical pattern of aggression should justify future aggression, it could as easily be argued (and would seem more in keeping with the framers' tradition of self-reflection) that America should seriously rethink this trend.

BACK TO FUJI AND TOOMS

There is a vast gulf—literally and figuratively—between neoconservative cynicism and the idealistic aspirations of airmen like Fuji and Tooms, whose vision of America is not one of a "Dangerous Nation" but rather of a beacon of democracy whose cause is freedom, not expansion.

As they recount their mission to kill Saddam Hussein, Fuji and Tooms do not use neoconservative buzzwords like "Pax Americana" or "benevolent hegemon." Indeed, in several hours of interviews with them, the word "neoconservative" itself was never mentioned, let alone the notion that their mission was the brainchild of a group of policymaking civilians plotting world domination. Instead, what one hears from Fuji and Tooms is a combination of personal pride at having been chosen for such a significant mission, a bittersweetness that the mission failed in its specific purpose, and throughout, an unflinching confidence that the mission was just a small part of America's larger purpose to spread democracy around the world.

"I look back on it now," Tooms recalls wistfully, "and it still seems like a dream to me. I mean, we tell the story about it. You sit down and talk with your kids. And you get some tough questions. You get asked by your daughter, 'Did you go out and try to kill Saddam Hussein?' And that's a tough one to answer to a little kid. But when we saw him captured on TV, sure, one side of me said, 'You know, I guess we didn't get him.' But in the end we got him."

Fuji echoes his wingman's bittersweet sentiment.

"March nineteenth," he exclaims boyishly, "is one for the history books—my personal history books. How many times in a lifetime does an individual get the opportunity to take the opening shot in a conflict that will liberate a people?"

Fuji's dreamlike words are made only more poignant by the unraveling of the war his mission launched. For in its tragic defiance of his hopes lies the brutal cost of the nation's drift over two centuries from a modest republic cautiously weighing the challenges of an empire to a superpower of unprecedented global audacity. Along the way, the American way of war has lost its way. A nation forged in a war of revolution against an empire has over time come to repeat the very errors from which it sought to learn—the runaway expansionism combined with weakening commitment to founding principles, the growing military that spirals on itself, thrusting the nation into conflicts of ever-increasing scope and depth.

Though the push toward militarism has been evolving since the nation's founding, it made an evolutionary leap with the entry into World War II, America's "good war," and the cauldron from which the nation emerged a superpower. Comparisons between America's intervention in Iraq and the fight against the Axis powers may provoke howls. But if the country is to come to terms with the manner by which our national charter has so decisively shifted toward the imperial, then a serious examination of the implications of her engagement in World War II is vital.

2

The Arsenal of Democracy

Men, this stuff that some sources sling around about America wanting out of this war, not wanting to fight, is a crock of bullshit. Americans love to fight, traditionally. All real Americans love the sting and clash of battle.

General George Patton
East Anglia, 1944

At first glance, George W. Bush, Franklin D. Roosevelt, and the wars each presided over might seem to have little in common. Roosevelt is widely seen as a national hero who oversaw a military, moral, and leadership triumph; Bush is the reverse on all counts. Yet there are parallels to how each president guided America into conflict and transformed the country's foreign policy profile. Before there was "a new Pearl Harbor," there was the original; and though World War II and Iraq differ vastly in purpose, scale, and effect, both exerted disfiguring pressure on the country's republican framework of checks and balances.

While no rational person can second-guess FDR's extraordinary achievement in thwarting the ravages of fascism in Europe and Asia, it can be fairly noted that unprecedented power was concentrated in the executive branch during his presidency, and that this power shift—as anticipated by the framers—was facilitated by the political and economic pressures of wartime.

World War II was an international triumph shadowed by domestic irony. The irony is deepened by the fact that, though Roosevelt is widely and justifiably seen as a heroic figure, it was on his watch that the nation underwent significant constitutional upheaval. His presidency thus teaches us that war itself—whether just or unjust—exerts disfiguring force on the republic's structural integrity. Even when a war is carefully considered, entered into as a last resort, and justified by external threats, it can still undermine the checks and balances, greatly empowering the executive while also making future war more likely. In this context, one can begin to see George W. Bush, his wars, and the vaulting power they have concentrated in the executive branch as both a fulfillment of Madison's and Jefferson's worst fears and an aftereffect of the prerogatives assumed by Roosevelt.

AMERICA FIRST

Though FDR's initial focus after taking office was on overcoming the Great Depression, he soon perceived the significance to America of rising tensions in Europe and Asia. As Robert Dallek notes in *Franklin D. Roosevelt and American Foreign Policy*, FDR's first inaugural address signaled his emphasis on domestic issues; yet the growing international crisis would gradually draw his focus outward.

FDR publicly espoused the isolationist inclination to "shun political commitments which might entangle us in foreign wars." In private, though, as early as 1933 he had begun to feel that war and U.S. involvement therein might be inevitable. Watching the rise of Japanese aggression toward China, and considering the prospect of Japanese aggression toward Russia, he wrote in 1933, less than six months after his first inauguration, that "the whole scheme of things in Tokio [sic] does not make for an assurance of non-aggression in the future."[1] Three years later, further developments overseas began to persuade FDR that Europe too was on a path to war: the Nazis had invaded the Rhineland in violation of the Treaty of Versailles; Mussolini had invaded Ethiopia and withdrawn Italy from the League of Nations, declaring his intention to "restore the glory that was Rome"; and civil war had broken out in Spain, with the Germans and Italians lending support to General Franco. FDR saw inevitable implications for America. Yet a vast majority of Americans remained staunchly isolationist.

When Ethiopia's emperor Haile Selassie I appeared before the League of Nations to beg its member states for help in halting Italy's assault, his despairing words echoed in a silence of global apathy. "I thought it to be impossible," the emperor lamented, "that fifty-two nations, including the most powerful in the world, should be successfully opposed by a single aggressor." He then asked a question that cut to the heart of the matter for America: "Have the signatures appended to a Treaty [i.e., establishing the League of Nations] value only insofar as the signatory Powers have a personal, direct and immediate interest involved?"

The isolationism FDR faced in his first years in office was less an organized ideology than a generalized apathy toward foreign engagement. Over time, though, as tensions in Europe and Asia rose, that apathy morphed into a more pointed opposition toward American entry into the war. This shift was facilitated by the America First Committee, a pressure group that galvanized the spirit of isolationism into a powerful national movement. A September 1939 Gallup Poll (taken within days of Hitler's invasion of Poland) found that 90 percent of American adults wanted to keep out of the war.[2] By 1940, this figure had dropped only slightly, to 88 percent; isolationist sentiment was resilient.

As Donald E. Schmidt writes in his 2005 book, *The Folly of War*, FDR's management of the country's disposition toward war through the late thirties was an increasingly delicate balancing act. "Walking on eggs," as he called it in a letter to the governor general of Canada,[3] FDR developed a clever strategy to kill two birds with one stone. As a prelude to war itself, he undertook to make America "the great arsenal of democracy." This entailed marshaling America's population, resources, and industrial capacities not only to build defensive capabilities but to become the leading supplier of weapons to the British and other Allies.

When Roosevelt asked Congress in 1935 for a defense budget of $1.1 billion, the largest peacetime defense budget in American history to that point,[4] his critics saw the move as a devious tactic to "entangle" the country overseas. In the spirit of the framers, they saw an ominous connection between FDR's increased inclination toward war and his "New Deal" of extensive social programs and federal investment. "Armies, and debts, and taxes," Madison had written in 1795, "are the known instruments for bringing the many under the domination of the few."[5]

War and government expenditure would lead, critics asserted, to the overgrowth of executive power and thus endanger the liberties for which the republic was founded.

Today, FDR is viewed so glowingly it's hard to remember that a large part of the population during the 1930s perceived him as a threat to the republic, a near monarch seizing unprecedented executive power. In 1935, columnist Mark Sullivan wrote that the following year might see "the last presidential election America will have. . . . It is tragic that America fails to see that the New Deal is to America what the early phase of Nazism was to Germany." The Republican Party likewise warned in December 1935 that "the coming election will determine whether we hold to the American system of government or whether we shall sit idly by and allow it to be replaced by a socialist state honeycombed with waste and extravagance. . . ."[6]

To restrain what they perceived as FDR's executive excesses, his critics in Congress secured the passage of a Neutrality Act, imposing limits on American involvement abroad. Between 1936 and 1939, three revisions of this act were passed. The revisions were a series of fits and starts, two steps forward, one step back—a dance between the executive and legislative branches in which Congress sought to codify strict American neutrality while FDR sought executive discretion to determine whether an international situation warranted an exception thereto.

The first Neutrality Act, of 1935, legislated congressional demands for a "mandatory neutrality law" that would act as an embargo on the export of "arms, ammunition, and implements of war" to overseas belligerents. Even so, it vested in the executive the power to define which arms, ammunitions, and implements would fall under the embargo. The 1936 act gave the president even more latitude, granting him the license to "proclaim" a state of war between countries and thus label them "belligerents" for the purposes of the act, yet prohibited the sale of weaponry or financial assistance to belligerents. In response to the outbreak of civil war in Spain, the 1937 revision closed loopholes that had allowed for the sale of weaponry and the offer of monetary aid to countries engaged in civil conflict. The act had up to then covered only war between countries.

The final revision, of 1939, reflected the most heightened tensions yet between FDR and the isolationist America First Committee. It arose in response to Hitler's invasion of Poland. Though FDR would have preferred to see the Neutrality Act repealed, he recognized the improbability of that and instead sought the addition of a "cash-and-carry" provision to the law. This would allow America to supply war matériel to belligerents, so long as it was on a cash basis and no American vessel was involved in the transaction. As Dallek recounts, the outbreak of war in Europe made Americans more open to consider an adjustment of their commitment to neutrality, yet FDR proceeded with great caution, recognizing that public sentiment remained vehemently opposed to official U.S. entry.[7] Even so, America First moved into high gear, mounting a massive radio and mail campaign "to disseminate the impression that the President will, if not restrained, get the country into war."[8] Congress granted the cash-and-carry provision, but also placed further restrictions on U.S. ships sailing into conflict areas.

Though framed as a debate over America's role outside her borders, the battle between FDR and Congress over neutrality was equally about U.S. domestic policy and the balance of power between the branches. For both FDR and his adversaries, the issue came down to whether the executive or the legislative branch would maintain greater control over if and when to make exceptions to the principle of neutrality. This boiled down to which branch had the greater power to make war—a question that underpinned American history to that point and continues to do so to this day. By demanding discretion over the Neutrality Act, FDR sought to concentrate that power in the executive branch. By instead seeking "impartial" Neutrality Acts (i.e., without presidential discretion), members of Congress sought to honor Jefferson and Madison's intention that Congress act as a "check to the Dog of war." As California senator Hiram Johnson expressed this effort in 1937: "I will try to prevent the President's sinister grasp of . . . the war-making power."[9]

With the Japanese attack on Pearl Harbor on December 7, 1941, the neutrality debate became academic. Overnight, public opinion turned virtually unanimous toward support for American entry. The America First Committee lost currency, and a vindicated FDR acquired unprecedented power to prosecute the war. The "great arsenal of democracy" he had sought to build throughout the 1930s would suddenly have its day, not only to promote domestic economic growth and provide indirect support to America's allies but also as a force for America's direct expansion on the world's stage—a quantum leap for the American way of war. World War II likewise catapulted FDR from controversial to iconic status. The debates over executive power faded into memory as the imperatives of U.S. security united the country. Yet, as time has borne out, those originally suspicious of FDR's machinations may not have been all wrong.

IF ROOSEVELT HAD A RICHARD PERLE

It would have to have been Commander Arthur McCollum, a foreign policy adjutant who vigorously promoted entry into the war. In 1940, while serving as an officer in the Far Eastern section of the Office of Naval Intelligence (ONI), McCollum wrote an "eight-point plan" that called for the United States to provoke Japanese aggression in order to turn public opinion in favor of entering the war. It has come to be called the McCollum Memo.

The memo remained classified until 1994, when historian Robert Stinnett used the Freedom of Information Act to secure its release while researching his controversial 2000 book *Day of Deceit*. Since then, the McCollum Memo has stimulated controversy among a handful of revisionist historians of Pearl Harbor, but it is still largely unknown by the general public. It not only suggests that FDR made America an "arsenal of democracy" in the late 1930s, but that members of his administration understood long before Pearl Harbor (as Bush's neoconservatives later would with 9/11) that without such an attack, America could not be put on a war footing.

McCollum wrote his memo more than a year before Pearl Harbor. It was submitted to his superiors, Captains Walter Anderson and Dudley Knox, on October 7, 1940. Like the "new Pearl Harbor" reference in the 2000 PNAC report, the McCollum Memo recommended significant changes to America's defense posture, yet recognized public opinion to be unready for such change in the absence of an attack. McCollum argued that "prompt aggressive naval action against Japan by the United States" would offer several benefits to the United States, yet "it is not believed that in the present state of political opinion the United States government is capable of declaring war against Japan without more ado."[10] He went on to recommend eight steps to guide America into war, concluding in his memo's most controversial phrase, "if by these means Japan could be led to commit an overt act of war, so much the better."

While there is no hard evidence that the memo was ever read by Roosevelt, Anderson and Knox were two of FDR's key military advisers. It would therefore seem hard to believe that the president could have been entirely unfamiliar with McCollum's ideas.

With the release of the memo, McCollum has grown from a key figure in the perceived failure by the Roosevelt administration to have anticipated Pearl Harbor to one of greater intrigue, associated with the idea that, far from failing to anticipate such an attack, FDR and his advisers may have cunningly maneuvered America into war with Japan by working to provoke it. As with neoconservatives in the Bush administration like Perle and Wolfowitz, suspicions have arisen about McCollum's influence on FDR's national security decision making. To judge by a quick Google search of the two words "McCollum Memo," these suspicions tend to be overblown, depicting the memo as the smoking gun of a conspiracy at the highest level to provoke an act of war by Japan. These overly strident claims likewise provoke overly strident dismissals, so that the deeper significance of the McCollum Memo tends to be lost. Keeping in mind that no single memo by a midlevel functionary should be given too large a role in the shaping of a president's policy, the McCollum Memo nonetheless demands attention.

In his definitive 1980 book *At Dawn We Slept*, the late military historian Gordon W. Prange portrays McCollum as just one of several intelligence functionaries who either missed, misread, or mishandled indicators of Japan's intent to conduct a surprise attack. Roberta Wohlstetter, in her book *Pearl Harbor: Warning and Decision,* portrays McCollum simply as a cog in the broken machine of American intelligence handling—a case study in why the machine needs to be better organized, managed, and centralized. That critique of American intelligence practices is cited as the motivation for creation of the Central Intelligence Agency in the aftermath of the war. Yet Wohlstetter's portrayal of McCollum, like Prange's, is incomplete.

In a posthumously written introduction to Prange's *At Dawn We Slept*, Donald Goldstein and Katherine V. Dillon maintain that "space did not allow treatment of the revisionist thesis that President Roosevelt wanted and either permitted the attack or deliberately engineered it to bring the United States into World War II by 'the back door.' " They also cite Prange's argument that "neither the evidence nor common sense justified this view of the matter."[11] It is worth noting that at the time of Prange's death in 1980, the McCollum Memo remained classified. One wonders whether, if Prange had known of it, he might have come to a different conclusion.

Stinnett uses the McCollum Memo as a cornerstone of his analysis in *Day of Deceit*. He portrays McCollum not just as an intelligence functionary in the processing of Japanese cable traffic but as being involved in the shaping of U.S. foreign policy long before the attacks.

According to Stinnett, McCollum's life path prior to his writing of the memo gave him an intimate understanding of Japanese society. He was born to American missionary parents in Nagasaki in 1898, and Japanese was his first language. McCollum returned to America in his teens but, after graduating from the U.S. Naval Academy, he returned to Tokyo. There, in 1923, as a naval attaché to the U.S. Embassy, he had the unique distinction to be invited to instruct Crown Prince Hirohito, Japan's future emperor, in dancing the Charleston.[12] There's an irresistible irony in the picture of a young U.S. naval attaché teaching dance steps to the future emperor of a nation with which, seventeen years later, he would help guide America to war.

McCollum's 1940 memo advocated the following eight foreign policy measures, designed, in his words, to compel Japan "to commit an overt act of war":

A. Make an arrangement with Britain for the use of British bases in the Pacific, particularly Singapore.
B. Make an arrangement with Holland for the use of base facilities and acquisition of supplies in the Dutch East Indies.
C. Give all possible aid to the Chinese government of Chiang Kai-Shek.
D. Send a division of long-range heavy cruisers to the Orient, Philippines, or Singapore.
E. Send two divisions of submarines to the Orient.
F. Keep the main strength of the U.S. fleet now in the Pacific in the vicinity of the Hawaiian Islands.

G. Insist that the Dutch refuse to grant Japanese demands for undue economic concessions, particularly oil.
H. Completely embargo all U.S. trade with Japan, in collaboration with a similar embargo imposed by the British Empire.

According to Stinnett, FDR implemented all eight measures, and this haunting fact serves as the basis for Stinnett's thesis that FDR conspired both to provoke an attack by Japan and then to cover up having done so.

Though Stinnett's claims are inflammatory, he is not alone in seeking to revise the history of Roosevelt and Pearl Harbor. Some have argued that Roosevelt knew that the attack was imminent and allowed the ships and forces at Pearl Harbor to be devastated. This argument draws on circumstantial evidence such as the fact that certain revealing Japanese telegrams and radio transmissions were ignored, and that U.S. intelligence officers who observed files being destroyed in the courtyard of Honolulu's Japanese consulate a week before the attack did not sound an alarm.[13]

There is also the fact that McCollum was by no means the only American official on record as anticipating the utility of a first strike by Japan.[14] Secretary of War Henry Stimson summarized in his diary entry for November 25, 1941, a meeting with the president and his War Cabinet, in which FDR reflected that "we were likely to be attacked as soon as next Monday," and that "the question was how we should maneuver them into the position of firing the first shot without allowing too much danger to ourselves." In 1946, when Congress investigated the events of Pearl Harbor, Stimson's use of the word "maneuver" naturally lit off a firestorm of criticism among FDR's opponents.

Republican senators Owen Brewster of Maine and Homer Ferguson of Michigan argued that the president, instead of seeking a declaration of war by Congress, "chose an alternative of waiting for an overt act by Japan." Journalist George Morgenstern, author of *Pearl Harbor*, published in 1947, which was the first highly controversial reexamination of the attacks, went further, charging that FDR and his advisers "reckoned with cold detachment the risk of manipulating a delegated enemy into firing the first shot, and they forced 3,000 unsuspecting men at Pearl Harbor to accept that risk."[15]

In a written statement to the investigating committee in March 1947, Stimson sought to clear up the confusion his diary entry may have caused, but ended up only deepening the impression of an official strategy to produce a first strike by Japan. "In spite of the risk involved, however, in letting the Japanese fire the first shot," Stimson wrote, "we realized that in order to have the full support of the American people it was desirable to make sure that the Japanese be the ones to do this so that there would remain no doubt in anyone's mind as to who were the aggressors."[16]

To complicate matters further, Stinnett explains that "on November 27 and 28, 1941, U.S. military commanders were given this order: 'The United States desires that Japan commit the first overt act.' According to Secretary of War Henry L. Stimson, the order came directly from President Roosevelt."[17] This particular citation is haunting for its use of the same formulation "overt act" that appears in the McCollum Memo. If Stimson is correct that the order came from FDR, this might suggest that FDR was at least superficially familiar with either McCollum's memo, its underlying strategy, or even its specific language.

Beyond Stimson, Stinnett cites other military men intimately involved with Pearl Harbor who have challenged the official story in the years since. Among them are Admiral James O. Richardson, who served as Commander in Chief of the Pacific Fleet (CINCPAC) from 1940 to 1941, and his successor Husband Kimmel, who was in command at the time of the Pearl Harbor attacks. Richardson had in fact been replaced by Kimmel for the very reason that he had been outspoken about the deployment of the fleet to Pearl Harbor in the first place.

In April 1940, six months prior to McCollum's submission of his eight-point plan, the recommendation of its sixth item—"Keep the main strength of the U.S. fleet now in the Pacific in the vicinity of the Hawaiian Islands"—had already been ordered. Significant portions of the fleet were deployed to Hawaiian waters for the purposes of an annual training exercise. Upon completion of the exercise, the Roosevelt administration opted to keep the fleet based at Pearl Harbor. In a May 1940 meeting, FDR met with his secretary of state Cordell Hull and Navy Secretary Frank Knox to discuss the permanent basing of the fleet in Hawaii. Richardson, who was CINCPAC at the time, could see no rationale for doing so, and he made his objections known. He was opposed for several reasons, including Pearl Harbor's lack of training facilities, ammunition, and fuel supplies, and the lack of support vessels. He also believed his fleet was being used in an unconscionable strategy to lure the Japanese. "He would not sacrifice his ships and men to what he saw as a flawed policy," Stinnett explains.

Richardson even secured a one-on-one meeting with FDR, at which he voiced his concern that his fleet was being placed in harm's way as a target for Japanese attack. He even asked FDR point-blank, "Are we here as a stepping-off place for belligerent activity?" Though FDR assured him otherwise, Richardson remained unconvinced. He was removed from his post in February 1941, replaced by Admiral Kimmel.

Kimmel was not privy to Richardson's discontent about the basing. Worse still, information available at the time about potential Japanese aggression against Pearl Harbor was actually kept from Kimmel, intelligence that would have been vital for preparing the fleet for attack.

In his 1955 book *Admiral Kimmel's Story*, Kimmel makes the case that the "withholding [of] vital information from our commanders at Pearl Harbor has never been explained," and that this withholding was in his view a component of "the strategy of maneuvering the Japanese into striking the first blow at America." Though Kimmel attests this strategy was unknown to them at the time, he infers that the Departments of War and of the Navy, "responsible only to the President of the United States," failed to provide him with necessary information. He goes on to insinuate that "it is impossible to believe that both these agencies of such proved reliability and competence should simultaneously and repeatedly fail in such a crisis."[18]

Indeed, there is overwhelming evidence that tremendous stores of information about Japan's preparations for Pearl Harbor never reached Admiral Kimmel. In the fourth chapter of his memoir, matter-of-factly entitled "Information Withheld and Its Significance," Kimmel cites a chilling array of intercepted Japanese cable traffic that was either "withheld from me" or "never supplied to me." Of particular importance were "intercepted dispatches between Tokyo and Honolulu on and after September 24, 1941, which indicated that a Japanese move against Pearl Harbor was planned in Tokyo." Had these been shared with him, he argues, they "would have radically changed the estimate of the situation made by me and my staff."[19]

Kimmel's scathing criticism of the chain of command has been written off historically as the embittered defense of a man blamed for America's lack of preparation. In January 1942, just five weeks after the attacks, a five-member commission headed by Supreme Court Associate Justice Owen Roberts concluded that full responsibility lay with Kimmel and Army General Walter Short for having failed in their duties to be better prepared for such an attack.[20] Upon reading the commission's report, Admiral Richardson condemned the scapegoating of Kimmel and Short as "the most unfair, unjust, and deceptively dishonest document ever printed by the Government Printing Office."[21]

Regrettably, the debate over Pearl Harbor has devolved through the years into a contest not only between FDR admirers and detractors, but between conspiracy theorists and those who reflexively dismiss conspiracy theories per se. The conspiracy theorists overinterpret the circumstantial evidence to say that FDR not only anticipated and provoked the attack but even knew the details of where and when it might occur. Skeptics dismiss any chance of FDR having known, citing his heroism and the fact that the evidence is so circumstantial. A more thoughtful view is that FDR was more inclined to enter the war than most Americans and may even have pursued policies in support of America's allies that were inflammatory, but that is a far cry from his having known in specific about the attack itself.

Stinnett's *Day of Deceit* was received by critics as a late hit on FDR's legacy. In a scathing review in *The New York Review of Books*, intelligence historian David Kahn played the role of mythbuster, devoting the majority of his 2,500 words to challenging certain of Stinnett's claims on technical grounds. In an ensuing published debate between them, one finds oneself aswim in shop talk between two obviously well qualified scholars—one with highly specialized knowledge of the intelligence world in general and the other who has devoted vast energies to the particular study of the intelligence surrounding Pearl Harbor. Ultimately, the debate between them suffers from too much time having passed for either side to prove his case dispositively. For each of Stinnett's theories, Kahn has a quick retort, and for each retort, Stinnett has a complicating ripple.

For example, Kahn notes that two of the steps enumerated by McCollum (steps "C" and "H") "reflected longstanding American policies in support of China and opposition to Japan's aggression and fascism."[22] This is true, but it ignores the clear fact that for these eight steps to have been committed to paper by McCollum more than a year before Pearl Harbor, submitted to his superiors, and then, whether by consequence or coincidence, implemented by FDR is at least noteworthy. Stinnett may have needlessly invited resistance to his inquiry by trying to marshal the facts into an overly ambitious argument. And Kahn may be right in his criticism that "Stinnett is such a passionate believer in conspiracy that he is unwilling to consider the countervailing evidence. He is offering not a theory but a definition, which cannot be contradicted." To a guy with a hammer, of course, everything looks like a nail, and there is a sense in *Day of Deceit* that Stinnett may have become too inclined to suspect a conspiracy around every turn. But this does not detract from the remarkable window that the McCollum Memo provides into the cold and shadowy calculus with which national security decisions may be considered.

By featuring the McCollum Memo so prominently, and drawing attention to the extensive parallels between its recommendations and the policy decisions undertaken by FDR, Stinnett does not demonstrate that FDR was a "traitor," as Kahn suggests. Rather, he illuminates that statecraft, even when undertaken by a heroic figure, is a shadowy business, and that unjust means may at times be seen as justified for achieving a vital end. In this sense, *Day of Deceit* demonstrates that it is possible to hold FDR in the highest esteem while recognizing that the country's entry into World War II was more premeditated than is generally understood.

Despite obvious differences, comparisons to the Bush administration's march to war in Iraq are enlightening. While conspiracy theorists have deduced from the 2000 PNAC Report that Richard Perle and his neoconservative compatriots in the administration not only saw the potential utility of a "new Pearl Harbor," as the memo suggests, but actually looked the other way, available evidence is insufficient to support this view. There is some evidence to suggest that while the attacks might have been thwarted by information available to the CIA and FBI, the hijackers were not apprehended due to a number of communication lapses between and within those agencies.[23] Still, it is clear that, like McCollum, the neoconservatives were willing to promote a dark calculus about America's national interest—one that included the need to provoke a foreign attack to move domestic public opinion—and that they were then willing to exploit the national sentiment provoked by 9/11 to serve a prior agenda—distorting the truth about the threat posed by Saddam in order to gain the nation's support for war.

While there is evidence of secret maneuvers resulting in America's entry into both World War II and Iraq, a glaring difference is, of course, that in World War II, America faced adversaries that were in fact actively threatening her national interests. Another crucial difference is that World War II involved a draft and significant sacrifice for the vast majority of the population. With Iraq, the case for war was predicated in large part on the promise of a quick and painless victory. Ironically, the distance America has traveled in her conception of when to go to war, and the nature of the sacrifice required, is the result of powerful forces unleashed by the development of America's warmaking capacity to fight World War II.

THE FURY OF AN AROUSED DEMOCRACY

The term "American way of war" was used by British historian D. W. Brogan in 1944 to describe what he saw as America's innovative contribution to the history of warmaking in World War II. Before Pearl Harbor, FDR's "great arsenal of democracy" made America a supplier of arms to America's allies. Following the attack, the arsenal turned inward, becoming an invincible tool for America's own prosecution of the war and, ultimately, the driving force in a far-reaching transformation of American society. In both the Pacific and in Europe, FDR's mobilization of the American people, economy, and industrial capacities not only proved decisive for victory but set the stage for America's international posture for the latter part of the twentieth century.

In Brogan's eyes, what distinguished the American military was that it was "mechanized like the American farm and kitchen (the farms and kitchens of a lazy people who want washing machines and bulldozers to do the job for them)." Combining low-cost mass-production methods with faster means of delivering materiel to the battlefield, America first equipped her allies to fight the Axis powers before then marshaling that same strength to secure her own victory.

"War is a business, not an art," Brogan wrote. "They [the Americans] are not interested in moral victories, but in victory . . . the United States is a great, a very great, corporation whose stockholders expect that . . . it will be in the black."[24]

At its best, the American way of war represented the harnessing of America's industrial strength and large population for the fight against fascism. Following World War I, the United States had demobilized to the point that by 1939, the country had only 180,000 troops, the lowest level of enlistment since the end of the Civil War.[25] To remedy this, Army Chief of Staff General George C. Marshall requested the first peacetime conscription in the nation's history. Under what became the Selective Service Act of 1940, millions of Americans were drafted. By the war's end, the number of those serving had skyrocketed from roughly 180,000 to 12 million.[26] Alongside this meteoric increase, U.S. industry also experienced an unprecedented boom.

Michael Sherry summarizes this industrial explosion in his book *In the Shadow of War*:

> Manufacturing output doubled between 1940 and 1943. Armaments production increased eightfold between 1941 and 1943, to a level nearly that of Britain, the Soviet Union, and Germany combined. Output of ships, often by remarkable assembly-line methods, was staggering. Most telling was success in technically advanced fields: aircraft production zoomed from 5,856 in 1939 to 96,318 in 1944—more than double what any ally or enemy produced, even though the United States made bigger planes.[27]

"Hitler should beware," declared General Dwight D. Eisenhower at the war's outset, "the fury of an aroused democracy."[28] And indeed, American victory over the more monolithic and oppressive powers of Germany and Japan seemed a triumph of the power of unleashed human imagination, energy, and industry over the more regimented and repressive exploitation of human activity overseas. Nowhere was this more poignantly demonstrated than in the enormous advantage America reaped through the employment of female and minority labor in the war effort. Between 1940 and 1945, the female workforce grew by 50 percent, from 12 million to 18 million. During these years, the number of jobs for black Americans in the Army also jumped dramatically, from 5,000 to 920,000.[29] Whereas "Rosie the Riveter" and prizefighter-turned-soldier Joe Louis became national symbols for the expanded role played by women and minorities, the Germans were committed to keeping women out of the workforce and annihilating the very minorities whose labor they might otherwise have exploited.

As Sherry explains, World War II "diminished ethnic and religious cleavages, in part because they were subordinated, at least in theory, to 'the idea that what united Americans was a great deal more important than what divided them.' "[30] If America was a melting pot, the fire of war seemed to turn up the heat, melting away barriers that had persisted in fostering division contrary to America's ideals.

"Hitler was the one," recalled one African-American, Fanny Christina Hill, in her oral history published in 2003, "that got us out of the white folks' kitchen."[31]

Indeed, for many Americans, the experience of World War II wedded the idea of a triumphant role for America on the world's stage with an idealistic vision of America as a haven of liberty and multiculturalism. The unity, diversity, industry, and independence required to win the war were all qualities associated with the nation's founding. And so it was that America seemed to triumph abroad when she fulfilled the aspirations set forth by her framers. Under duress, the nation could live up to the idealism of its principles (too often unfulfilled in its daily routine), and the irresistible poetry of this made a deep impression on the national psyche—one that persists in some form to this day.

At its worst, World War II's development of the American way of war led to an overemphasis on warmaking as a part not only of foreign policy but of American life as well. As the term "American way of war" implies, World War II wove the idea of "war" inextricably into the fabric of the American way itself. Before the war even began, industrial mobilization started to reshape the U.S. landscape, creating winners and losers in the new wartime economy. Western states, fueled by the needs of the Pacific theater, grew in wealth, employment, and population, while small rural areas, such as much of New England, suffered losses, their people migrating westward for jobs and their prevailing industries weakening. In a striking example, ten percent of all federal money spent during the war was spent in California alone.[32] Eastern states suffered during the same period. In the words of one observer, "it was [as] if someone had tilted the country: people, money, and soldiers all spilled west."[33]

The wartime prosperity of a state and, by extension, its people was determined by the degree to which the state's industrial base was applicable to military purposes. When the war was over, industries that had sprung up did not just close their factory doors but instead adapted their products to service the postwar moment. This led to the perpetuation of a wartime economy. In a spirit of postwar military Keynsianism, many defense industrial products were simply refitted to serve postwar civilian uses (radar, duct tape, jet aircraft). These modern marvels were seen as happy by-products of military-industrial research and innovation, making defense development seem indispensable even to the peacetime progress of the nation.

This phenomenon has become a self-perpetuating one in the years since, diverting an ever-increasing disproportion of national resources from vital areas of national need into the most blunt instrument of national power: the military. As Eisenhower and others have warned, this diversion risks weakening from within the very country the defense spending seeks to defend from without. The longer this cycle continues and the more parts of the system adapt to fit it, the harder it is for the country to extricate itself from its implications.

THE BATTLE FOR MEN'S MINDS

While defense sector jobs and technological progress before and during World War II wove increased militarism into the nation's daily life, Hollywood wove the same into the national imagination. Collaboration between Hollywood and the military dates back almost to the dawn of celluloid. In 1915, West Point provided advisory and artillery support to D. W. Griffith for the making of *The Birth of a Nation* and nine years later provided Griffith with 1,000 cavalry troops for his epic *America*.[34] But the alliance between Hollywood and the military after Pearl Harbor was closer than ever. In forming his strategy for World War II, General

Marshall decided that what America lacked in troop strength to defeat the Axis powers it could make up for through a sense of purpose. In early 1942, he asked Hollywood director Frank Capra to use his filmmaking talents to communicate America's cause to new recruits.

"He told me we were raising a very large army," Capra would later recall, "and that we were going to try to make soldiers out of boys who, for the most part, had never seen a gun. They were being uprooted from civilian life and thrown into Army camps. And the reason why was hazy in their minds. . . . 'And that, Capra, is our job—and your job. To win this war we must win the battle for men's minds.' "

Marshall said that he wanted Capra to produce a series of films to "explain to our boys in the Army why we are fighting, and the principles for which we are fighting."[35] Capra accepted the commission and began work on a series of indoctrination films that came to be called *Why We Fight*.

The *Why We Fight* series helped forge an American military identity to compete with the concept being promoted by the Axis powers. Made largely through the reediting of confiscated Axis newsreels, the films depicted the war as "a fight between a free world and a slave world," with no doubt as to what side America was on. In contrast to the monolithic *Ubermensch* image promoted by Germany and Japan, Capra enlisted some of Hollywood's brightest lights—including director John Huston, cartoonist Dr. Seuss (then Theodore Geisel), and voice-over artist Mel Blanc—to portray the strength of America's military as a result of its diversity, humanity, and the rightness of its cause. "Private Snafu," a cartoon character created by Dr. Seuss and spoken by Mel Blanc (using the same voice he would later use for Bugs Bunny), became the prototype for this populist vision of the American soldier. SNAFU is a playful military acronym for "Situation Normal All Fucked Up." Private Snafu was the soldier who gets it wrong in every situation. As such, he becomes an unlikely hero, helping America defeat the enemy not through an advantage in might or cunning, but rather through the implementation of a superior ideology by good working people in the field.

In Snafu's image, America became a motley band of ne'er-do-wells, bound invincibly together by the righteousness of their common cause. That they are multiethnic and nonconformist becomes a reflection not of weakness but of the greater values of the more open society they represent. As such, the *Why We Fight* films cast America's role in World War II in terms of the larger global conflict between freedom and slavery, light and dark, good and evil. *Why We Fight* cemented in the popular imagination what FDR's American way of war was institutionalizing into daily life. Warmaking itself was reinvented in an American mold, overcoming Americans' founding disinclination toward war, and winning popular support not only for the war effort but for a new and expanded way of seeing America on the world stage.

Taken together, these factors partially account for why so many of the socioeconomic innovations in the American way of war outlived the timeframe of World War II, making war such a central part of American life. While developments in defense technology made war more practicable and provided much needed jobs to a depressed economy, progressive recruitment policies made the war a triumphant fulfillment of America's promise over its more oppressive enemies overseas. Such prosperity and attractive folklore helped candy-coat a set of shifts in the nation's separation of powers that might otherwise have offended public sentiment.

Added to this, of course, was the cult of personality that emerged around FDR himself. Initially underestimated, his vaulting success after Pearl Harbor at unifying the nation and securing victory imparted to his ideas a lasting resonance in the minds of the American public. For a country that once shied away from war, the American way of war had done more than simply win World War II—it had made war the American way.

BUILDING THE WORLD OF TOMORROW

Beyond a shift in the American public's view of war, World War II also represented a shift in America's political economy, producing unprecedented closeness between the federal government and corporate America. Relations between these two had been strained for some time, reaching their nadir with the crash of 1929 and ensuing depression. As FDR campaigned for president in 1932, he stated his intention to deploy the power of the federal government to forge a more socialized society with outright contempt for the corporate sector and its abuse of the

American people. America's industrial giants, FDR argued, "have been moved less by calm analysis of the needs of the Nation as a whole than by a blind determination to preserve their own special stakes in the economic order."[36] By fingering the corporate sector as having failed the American people, FDR drew clear battle lines between government and industry. Despite his own wealthy origins, he assailed the corporate elite as "economic royalists," who "carved new dynasties . . . new Kingdoms" built upon a system of exploitation, monopoly, and control "undreamed of by the Fathers."[37]

"Against economic tyranny such as this," FDR declared, "the American citizen could appeal only to the organized power of government. The collapse of 1929 showed up the despotism for what it was. The election of 1932 was the people's mandate to end it. Under that mandate it is being ended." Accordingly, FDR passed the National Industrial Recovery Act of 1933, which gave the government power to regulate competition between companies in the private sector, setting rules for pricing minimums, non-compete agreements, and restrictions on production. In 1935, he passed the National Labor Relations Act, which removed legal barriers to labor organizing against big business. That same year, he established the Works Progress Administration (WPA), providing jobs to almost 10 million Americans in public service.

Over the ensuing decade, as FDR sought through his New Deal policies to make Americans increasingly see the government as the engine for their personal betterment, industry fought to do the same. Companies spent vast sums to produce and advertise products claiming to be instrumental in improving the lives of everyday people. New York City's 1939 World's Fair was the pinnacle of these private sector countermeasures. Under the slogan "Building the World of Tomorrow," the fair was an opportunity for corporate America to mend its relations with the public. By 1939, FDR's government had all but replaced the private sector as the nation's engine of economic growth. Companies exhibiting at the fair sought to retake a more central role.

To this end, General Motors spent several years preparing its thrilling Futurama ride, in which fairgoers could ride through a dreamlike vision of the future complete with thousands of GM cars, superhighways, and other fruits of American industry. It was, as Roland Marchand describes in *Creating the Corporate Soul*, "a serious look at the nation's future—

through General Motors' eyes."[38] Not to be outdone, RCA used the fair to unveil television. DuPont introduced nylon.

The message from corporate exhibitors was simple: the key to a hopeful and prosperous future lay not in FDR's New Deal but in the advances made possible by corporate America.

With the rising threat of war in Europe and then the sudden exigency of Pearl Harbor, this tug-of-war between industry and government for the hearts of the American consumer became academic. Just as it melted certain ethnic, religious, and gender distinctions, the sudden survival needs of wartime production forged a new relationship of unprecedented harmony between the two sectors. Government needed industry, industry needed government, and, above all, America needed both to cooperate unreservedly to secure victory. However it was intended, this alliance gave the defense apparatus a life of its own in influencing public policy.

"Tentative terms for a lasting business-government partnership were set by the war," writes Michael Sherry in *In the Shadow of War*. "Government (especially the executive branch) and business (especially large corporations) would be the senior partners in the firm. Congress would help set policy and broker disputes but would function more as an arena for conflict than as a decisive force itself."[39] Ironically, to fight fascism in Europe and Asia, FDR's America forged an alliance between government and the corporate sector that in many ways took its cue from the very systems it sought to defeat. "Fascism should more appropriately be called corporatism," wrote Italian philosopher Giovanni Gentile in a definition espoused by Mussolini, "because it is a merger of state and corporate power."[40] Even in his own "Simple Truths" address to Congress in 1938, FDR had defined Fascism as "ownership of government by an individual, by a group, or by another controlling private power."[41] While the despots of Germany and Japan had all marshaled the power of their industrial giants—from I. G. Farben to Deutsche Bank, Nissan, and Mitsubishi—to arm their campaigns of aggression, America's elected head of state would, for different purposes, mobilize U.S. industrial might.

Though this executive-corporate alliance would in no way lead to the kind of internal atrocities associated with fascism, it nonetheless exerted damaging influence upon the separation of powers. What it produced was a symbiotic relationship between the executive branch and corporate America in which each simultaneously shelters and empowers the other at the expense of the separation of powers. While the executive provides the corporation with a national security basis on which to market its products under the cover of executive privilege and prerogative, the corporation arms the executive with the research, development, and production power to advance his warmaking goals, regardless of Congressional opposition. Since the activities of a corporation are less vulnerable to public or congressional scrutiny than those of a public institution, the corporation affords the executive an added measure of shelter from such scrutiny. The prosperity that followed the war also provided cover. As Michael Sherry writes, "When military spending produced abundance, few Americans were inclined to quarrel over the relationships of power that resulted."[42] While this recipe had expanded the capacity of the Fascist powers to industrialize their acts of aggression, for the arsenal of democracy it produced a climate of decreased transparency and accountability and, ultimately, of unchecked executive power.

PLEASE, MR. SENATOR. IT'S TOO BIG FOR YOU

FDR served three full terms as president and was inaugurated for a fourth on January 20, 1945. By that time, he had in both the duration and scope of his presidency become the closest thing America had ever had to a monarch. The longest-serving president in American history, he had led the country out of the great Depression and through the most significant war in its history. Through his development of the New Deal and the arsenal of democracy, FDR had revolutionized the American way at home, and the American way of war abroad. In the process, the unprecedented degree of executive power he amassed inflicted both immediate and long-term damage to the carefully calibrated separation of powers. While FDR was not without his critics for this, even during his presidency, their worst fears were never realized. His New Deal did not turn out to be "the early phase of Nazism" that Mark Sullivan had predicted in 1935. And the election of 1936 did not result in a "dictatorship that mocks at the rights of the States and the liberty of the citizen," as FDR's detractors in the Republican Party had predicted.[43] Still, some of these fears were not entirely unfounded. During his White House years, FDR transformed the executive branch into an office of far greater power, secrecy, and autonomy than had ever been contemplated before.

Two notable examples of FDR's expansion of executive power are his effort to pass the Judiciary Reorganization Bill of 1937 and his decision in 1940 to run for a third presidential term. The 1937 bill was presented by Roosevelt as a simple effort to relieve the workload of federal judges. As originally written, it would have required that they must step down at the age of seventy and allowed for a total of fifty additional judges. The bill was FDR's response to a series of U.S. Supreme Court decisions overturning measures of his New Deal. Had it passed as originally put forward, it would have empowered FDR to appoint as many as six additional justices to the Supreme Court, leading his critics to accuse him of trying to "pack the Court" with like-minded jurists and thus undermine the separation of powers between the executive and the judiciary.[44] The bill was fiercely opposed by Democrats and Republicans alike, and in its final form it was stripped of the offending provisions.

Three years later, FDR further inflamed his critics when he broke from the precedent set by George Washington that presidential term limits be limited to two. By 1945, when FDR ran for his fourth term, the impression of an imperial presidency was hard to deny.

While FDR's effort to "pack" the Supreme Court and his decision to run for a third term were made prior to U.S. involvement in the war, once the war began, it became a catalyst for further upsets of the balance of power. On February 19, 1942, less than three months after the attack on Pearl Harbor, Roosevelt seized expanded executive power in the name of security when he issued Executive Order 9066, authorizing the U.S. military to forcibly remove persons with foreign enemy ancestry (both U.S. citizens and noncitizens) from their homes and place them in internment camps. This resulted in the internment of 120,000 people of Japanese descent, roughly 60 percent of whom were American-born U.S. citizens. That same year, FDR assumed additional executive power when he convened military tribunals to try accused German saboteurs captured inside the United States. The Supreme Court supported this expansion of executive power when it ruled in the landmark decision *Ex parte Quirin* to uphold Roosevelt's tribunals.

Roosevelt was by no means the first U.S. president to assert wartime executive authority to imprison American citizens at his own discretion. His decisions to intern Japanese subjects and try Germans by military tribunal followed Abraham Lincoln's controversial wartime precedent of suspending habeas corpus and imprisoning thousands of political adversaries at the outset of the Civil War. But the scale of FDR's Japanese internment was unprecedented. Presidents have issued executive orders since 1789, though their constitutionality is not fully clear. Roosevelt's Executive Order 9066 has been viewed in the years since as an overassertion of executive power and was officially and symbolically rescinded by Gerald Ford in 1976. Though the shock of Pearl Harbor may account for the sense of urgency that could produce so grave a measure, Executive Order 9066 remains nonetheless a stain on Roosevelt's legacy and a reminder of how quickly a nation at war can trade liberty for security.

Though Executive Order 9066 was an overt assertion of executive power, FDR asserted an even greater measure of power by more covert means. Indeed, nothing on FDR's watch was more challenging to the separation of powers than the secrecy with which the now infamous Manhattan Project was implemented. The project was so clandestine that, following FDR's death on April 12, 1945, his successor Harry S. Truman appears to have known relatively little of it. In his memoirs, Truman claims that it was only after Roosevelt's death that Secretary of War Henry Stimson advised him of "an immense project that was under way—a project looking to the development of a new explosive of almost unbelievable destructive power."[45] As David McCullough recounts in his biography *Truman*, while still a senator, the future president had written to Secretary of War Stimson to ask why the federal government was purchasing large tracts of land in Washington State. Truman was asking about land intended for secret Manhattan Project purposes. According to McCullough, Stimson found Truman to be prying into an area beyond his level of clearance and concluded that "under no circumstances was Senator Truman to be told anything more."[46]

Upon FDR's death, Truman would become president and commander in chief and be faced virtually overnight with the strategic and moral implications of the atom bomb. Roosevelt died just three weeks before the German surrender and so did not live to see the full triumph of his arsenal in Europe. America's industrial development, combined with George Marshall's "battle for men's minds," had indeed made America Roosevelt's "arsenal of democracy." Still, fighting in Asia continued, and this was the backdrop against which Truman learned about the bomb. "The victory won in the West," he declared following German surrender, "must now be won in the East."

From April 1 to June 21, 1945, the United States and Japan engaged in their last and bloodiest conventional battle of the war. The battle of Okinawa resulted in the deaths of over 13,000 U.S. and 70,000 Japanese troops, as well as more than 80,000 Japanese civilians.[47]

It has become generally accepted wisdom in the years since that the bombs dropped on the Japanese cities of Hiroshima and Nagasaki in August 1945 were necessary to end the war. But just as time has brought texture to the simplistic notion that Pearl Harbor was a total surprise, new information about the bombings of Hiroshima and Nagasaki reveals that there was more to them than purely "ending the war." Several historians, including Kai Bird, Pulitzer Prize–winning coauthor of *American Prometheus* and Gar Alperovitz, author of *The Decision to Use the Atomic Bomb*, have greatly informed the historical record on this incident. What their work reveals is that Truman's decision to use the bomb was at least partly guided by a desire to end the war with Japan in a way that would establish U.S. primacy over the Soviet Union in the postwar world. FDR's secret development of a bomb of such capacity for mass destruction, and Truman's subsequent decision to use it, changed forever the dynamic not only between America and the outside world but between the executive and the other branches at home.

Proponents of the bombings maintain that without them, the Japanese could not have been compelled to surrender, and that their continued fight would have incurred devastating American losses. Yet, as Alperovitz reveals, declassified Japanese telegraphs intercepted at that time showed that Truman and his advisers surely knew by 1945 that the Japanese were earnestly seeking a mediated end to the war.[48] By early July, Truman must have known that the only unshakable condition sought by the Japanese was that their emperor (seen by them as a direct descendant of God) be left in power and not subject to a war crimes tribunal—a condition the United States ultimately granted.[49]

Truman had, though, inherited from FDR a policy of accepting no less than unconditional surrender and he was intent on maintaining it. Unconditional surrender had been a point of contention among policymakers regarding the defeat of both Germany and Italy. Those opposed saw the demand as an overreach of America's international role—a form of nation building inconsistent with the framers' vision. Those in favor believed that anything less would signify a willingness to make deals with dictators. Allowing Mussolini, Hitler, or Hirohito to remain in power, they argued, would be unacceptable to the American people and an affront to the principles for which the war was fought.

Several of Truman's key advisers, however, including Secretary of War Stimson and Chief of Staff Admiral William D. Leahy, disagreed with this rigid perspective, urging Truman to soften his stance.[50] According to his diaries, Stimson himself tried three times in three weeks to persuade Truman to "clarify the surrender terms" for the Japanese in such a way as to let them know that their emperor would not be prosecuted.[51] Despite such objections, Truman remained insistent on unconditional surrender and saw the bombs as necessary for this purpose. "When the last Japanese division has surrendered unconditionally," he declared on May 8, 1945, "then only will our fighting job be done."[52]

On August 6, 1945, "Little Boy"—the first nuclear weapon ever used in warfare—was dropped on Hiroshima. Three days later, "Fat Man"—a more complex and powerful plutonium weapon—was dropped on Nagasaki. An estimated 200,000 people died in the two bombings. The Japanese surrendered within a week.

In his memoir, Admiral Leahy wrote: "It is my opinion that the use of this barbarous weapon at Hiroshima and Nagasaki was of no material assistance in our war against Japan. The Japanese were already defeated and ready to surrender because of the effective sea blockade and the successful bombing [of the mainland] with conventional weapons."[53]

Several other key insiders have voiced similar discomfort with Truman's decision. They include U.S. Fleet Commander Admiral Ernest King, Fleet Admiral Chester Nimitz, General Carl Spaatz, General Douglas MacArthur, and Brigadier General Carter Clarke. In *The Decision to Use the Atomic Bomb*, Alperovitz documents at least twelve instances at which one or another of Truman's key advisers entreated him to clarify the surrender terms.[54] They were urging him to signal to the Japanese that their emperor would not be deposed from power or tried as a war criminal. The perception was that with those assurances Japan would be inclined to surrender.

To varying degrees, these men all believed that the losses suffered by Japan by early summer 1945 (including the battles of Iwo Jima and Okinawa, the firebombing of Tokyo, and "Operation Starvation," an air campaign that crippled the country's logistics by mining its ports and waterways) would have compelled Japanese surrender before long.[55] Though it is unclear to what extent these individuals voiced their reservations at the time, each has in subsequent years publicized his feelings that the bombs were unwarranted, gratuitous, and even immoral.[56]

This perspective was summed up powerfully by Supreme Allied Commander Dwight D. Eisenhower, who would later write in his memoirs that he had expressed "grave misgivings" on the basis of his belief "that Japan was already defeated and that dropping the bomb was completely unnecessary."[57]

THE $2 BILLION QUESTION: WHY DID TRUMAN DO IT?

Speculating on Truman's motives is a risky business. It attempts to apply calm hindsight to a situation that was dizzying in its complexity and that above all, found Truman trying to come up to speed on a program of which he had previously been largely unaware. Still, the decision to use atomic weapons against Japan is so significant that it is necessary to try to understand what forces produced it. Though no such inquiry can produce a single, neat answer, an investigation has much to reveal about the origins and historical implications of Truman's decision.

Proponents of dropping the bomb argue that, however vast its death toll, it seemed a swift and sure way in a bloody wartime situation to end the war with Japan and avoid greater losses. Critics range from those who accuse Truman of having acted rashly, due to his inferior foreign policy skill relative to that of his predecessor, to those who think that the vast sums spent on the Manhattan Project pressured the fledgling president to deliver on its work. This dark suspicion was fueled by Truman's own words announcing the bombing of Hiroshima. "We have spent," Truman declared proudly, "two billion dollars on the greatest scientific gamble in history—and won."[58]

That Truman included this price tag in his first words of announcement implies that the cost was at least part of his calculation—that had the government gambled and lost, there would have been as much discredit to go around as there was glory for the success. The suspicion that the cost of the Manhattan Project played a role in the decision about the bombing was held not only by critics at the historical fringe but by Truman's secretary of war, Stimson, and by Admiral Leahy.

"It was my reaction," wrote Leahy in his memoir *I Was There*, "that the scientists and others wanted to make this test because of the vast sums that had been spent on the project. Truman knew that, and so did the other people involved."[59]

Whatever influence the immense cost of the Manhattan Project exerted on the new president, Alperovitz, Bird, and others have in recent years shed new light on a complex and previously classified series of events leading to the bombings that provides an even darker interpretation of Truman's thinking. Though the bombings of Hiroshima and Nagasaki might suggest that Truman simply ignored the calls by his key advisers to "clarify the surrender terms," there was a period of time during which this consideration was indeed a part of Truman's calculus. A close analysis of the events leading up to the bombings suggests the chilling prospect that Truman had indeed intended to soften his stance on unconditional surrender but then changed his mind after the successful Trinity test of the atom bomb in the New Mexico desert. As Bird, Alerpovitz, and others contend, this event may have altered Truman's strategic calculus about how best to end the war with Japan. Suddenly at work was not only the assurance of the bomb's power, demonstrated by the Trinity test, but a more long-term consideration of the bomb's role in a looming geopolitical contest with the Soviet Union.

The Soviets had, of course, been a vital partner in defeating the Nazis, and their aid in the fight against the Japanese had been a goal of FDR's inner circle. Yet it was only after the Soviets had made significant advances, culminating in the decisive victory in the gruesome battle of Stalingrad, that they were in a position to join the fight against Japan. At Yalta, in February 1945, Joseph Stalin had left no doubt of Soviet intentions, agreeing to enter the war against Japan within ninety days of German surrender. With Soviet involvement, the Japanese were sure to concede defeat.

Thus, once Germany fell on May 7, a two-part strategy formed inside Truman's Joint Intelligence Committee, based on the belief that if "the Japanese people, as well as their leaders, were persuaded both that absolute defeat was inevitable and that unconditional surrender did not imply national annihilation, surrender might follow fairly quickly."[60] The basis of this strategy had come from Prime Minister Winston Churchill who, at Yalta, had suggested a "mitigation" of the unconditional surrender doctrine in combination with a four-power surrender ultimatum to be presented to Japan.[61] It became increasingly clear over the months that followed that the Potsdam Conference, slated for July 1945, would be the setting for such an ultimatum.

According to Alperovitz, as Potsdam approached and Truman's advisers entreated him with increasing vigor to clarify the surrender terms, Truman began to sign on to a stick-and-carrot scenario in which the United States would indeed clarify the surrender terms at Potsdam, and then shortly thereafter, in mid-August (ninety days after German surrender), the Russians would enter the war. The Japanese, it was imagined, would receive their minimum term of surrender, see the futility of fighting Stalin, and fold.

The first evidence that Truman was amenable to this plan can be inferred from his official statement on May 8, 1945, following German surrender. Though uncompromising in tone, the statement represents a crucial departure from the rigidity of his previous stance. "Our blows will not cease," Truman declared, "until the Japanese military and naval forces lay down their arms in unconditional surrender."

Though Truman maintained the phrase "unconditional surrender," it is crucial to note that he had narrowed his demand from the unconditional surrender of the nation of Japan to the unconditional surrender of just "the Japanese military." The president went on to put an even finer point on this, explaining: "Just what does the unconditional surrender of the armed forces mean for the Japanese people? It means the end of the war. It means the termination of the influence of the military leaders who have brought Japan to the present brink of disaster. . . . Unconditional surrender does not mean the extermination or enslavement of the Japanese people."[62]

The next day, *The Washington Post* echoed the softening of the surrender terms, in effect lauding Truman's change in paradigm. "What we are suggesting, to be sure, is conditional surrender. What of it? Unconditional surrender was never an ideal formula."[63]

Between May 8 and July 15, as Potsdam approached, Truman's advisers made countless efforts to persuade him to qualify the unconditional surrender terms and Truman gave increasing signs of his openness to do so. At a meeting with his Joint Chiefs on June 18, when Admiral Leahy warned that unconditional surrender could make the Japanese "prefer to die fighting than accept military defeat," Truman seemed to concur, offering that he had for that very reason "left the door open for Congress to take appropriate action with reference to unconditional surrender."[64]

All of the months of debate over the surrender terms had culminated triumphantly in the drafting of the Potsdam Proclamation in which a crucial paragraph—paragraph 12—gave the Japanese comfort with regard to the maintenance of their emperor. It read:

> 12. The occupying forces of the Allies shall be withdrawn from Japan as soon as our objectives are accomplished and there has been established beyond doubt a peacefully inclined, responsible government of a character representative of the Japanese people. This may include a constitutional monarchy under the present dynasty if it be shown to the complete satisfaction of the world that such a government shall never again aspire to aggression.[65]

Despite its qualifying language, the paragraph represents an unmitigated capitulation to the desire of Truman's advisers that he soften the surrender terms. Its reference to "the present dynasty" was an unmistakable signal to Japan that the fate of their emperor and the soul of Japanese life would be theirs to determine. When Truman set sail for Potsdam aboard the USS *Augusta* on July 7, 1945, paragraph 12 was included in the draft proclamation traveling with him.

Yet in a development of historic significance, by July 26, when the Potsdam Proclamation was publicly announced, paragraph 12 had been altered, with the comforting passage about the Japanese emperor removed. Instead, it now read:

> 12. The occupying forces of the Allies shall be withdrawn from Japan as soon as these objectives have been accomplished and there has been

> established in accordance with the freely expressed will of the Japanese people a peacefully inclined and responsible Government.

What had changed?

The answer may at least in part lie in the successful Trinity test on July 16. When Truman was informed within hours of its success, the bomb seems to have shifted in his mind from a tool for ending the war with Japan to one that could establish America's primacy in the postwar global balance of power. Here, the analysis by Bird and Alperovitz goes to a dark place, revealing how America's posture toward a postwar Soviet Union may have been as much a motivating force behind the atomic bombings of Japan as the obvious desire to end the war.

From both his diaries and the minutes of meetings with Secretary of State James Byrnes and others, it is clear that Truman's mind after Trinity was on more than just Japanese surrender. His decision to use the bombs was apparently influenced by his sudden recognition of the strategic relevance of nuclear power to the postwar relationship between the United States and the Soviet Union.[66] His diary entry for July 18, 1945, for example, reveals his awareness of Japan's intention to surrender and yet his persistent view that the bomb was necessary.

Recording notes of a conversation at Potsdam with Churchill ("P.M.") less than three weeks before the bombing, Truman wrote: "Stalin had told P.M. of telegram from Jap Emperor asking for peace. . . . Believe Japs will fold up before Russia comes in." Then, in an excited tone, Truman added: "I am sure they will when Manhattan appears over their homeland."[67] He would seem to have already decided to use the bombs, despite Churchill's optimism regarding Japanese surrender.

Referring to the development of the bomb, Truman noted in his diary that day that he would "inform Stalin about it at an opportune time." That time came the next day during a break at Potsdam. On the back of a photo taken of them together, Truman wrote a boastful caption for the picture ". . . in which I tell Stalin we expect to drop the most powerful explosive ever made on the Japanese. He smiled and said he appreciated my telling him—but he did not know what I'm talking about—the atom bomb!" [emphasis Truman's] In addition to the aggressive spirit with which he anticipated the effect of the Manhattan Project on Japan, Truman's caption reveals that he harbored an almost playful sense of rivalry with America's erstwhile ally Stalin over the possession and planned use of the bomb.[68]

A month later, less than two weeks after the bombing, Albert Einstein, whose letter to FDR virtually launched America's atomic program, confessed publicly that he "deplored" America's use of the bomb and suspected it was "carried out to end the Pacific war before Russia could participate."[69] Einstein's reproach opens the door to the complex calculus with which Truman, without the knowledge of Congress or the American people, made the decision not only to use a weapon of mass destruction but to launch a preemptive show of force against a potential future adversary.

From a foreign policy perspective, the use of the bombs killed two birds with one stone—ending the war with Japan while firing the first shot in the Cold War against the Soviet Union. Strategic as Truman's decision in that regard might have been, the bombings of Hiroshima and Nagasaki are an extreme case of the kind of self-perpetuating militarism feared by the framers.

To be fair to Truman, one must recall that the path to Hiroshima and Nagasaki began in the concentration of executive power by FDR. Since as a senator and then vice president, Truman knew little or nothing about the Manhattan Project, he could not upon FDR's death have known FDR's full intentions for the bomb. Since FDR died before German surrender, Truman also could not have known what FDR might have done in the situation he now faced.

Though one can never know if Roosevelt would have used the bombs, it was his restructuring of the power of the executive that afforded Truman a zone of secrecy from which to launch the attacks, despite the better judgment of so many of his best advisers and without the knowledge of Congress or the American people.

Ever since the bombings, it has become conventional wisdom that, without them, one million American lives might have been lost, thus justifying the more than 200,000 Japanese lives taken. Yet, in his groundbreaking essay, "Seizing the Contested Terrain of Early Nuclear History," historian Barton Bernstein documents a shadowy enterprise in which Harvard University president and Truman adviser James Conant engineered the drafting and release of a February 1947 article in *Harper's Magazine* (attributed to former Secretary of War Stimson) that asserted this "one million" man figure. The only official estimate of potential U.S. losses available at the time, however, had appeared in a June 15, 1945 memo by the Joint War Plans Committee, which assumed a worst-case scenario of 20,000 to 46,000 American lives, a far cry from one million. By exaggerating the risk of not using the bombs, Conant shaped for decades the public's understanding of the necessity of the bombings and thus legitimized the atomic program that produced them (with all its secrecy and implications for expanded executive power) as a new and necessary component of the American way of war.

AND LET'S NOT FORGET ARTHUR MCCOLLUM

In this discussion of Hiroshima and Nagasaki, as is so often the case, there's an admitted tendency to focus more on Hiroshima. Indeed, Nagasaki often seems a historical footnote to Hiroshima. And yet it holds special poetry. Since the full geopolitical fallout of Hiroshima had not yet been felt when Nagasaki was bombed, there is a feeling of senseless overkill. Further, because the bomb used for this second attack was so much more powerful than that at Hiroshima, one gleans a haunting sense of a technological test being conducted at the cost of 80,000 Japanese lives.

Finally, Nagasaki returns us to Arthur McCollum who, in his infamous eight-point memo, advocated U.S. entry into a war that, however necessary, came to destroy his birthplace. When one recalls McCollum's upbringing in Nagasaki by Baptist missionary parents, and the image of him teaching the future emperor to do the Charleston, a particularly poignant irony is spotlighted. In a sense, McCollum's story is a metaphor for America herself, for just as the atom bomb shook his birthplace beyond recognition, so, too, it fundamentally challenged America's own foundations. Though in so many ways the war was a victory wrought from the democratic energies of the nation, it unleashed the opposing forces of executive overreach and militaristic aggression that would shape American policy for decades to come.

3

Fear in the Night

The connection between the discovery of gunpowder and the overthrow of feudalism by the bourgeoisie has been pointed out . . . and though I have no doubt exceptions can be brought forward, I think the following rule would be found generally true: that ages in which the dominant weapon is expensive or difficult to make will tend to be ages of despotism, whereas when the dominant weapon is cheap and simple, the common people have a chance. Thus, for example, tanks, battleships and bombing planes are inherently tyrannical weapons, while rifles, muskets, long-bows and hand-grenades are inherently democratic weapons.

George Orwell
"You and the Atomic Bomb"
October 19, 1945

1947 was a big year for America. On July 4, the *Roswell Daily Record*, the local paper of a small ranching community in southeastern New Mexico, revealed that an "unidentified flying object" had crashed near the Roswell Army Air Field outside of town. A press release was issued by the air field staff on July 8, then mysteriously changed on July 9, giving birth to a half century of conspiracy theories, books, and movies suspecting an intergalactic cover-up. The same year, DeForest Kelley, who would later play the legendary Dr. McCoy on the hit TV series *Star Trek*, would make his silver screen debut in the mystery thriller *Fear in the Night*.

All across America, fear was in the air. As South Dakota senator Chan Gurney declared in the *Congressional Record* of March 5, 1947, "To best describe in one word the feeling of peoples all over the globe in this year of 1947, I would select the one word 'fear.' There is fear of war, fear of starvation, fear of the spread of tyrannical government. The world is stumbling through black clouds of fear for the future, generally."

Just two years since its glorious triumph in World War II, America had become a paranoid giant. Whether from outer space or across the sea, Americans feared that the republic was in peril. Despite their victory over the Axis powers, President Truman and his advisers now confronted an aggressive Soviet Union poised to arm itself with atomic weapons and determined to promote the spread of communism beyond its borders.

The establishment of the United Nations in 1945 was inspired by the imperative to ensure that no such devastating war could ever happen again. "We all have to recognize," Truman declared at the drafting of the UN Charter, "no matter how great our strength, that we must deny ourselves the license to do always as we please."[1] With these words, Truman officially reversed both America's long tradition of isolationism and decreased her latitude to act unilaterally, aligning America's interests more closely with those of Europe than ever before.[2]

The rising fear of another war was both real and manufactured. Though the Cold War was fueled at times by exaggerated estimates of Soviet strength, Stalin's progress across Europe between 1945 and 1946, from Prussia to Königsberg, and finally to Berlin, was an undeniable cause for concern. The Red Army left behind occupying forces that either imposed military rule, or fostered homegrown Communist governments. Soviet general Chernyakhovsky warned in January 1945, "There shall be no mercy—for no one . . ."[3]

Though Stalin's expansion of Soviet-controlled territory was for the moment restricted to Europe, his rhetoric expressed global ambitions. On February 9, 1946, he issued what seemed a de facto declaration of war against capitalist nations. "The development of world capitalism," he declared at Moscow's Bolshoi Theater, "proceeds not in the path of smooth and even progress but through crisis and the catastrophes of war." A war of words with the West ensued, with Winston Churchill on March 5 coining the phrase "iron curtain" in a stirring speech warning of the Soviet threat, and Stalin responding by comparing him to Hitler.[4] With the horrors of atomic war burned so recently and indelibly in the public mind, these rising passions fueled public hysteria over the prospect of a nuclear holocaust.[5] Truman and his administration determined that a more assertive U.S. foreign policy was required, but they faced a renewed domestic spirit of isolationism that had compelled a rapid demobilization of U.S. forces at the end of the war.

Truman's secretaries of war and of the Navy had warned him in October 1945 that demobilization would undermine America's hard-won global position, but Truman could not contain public and congressional demands. Between 1945 and 1947, America's armed forces shrank, in today's dollars, from 12 million to just 1.5 million. Annual defense spending plummeted from $775 billion in January 1945 to $113 billion in 1947. Yet the growing Soviet threat would soon compel a renewed military buildup.

THE DOMINO THEORY

1947 was also the year that the House Un-American Activities Committee began its "Red Scare" hearings into alleged Communist activities in Hollywood, and Truman introduced a "loyalty oath" program to investigate the political affiliations of federal employees and require them to put assurances regarding the same in writing. Runaway fears led to the creation of federal civil defense programs and the marketing of fallout shelters. "Once upon a time," warned the narrator of a U.S. military film on the Soviet threat, "your hometown was safe. But not now! It is possible for a rocket to strike your home. Right now! Today! Right now! And, what defense remains? Strength! Strength! Ready if we need it!"[6]

Ironically, as Americans looked ever more fearfully to the skies and across the sea, the greatest threat to the republic was actually emerging from within. On February 27, 1947, behind the closed doors of the White House Cabinet Room, a new chapter of American foreign policy was being written, with fateful long-term consequences.

"The continual effort and alarm attendant on a state of continual danger," Alexander Hamilton had written in *The Federalist Papers*, "will compel nations the most attached to liberty to resort for repose and security to institutions which have a tendency to destroy their civil and political rights. To be more safe, they at length become willing to run the risk of being less free."[7] Fulfilling Hamilton's prophecy, the Truman Doctrine, born that February day in the Cabinet Room, set in motion an overhaul of America's foreign policy establishment—one that would expand America's role abroad and fundamentally alter her separation of powers at home.

The Soviets had already exerted pressure over the whole of Eastern Europe. Both Turkey and Greece now faced Communist threats. Stalin was pressing Turkey to forfeit land for Soviet bases in the Turkish Straits, and Greece was contending with a brutal Communist rebellion. Five decades later, when Saddam Hussein fashioned himself in Stalin's image, the comparison lay in more than just the mustache and dour demeanor. For, like Stalin, Saddam was a strange bedfellow to America and Britain, who would outlive his usefulness and become a threat.

Unlike Saddam, though, Stalin represented a real and formidable threat to his neighbors and, potentially, to the security of the United States. The February 27 meeting, which included President Harry Truman, Under Secretary of State Dean Acheson, and a bipartisan group of congressional leaders, was a watershed moment in the history of U.S. foreign policy as the Truman administration sought to address the threat. Acheson explained that six days earlier, British officials in Washington had alerted the State Department that war-ravaged Britain could no longer provide financial support to the governments of Greece and Turkey and asked the United States to provide such aid in their stead. The British leadership believed the Communist guerrilla rebellion in Greece was an extension of Stalin's policy of expansion and oppression.[8] Furthermore, if the Soviets gained control in Greece and Turkey, they would also gain access to the eastern Mediterranean, and from there to Western Europe. After two-facing the United States at Yalta and imposing an iron fist over Poland and Eastern Europe, Stalin seemed a major threat, no longer to be appeased.[9] However legitimate these concerns, the request by British officials for U.S. assistance to Greece and Turkey held both great symbolic and practical implications. It was an implicit admission by the British that they had been replaced by America as a power of global scope, a kind of passing of the torch of empire.[10]

The notion of "pulling British chestnuts out of the fire" at first fell on deaf ears. Then Acheson warned that there was more at stake than Greece and Turkey. If these states fell to the Communists, he argued, others might fall in an ominous chain reaction, an analysis that came to be known as the "domino theory."[11] The argument sparked fear in the room and set the Truman Doctrine in motion.

Two weeks later, on March 12, Truman appeared before a joint session of Congress to request $400 million in military and economic aid for Greece and Turkey. At the February 27 Cabinet Room meeting, Republican senator Arthur Vandenberg had advised Truman that if he wanted to win the support of the Republican-controlled Congress for this kind of expenditure, he would have to "scare the hell out of the American people." Truman's March 12 speech to Congress sought to do just that.[12] "The gravity of the situation which confronts the world today necessitates my appearance before a joint session of the Congress," the president warned. "The foreign policy and the national security of this country are involved."

Declaring that the "very existence" of the Greek state was at risk and that Turkey's security was vital to the "preservation of order in the Middle East," Truman made Acheson's domino theory the foundation of his argument for a new U.S. foreign policy. "I am fully aware of the broad implications involved if the United States extends assistance to Greece and Turkey," he said. "I believe that it must be the policy of the United States to support free peoples who are resisting attempted subjugation by armed minorities or by outside pressures."[13]

The Truman Doctrine was a sea change, the most significant expansion of American foreign policy since the Monroe Doctrine of 1823. Monroe had broadened America's military mandate from self-defense to the defense of all free peoples in the western hemisphere. The Truman Doctrine went further, interpreting a threat to free people anywhere as a threat to America. This loosened definition blurred the line between peacetime and war, effectively calling for permanent military preparedness, and expanding America's peacetime involvement around the world beyond anything previously contemplated.

FAST-FORWARD SIXTY YEARS

The developments of 1947 have been all but forgotten by the American public. But not by Colonel Lawrence Wilkerson. Born in 1945, just as the war was coming to a close, Wilkerson is too young to recall the events of 1947 firsthand. But sixty years later, they are at the forefront of his thoughts and the heart of his curriculum. Today, Wilkerson is a professor of national security policy at the College of William and Mary. He teaches his students that the transformation of American foreign policy set in motion by the Truman Doctrine, and particularly the passage of the National Security Act of 1947, has produced unintended negative consequences for the balance of powers among the executive, legislative, and judicial branches. Initiated as an effort to improve U.S. military preparedness and coordination as well as the nation's ability to gather intelligence on foreign threats, the act established a National Military Establishment, an independent air force therein, the National Security Council, and the Central Intelligence Agency. In doing so, it has concentrated increased warmaking power in the executive branch without providing for effective checks in Congress or the judiciary on that new power.

Despite his professorial civilian dress, Wilkerson is best known as an Army man who rose in the ranks to become chief of staff to Colin Powell, a post he held for the last sixteen of his thirty-five years in the Army. Along with Powell, Wilkerson joined the Bush administration in 2001 and left in January 2005.

Nine months later, on October 25, 2005, Wilkerson published an op-ed in the *Los Angeles Times* that was arguably the most outspoken attack levied at the Bush administration by a former insider. In it, he described the self-acknowledged "cabal" led by Cheney and Rumsfeld, as one whose "insular and secret workings" resembled the decision-making process "one would associate more with a dictatorship than a democracy." Wilkerson takes exception to a wide range of abuses of power by the Bush administration, but the breaking point for him came amid revelations of detainee abuse, which he sees as a gross violation of American principles and standard procedures.

On July 21 of that year, Cheney had met with three senior Republicans on the Senate Armed Services Committee to urge them to block legislation that would prevent the continued "cruel, inhuman or degrading treatment" of detainees by the U.S. military. "That was the straw that broke the camel's back," Wilkerson recalls. "A vice president—arguably the most powerful in our history—in public, advocating torture. Unprecedented."[14]

If Wilkerson had any second thoughts about his bold attack on the vice president, they were quickly put to rest. The very next day, Cheney appeared on Capitol Hill in a visit that earned him the title "Vice President for Torture" on the editorial page of *The Washington Post*. Joining a Republican Senate luncheon, he restated his case for greater latitude for the administration to authorize torture.

Wilkerson was appalled. "Who understands the perversion of American values better than a person who's been part of that perversion?" he asks with a raised eyebrow and the boyish South Carolina lilt he's never lost. Wilkerson chooses the word "perversion" advisedly, for it was the detainee abuse scandal at Iraq's Abu Ghraib prison that compelled him to oppose the omnipotent Cheney over the administration's detainee policies.

YOUR BEST KILLERS

Wilkerson's account of the fight within the administration over Abu Ghraib speaks volumes about just how out of balance executive power—and the potential for abuse of that power—has swung. In April 2004, just before the photographs of abuse at Abu Ghraib were made public, Powell alerted Wilkerson that a scandal was about to erupt and that he wanted a dossier of every document that could shed light on how the events at Abu Ghraib came to pass. Along with Powell's legal adviser William Taft IV (grandson of the twenty-seventh president), Wilkerson spent the next eighteen months conducting an exhaustive study. "We got our hands on all the documentation we could and interviewed people in a nonattribution environment. No press. Just military. And I began to absorb more and more of what was happening on the ground and not just Iraq, but Afghanistan, in Cuba at Guantánamo and other places."

For Wilkerson, the investigation was more than an assignment. Unlike Cheney and others, when Wilkerson speaks of torture, he speaks from experience of its effects and implications. As a first lieutenant, Wilkerson was deployed to Vietnam in March 1969 and spent a year in combat.

"When you ask somebody to kill people for the state, particularly for a democracy, you're asking them to do something that's not necessarily out of their character—because every man can be a beast—but something contrary to their upbringing and education. When you do that, you need every rule, every tool in your kit bag to keep them from going overboard." It was in Vietnam that Wilkerson encountered firsthand "how bad policy flows downstream from the top.

"Often in your platoon, your best killers, your best warriors are those who will become your beast. They will become people who will kill little girls and boys, and burn villages. We operated many times in 'free-fire zones' where you'd shoot anything that moved. When I first took over the platoon, there were occasions where we did that, and it had been little girls, women, boys.

"So I have a particularly poignant understanding of the tools the lieutenant or captain on the ground needs to have available to him to keep people from going beyond the laws of war, the Geneva Conventions, as was done in Abu Ghraib, Bagram, Afghanistan, and Guantánamo. That's the reason I had this gut-level reaction when I learned what was going on."

Perhaps the most stirring image of all those leaked from the secret world of horror at Abu Ghraib was that of a hooded detainee, perched on a wooden crate, arms outstretched in a Christ-like pose, with wires attached to his genitals, hands, and feet. For an administration that had gone to lengths to reject public accusations that the Iraq War was motivated by the president's own personal religious zeal, the symbolism could not have been worse. But for Wilkerson and others versed in the particulars of American warfare—particularly of the interrogation techniques of past wars—the pose was all too recognizable and revealed much about the origins of the scandal. "The Vietnam," as the pose is called in intelligence circles, is a standard technique of torture that harkens back to the Vietnam War. Its reappearance told Wilkerson that the "flunkies" perpetrating this form of abuse were not reinventing the wheel but receiving instructions from older, more seasoned officers.[15]

"I'd had it." Wilkerson shakes his head. "By the time I got to October

2005, I couldn't walk into a courtroom under rules of evidence and prove that anybody had done anything so that they would go to jail, *because that's not the way it works at those levels of power.* But I knew in my heart that it had been condoned at the highest levels of our government, particularly by the vice president of the United States and the secretary of defense. It was not bad apples. It was policy."

TAKING THE GLOVES OFF

Wilkerson's attack on the vice president and Cheney's defiant follow-up were the public expression of long-standing internal tensions within the administration. As Karen DeYoung writes in *Soldier*, her sweeping biography of Colin Powell, differences within Bush's cabinet, present from the outset, calcified after 9/11 into clearly drawn battle lines.

"A growing antipathy," DeYoung notes, "between Powell and the State Department, on one side, and Cheney, Rumsfeld and their senior staffs, on the other, extended far beyond specific policy disagreements. It was institutional, ideological and even personal."[16] The differences inside the administration had reached such a point that even neoconservative ally William Kristol wrote six months after the start of the Iraq War that the administration was in a state of "civil war."[17]

The conflict between the State Department on one side and the Pentagon and vice president's office on the other preceded the march to war in Iraq. "There was clear friction over the North Korean situation in the six-party talks," Wilkerson notes. "Clear friction over U.S.-Iran policy. Clear friction in general over U.S.-European policy. And Powell spent much of his energy trying to keep the transatlantic relationship from splintering even worse than it did." The results of Powell's efforts were mixed. While he did not prevail in efforts to shape U.S. policy on Iran, Wilkerson argues that Powell was successful in fighting Cheney and Rumsfeld's impulse to make China "the new Soviet Union." Following the collision of an American and Chinese plane on April 1, 2001, over the South China Sea, the president sided with Powell in valuing China's economic importance too highly to support Cheney and Rumsfeld's adversarial approach.

According to Wilkerson, these and other areas of disagreement between the camps all seemed like customary intellectual fair play—healthy, Socratic debate between competitive players—until Abu Ghraib. Wilkerson argues that Abu Ghraib represented "the culmination of a colossal battle within the statutory decision-making process" over the treatment of detainees. Simply put, the Cheney/Rumsfeld camp after 9/11 wanted "to take the gloves off" in the war on terror, while Powell and company sought to uphold customary U.S. wartime standards.

This standoff intensified when Bush, supported by a compliant Justice Department, sided with the Pentagon against the State Department in declaring the Geneva Conventions inapplicable to al Qaeda and the Taliban. In response, a flurry of internal memoranda revealed passionate debate between opposing voices within the administration.

Cheney's no-holds-barred approach was summarized in a January 22, 2002, memo drafted for presidential counsel Alberto Gonzales by Assistant Attorney General Jay S. Bybee. The memo argues that neither domestic law (the War Crimes Act) nor international law (the Geneva Conventions) would constrain the United States in its handling of al Qaeda prisoners. It also asserted that President Bush had constitutional authority to "suspend our treaty obligations toward Afghanistan" because it was a "failed state."[18]

Powell disagreed, arguing that the Geneva Conventions should apply to al Qaeda and the Taliban. In a January 25 memo to Gonzales, he maintained that the no-holds-barred approach would "reverse over a century of U.S. policy and practice . . . and undermine the protections of the law of war for our troops, both in this specific conflict and in general." He also warned of significant "negative international reaction," which would make "military cooperation more difficult to sustain." Most pointed, he warned that such an approach would "make us more vulnerable to domestic and international legal challenges and deprive us of important legal options," rendering it likely that the administration "will be challenged in international fora (UN Commission on Human Rights; World Court; etc.)."

On February 7, the White House declared that the Geneva Conventions would in principle apply to the conflict in Afghanistan, but that the Taliban and al Qaeda would specifically not be granted prisoner-of-war status. The argument was that the groups did not represent a state and thus did not enjoy the protection of the Conventions. "The President's decision," Wilkerson recalls, "was a compromise between the need to maintain security on the one hand and our traditional, political, and cultural values on the other—between the national security state and the republic. It wasn't the compromise Powell would've recommended. But at least it was a compromise. It wasn't a wholesale abandonment of everything we stood for."

So what happened?

"What happened," Wilkerson explains, "was that underneath that memo the secretary of defense, with the cover of the vice president, went out and executed what they'd argued for all along. *The gloves were off.*" Cheney and Rumsfeld had, he asserts, subverted the president's stated policy. Six years later, in a 2008 exposé, ABC News would reveal that, despite the administration's claims that detainee abuse practices were the work of bad apples at lower levels of the command chain, "enhanced interrogation techniques" had in fact been discussed by a "principals committee" that included the president, Cheney, Rumsfeld, Rice, and even Powell.[19] According to Wilkerson, though, these meetings were highly orchestrated and the information discussed in them was of a very narrow focus. From Powell's point of view, Wilkerson says, the unusual techniques discussed that were inconsistent with longstanding norms and international legal restrictions regarding intelligence practices, "were discussed only in connection with certain exceptional high-value al Qaeda suspects and were only to be carried out in secret by the CIA."

According to Wilkerson, Powell's ultimate shock over the details of Abu Ghraib was compounded by what it revealed on a personal level for him—that Cheney and Rumsfeld had conspired to make an end run around his judgment and authority. Despite Powell's clear concerns, Rumsfeld and Cheney had drawn license from those "principals" meetings to "find ways to create a legal fabric for themselves to be able to engage in the same kind of activity the CIA had been authorized in rare cases to engage in, but to do so with the military. Rumsfeld wanted his own hand in the intelligence process, so he authorized people to do the same kinds of things across the military structure where people were being detained." In effect, Rumsfeld and Cheney had taken off the gloves not only in their treatment of the detainees but in their treatment of the statutory national security decision-making process, and specifically Powell's authority in it. Faced with the compromise forged by the president out of their disagreement with Powell, they had simply gone around it.

Recognizing that Powell's participation in the now infamous "principals" meeting makes him in some respect an accomplice to the decision to have authorized such questionable practices, Wilkerson offers a sober assessment of his former boss' accountability. "You can criticize Powell for participating in the narrowly conceived program as it related to the CIA and certain high-value suspects," Wilkerson concedes. "But you can't criticize him for knowing or participating in the migration of that program and its parameters into and across the armed forces. That responsibility rests with Rumsfeld and Cheney alone."

Following Bush's election in 2000, Powell was the president's first cabinet choice. He was also the one with the greatest star power and credibility. In a December 20, 2000, op-ed entitled "Powell, A Serious Man to Be Tested Before Long," Thomas L. Friedman of *The New York Times* expressed the widely held view that the revered former chairman of the Joint Chiefs ran the risk of "towering" over the president. Yet, as demonstrated by the Abu Ghraib saga, "the most trusted man in America" found himself and his team marginalized by Cheney, Rumsfeld, and their network. How could such a "towering" figure lose so much currency?

That Cheney and Rumsfeld were able so deftly to work around Powell is in large part a result of the National Security Act's seismic shift of power away from the State Department and of the creation of a labyrinthine structure of power within the Department of Defense established.

THE INCREDIBLE SHRINKING STATE DEPARTMENT

No image captures more pointedly the mysterious State Department career of Colin Powell than that of the secretary making the crucial argument before the United Nation in the administration's case for war in Iraq—a war that by all accounts he approached with greater caution than his more hawkish colleagues. Though his decision to throw his formidable credibility behind the president's call for war would prove instrumental in galvanizing public support, it was on a deeper level a far cry from the Powell the public expected to see, holding his own against his formidable administration colleagues. Instead, it appeared that the soldier had bowed to the authority of outspoken civilians, finding himself in a position he would later describe as the low point of his career.

For the public, as for Karen DeYoung, Powell's marginalization to a backseat role in the administration seemed to derive from the fact that he is, above all, a soldier for whom deference to authority is primary. Wilkerson emphasizes a different aspect of the story. The national security developments of 1947, he contends, have both directly and indirectly fostered a national security decision-making structure that tilts away from the State Department and favors military problem solving in foreign affairs.

"We created the national security state," Wilkerson nods gravely, referring to the passage of the act. In doing so, America tipped the balance toward militarism. "Marshall, Eisenhower, Truman, [James] Forrestal, and others," he explains, "understood that the power America was going to wield from 1945 on was going to be very different from the power it had wielded pre-1941. And that the apparatus for wielding that power was not quite up to the task."

Chalmers Johnson, a former consultant to the CIA's Office of National Estimates, and most recently the author of *Blowback* and *The Sorrows of Empire*, portrays the events of 1947 as pivotal to America's evolution from a modest republic to a global hegemon: "The American government was transformed after World War II once Harry Truman had driven us into the Cold War with the Truman Doctrine. We begin at this time to transform our government in such a way that it simply overwhelms the structure that was created in the Constitution of 1787."[20]

In practical terms, the National Security Act sought to address the increased security demands of the Truman Doctrine and the world of new challenges such an expanded national security mandate implied. Before its passage on July 26, the act was fiercely debated by members of Congress in the summer of 1947, and it is from their various voices that one can divine the conflicting network of motives and considerations from which the act emerged in its initial form. Though there were any number of less overt motivations and dynamics underlying it, the act on its face had three basic purposes.

The first and most widely acknowledged purpose was, in the words of Illinois Democrat Charles Price, "to increase the efficiency of the military organization."[21] This meant both improved coordination and cooperation between the military branches and a commitment to greater readiness, with a particular eye to the new significance of airpower in future wars. At that time, the armed services consisted of the Army, run by the War Department, the Navy, a department unto itself, and the Air Command, which had theretofore fallen under the control of the Army.

One of the crucial lessons learned from World War II had been that interservice rivalries and non-cooperation among the services had accounted for what Eisenhower called "unreadiness" that had needlessly cost American lives and wasted substantial funds. As the Cold War dawned, these rivalries were resurfacing with a vengeance, with the various services vying for national security resources and, in particular, control of the Army Air Command.[22] The situation cried out for remedy and the National Security Act sought to provide one by creating an independent Air Force and by unifying and better organizaing it and the other services under one roof.

The second acknowledged purpose of the act was to provide for better intelligence gathering, analysis, and dissemination processes in an effort to correct for the perceived intelligence failures that allowed the sneak attack on Pearl Harbor.

The third acknowledged purpose was, in the words of Republican Congressman Edward Robertson of Wyoming, "to promote the national security by providing for the coordination of all elements of national security."[23]

With these goals, the act added several new instruments of foreign policy decision making and implementation to America's national security system. They included:

- the Defense Department and the Office of the Secretary of Defense, initially called the National Military Establishment, but changed to Department of Defense (DoD) in 1949
- the Central Intelligence Agency

- the National Security Council and the post of National Security Adviser
- the Air Force

To think that such an extraordinary list of policy instruments—all of which are now an accepted part of everyday life—was simply added to America's policymaking system from one day to the next is remarkable. Their addition, of course, was a development of sweeping—and to some extent unintended—consequences. While these additions may on paper seem straightforward, subtler motivations among members of Congress were at work that had as much to do with achieving an improved balance of power among the branches as with improving America's defense and intelligence system.

As the saying goes, a camel is just a horse built by a committee, and nowhere is this more true than in Washington. In the act's ultimate expression of its goals one sees the unmistakable marks of compromise between the competing agendas of those in Congress as well as between the legislative and executive branches more broadly. The two most significant underlying motivations, unstated in the language of the act yet unmistakable in its effect, were to rein in the power of the executive and to reduce the influence of the State Department as the dominant force in America's foreign affairs. Also at work were partisan agendas, notably among Republican opponents of FDR who had long been frustrated by his concentration of power.

When the Republicans took control of Congress in 1947, they moved quickly to try to reverse elements of FDR's executive tilt. The most notable step they took—and one which was implicitly a swipe at his long reign—was to propose what became the 22nd Amendment to the Constitution, limiting the number of consecutive terms a president may serve. (It would be ratified in 1951.) But beyond limiting the executive's time in office, Republicans in Congress wanted to constrain his decision-making power. Perhaps due to FDR's heroic status and recent passing, these deliberations in Congress do not name him. Instead, the debate was framed in reference to a 1919 bill regarding presidential powers that had been proposed but not passed. The intention was to constrain future presidents from making policy decisions as close to the vest as FDR had done. "During the war," remarks Wilkerson, "FDR had even kept his own Secretary of State Cordell Hull out of the most sensitive policy decisions he made," a style of decision making that Wilkerson describes as "knowing everything and telling no one anything." Despite FDR's revered status, many wanted to undo the sweeping wartime powers he had assumed. Wilkerson adds, "They didn't want the secrecy, the concentration of power, the lack of transparency in decisions of life and death."

So it was that in its efforts to provide for improved coordination of national security policy, the act established the National Security Council. By designating which members of government would serve on the Council (including the vice president, secretary of state, secretary of defense, and other "secretaries and under secretaries of other executive departments and the military departments"), Congress sought to give itself greater access to and influence over the president's formulation of foreign policy.

The second underlying motive of the act—to counterbalance the power of the State Department—was in part achieved through the creation of the DoD itself, a massive new counterinfluence within the executive branch. But it was furthered by the creation of the CIA as an intelligence apparatus inside the executive branch yet independent from any pre-existing department therein. Prior to World War II, U.S. intelligence activity was divided haphazardly among various departments of the government, with the State Department overseeing the lion's share, and some in Congress had faced difficulty during the war securing information from the State Department. According to Wilkerson, there was a strong feeling as America entered the Cold War that the State Department was too controlling and inept—that it had failed to protect the nation from the attack on Pearl Harbor, and was generally "ill-equipped to meet the nation's future intelligence gathering, analysis, and dissemination needs."

These underlying goals produced unintended consequences. While the State Department was surely weakened by the act—perhaps excessively—it would be hard to argue, sixty years later, that the effort to rein in the power of the executive has succeeded.

"The lesson is: *be careful what you wish for*," Wilkerson laughs. As his own experiences at the State Department painfully revealed, one effect of the act has been to dangerously diminish the power of State by comparison to the massive concentration of power in the Department of Defense. "Now the State Department is a thirty-billion-dollar department," he says, "and the Defense Department is a half-trillion-dollar department."

Wilkerson's lament is more than just that of an embittered former State Department official, more than just that of someone who watched his boss suffer indignities at the hands of men far less versed in the realities of war. Of all the monies spent today in the United States on foreign affairs, 93 percent passes through the Department of Defense and only 7 percent through the State Department. This simple statistic goes a long way in explaining why America finds herself so often turning to "the military instrument" to solve international problems.

Dangerously, too, in Wilkerson's eyes, the National Security Act has resulted in an accumulation of excessive power in the executive branch, with ineffectual checks on that power in the other branches. This accumulation of power is not in itself a necessary recipe for abuse, but the mechanisms set up by the act have too often tended toward that outcome. The Bush administration has pushed the limits of executive power and the individuals responsible for doing so are certainly to be faulted for their advocacy of excess. But they were empowered to do so—to have run roughshod over Colin Powell's authority and to have crafted a secretive plan for attacking Iraq—by the structural changes enacted by the act.

To understand the sum impact of the National Security Act, it is instructive to examine how these individual changes have influenced policy in the intervening years.

A Military Superorganization: The Exploding Pentagon

The National Security Act was intended, in its own words, "to provide a comprehensive program for the security of the United States" through "the establishment of integrated policies and procedures for the departments, agencies, and functions of the Government relating to the national security." Advocates thus argued for the establishment of "a Department of Defense, including the three military Departments of the Army, the Navy (including naval aviation and the United States Marine Corps), and the Air Force under the direction, authority, and control of the Secretary of Defense."[24] The provision was not without its critics. During the heated congressional debates over the act's passage, some in Congress and the media decried the risks of creating a "military superorganization." The military editor of *The New York Times*, Hanson Baldwin, asked: "How can we prepare for total war without becoming a 'garrison state' and destroying the very qualities and virtues and principles we originally aimed to save?" As Michael J. Hogan writes in *A Cross of Iron,* "Several [congressional] committee members expressed great alarm" about the centralization of power in the DoD. Democratic senator Warren R. Austin of Vermont warned of a military dictatorship.[25]

In the years since, the Department of Defense has become the behemoth that was feared, with, even by its own calculation, some 5 million employees[26] and an annual budget larger than the GDP of Russia.[27] The president's 2009 budget provides $515.4 billion for the DoD's base budget, and also requested $70 billion in funding to support its wars in Afghanistan and Iraq.[28]

One of the largest office buildings in the world to this day, the Pentagon is home to over 20,000 employees. Construction of the 6.6 million-square-foot building began three months before Pearl Harbor, on September 11, 1941, and was completed on January 15, 1943, in order to handle the huge mobilization required to fight World War II. Intended to serve as a temporary military headquarters, FDR hoped it would later serve as a national archive. "The War Department will doubtless object to giving up the Pentagon building," he said, "but it is much too large for them, if we get a decent peace."[29] The construction of a building as monumental as the Pentagon to house the DoD is a perfect metaphor for the sea change from the emergency posture of World War II to the posture of permanent preparedness of the Cold War.

The Pentagon has virtually exploded in scale over the past sixty years. According to its own Web site, the DoD "manages an inventory of installations and facilities" consisting of "several hundred thousand individual buildings and structures" at home and in over 163 foreign countries, covering "over 30 million acres of land."[30] The sheer scale of the department in personnel, physical breadth, and economic wealth explains at least in part how it is able simply to overwhelm other departments within the executive branch (e.g., State) and to exert irresistible pressures upon policymakers.

Magnifying this power further is its concentration into the hands of a single civilian, just as critics feared at the time of the act's passage. This issue was one of the most heated points of contention in the debates of 1947, with the act's congressional opponents citing the danger of creating an "American Gestapo" and "domination by a group of military professionals." Yet power was concentrated even further in the Office of the Secretary of Defense, and within the bureaucracy of the Pentagon, when the act was amended in 1949. Prior to this amendment, each branch—Army, Navy, and Air Force—had its own cabinet-level secretary reporting directly to the president. With the 1949 amendment, this cabinet-level status was withdrawn. Only the secretary of defense was now a cabinet-level official. The act's advocates believed that establishing such a centralized structure would solve the problem of interservice rivalries. Not only had those rivalries impeded the prosecution of the war, but they had also prevented the Departments of War and Navy from providing Truman with a requested postwar plan for the proposed size and structure of the military.[31] Nonetheless, assigning such awesome warmaking power to a single appointee of the president, this amendment further tilted the delicate balance between the branches toward the executive, giving the president an unprecedented level of control over the national security agenda.

For many Americans, the path from 9/11 to Iraq shed new light on the inner workings of the Defense Department. Ever since the crash of American Airlines Flight 77 into the Pentagon's western wall exposed the concentric network of rafters and joinery constructed in the 1940s, the building's inner workings have been the subject of increased public awareness. The complex array of agencies operating under the auspices of the secretary of defense has come to light, from well-known ones like the Defense Intelligence Agency and the National Security Agency to lesser known ones (some of which are now defunct), like the Office of Special Plans, the White House Iraq Group, the Defense Policy Board, and the Office of Strategic Influence. The secretary of defense today presides over a vast military bureaucracy (much of it invisible from the outside) that enables him to carry out the directions of its "ultimate authority"—namely, the president of the United States—with limited involvement from Congress.

If a president is inclined toward military action (as Madison and Jefferson suspect all executives are), he is afforded one-stop shopping by the mechanisms of security policy and military power available to him through this vast bureaucracy. The Pentagon is a self-sufficient and full-service foreign policy instrument that can provide intelligence and expert analysis and then, on the basis of these, advocate, plan for, and ultimately implement military action solely at the will of the president. This enables a president to circumvent the inconvenience of achieving consensus among disparate voices even inside his own administration, including whatever dissent might be voiced by the diplomatic corps at the State Department. Which returns us to the twisted tale of Colin Powell's fateful appearance before the United Nations wielding faulty intelligence to make the case for war.

"Colin Powell is not an intelligence person," Wilkerson points out. "He's not an intelligence professional. He had to spend five days at Langley and two days in New York City in briefings with George Tenet [then head of the CIA], John McLaughlin, and others. He had to rely on them for his information. And he did. And like me he rues the day he did. But the bigger question is why was Tenet so incredibly reassured? Why did he call it 'slam-dunk'? 'Iron-clad'?"

Wilkerson's question points to the fallibility of the decision-making process as designed by the National Security Act. Much of what has been written about the handling of intelligence in the lead-up to the Iraq War revolves around neoconservative influence in the Bush administration. Wilkerson shares this concern yet sees it as a demonstration of the national security system's larger susceptibility to abuse from any group with its own privately held agenda.

Information has always been central to warmaking—from the intelligence that leads to war to that which guides its planning, to that which leads to surrender or victory. In an information age more than ever, information is central not only as the stuff on which military decisions are based but as a weapon in its own right. As intelligence grows increasingly central, the proliferation of specialized informational offices within the Pentagon, such as the now notorious Office of Special Plans, increases the chance that intelligence will be invisibly crafted to suit preordained purposes.

A common strategic precept among military planners holds that oppositions shape each other. Thus, as international terror increasingly assumes an elusive, decentralized, cellular structure—one not focused in a single state or state-sponsored entity but rather spread across a tapestry of interwoven threads—so too the military command structure of its adversary is assuming a more complex, elusive, and cellular form. This may go some way toward explaining the emergence during the lead-up to the Iraq War of a litany of previously unknown offices inside the Pentagon—small splinter cells working under the auspices of the secretary of defense "offline" from the officially recognized organizational structure of the DoD. Among these splinter groups none was more notorious than the all-too-Orwellian Office of Special Plans, conceived by Under Secretary of Defense Paul Wolfowitz to find evidence to support what Wolfowitz, Rumsfeld, and others privately sought to prove: that Iraq was linked to 9/11 and posed an ongoing threat to the United States.

Of course, a good deal of the intelligence used to make the case for war was gathered by the CIA, and George Tenet's assertion that the information collected comprised a "slam-dunk" case is widely seen as pivotal. Yet a closer look at the dynamics set up by the creation of separate intelligence-gathering operations within the DoD, under no obligation to coordinate or be in any way subservient to the CIA, reveals how the intelligence provided by these disparate sources is nonetheless quite closely linked.

Lieutenant Colonel Karen Kwiatkowski, who served in the Air Force from 1978 to 2003 and spent her last five years of service at the Pentagon, watched firsthand as the Office of Special Plans gained a dangerous level of influence over the Pentagon's intelligence-gathering processes and, by extension, over how this intelligence was used to support the administration's case for war. Kwiatkowski spent the last of her twenty-five years of service at the DoD's Near East and South Asia Directorate, whose purview included Iraq policy until it was marginalized by the newly formed Office of Special Plans. Today, Lieutenant Colonel Kwiatkowski lives in the Shenandoah Valley with her family, where she raises horses and, like Wilkerson, teaches college.

With the same blunt ease she might use to explain corruption in the horse trade, Kwiatkowski reveals two ways that members of the Bush administration seeking war with Iraq jerry-rigged the intelligence process. The first involves pressure by members of the administration upon existing intelligence agencies to "manufacture the *right kind* of actionable intelligence" supporting the need to overthrow Saddam Hussein.[32]

"Intelligence producers," she explains, "don't like to make radical statements, go out on a limb. They tend to be cautious and conservative." Kwiatkowski maintains that in 2002, "the CIA and the DIA [Defense Intelligence Agency] in particular were producing information that was far more conservative than anything in President Bush's speeches," and that, in response, pressure was exerted upon them "to tell them what they want to hear."

"The way the intelligence system works," she explains, "is that the DIA and CIA and the various other agencies each have an identified policy customer for whom they produce intelligence. It doesn't matter what administration we're talking about, if that customer's not pleased with the intelligence, the intelligence producer runs the risk of becoming marginalized."

In answer to Wilkerson's $64,000 question of why George Tenet saw the intelligence about Saddam as "slam-dunk" and why he spent seven days convincing Colin Powell of its legitimacy, Kwiatkowski's description of the pressure on intelligence producers to "satisfy their customers" is haunting. "There are thirteen different intelligence agencies," she explains. "You don't tell 'em what they want to hear, and they will go to other sources." With such an explosion of agencies, it's a buyer's market for intelligence, with each agency competing to outstrip the others to make its product more attractive to the "customer."

According to Kwiatkowski, the Bush administration's creation of its own intelligence instruments to "cherry-pick" certain types of information that supported their case for war both intensified this competitive market pressure and showed favoritism toward certain kinds of intelligence product. An instrument like the Office of Special Plans, which was in effect a joint venture between certain neoconservatives in the Pentagon (Bill Luti, Douglas Feith, Stephen Cambone) and their allies inside the Office of the Vice President (Dick Cheney, Scooter Libby), put pressure on the CIA to produce and approve intelligence of a specific nature. Presumably, it was in this slanted competition with other intelligence producers that Mr. Tenet—even in his purportedly independent capacity at the CIA—was inclined to produce his own brand of supportive intelligence. And when even this didn't satisfy, to declare the product cobbled together by the DoD's Office of Special Plans and the Office of the Vice President "slam-dunk" and to tell Powell as much.

So it was that the Pentagon's capacity to expand its own internal bureaucratic complexity and critical mass, and to do so in cahoots with compatriots inside the executive branch, generated a groundswell of support for the case for war. "In the staff meetings we had in the summer of 2002," Kwiatkowski recalls, "it became clear to me that this war was going to happen. An invasion of Iraq, a toppling of Saddam Hussein, was basically the given. It was just a matter of getting the American people up to speed and getting them behind this effort. Any other means by which Iraq could be dealt with were not discussed."

Shedding awkwardly harsh light on the roots of Wilkerson's perception of an emasculated State Department, Kwiatkowski adds that beyond the unspoken inevitability of the Iraq War, there was articulate communication by Defense Department appointees about how to get "resistance from the State Department to go away. How do we eliminate State Department resistance?" Alongside this effort, Kwiatkowski also recalls the conversations focusing on "how to ensure that the NSC, and the media, and the president *say the right things*."

Kwiatkowski's firsthand experience confirms the claims of Seymour Hersh in his October 27, 2003, *New Yorker* article entitled "The Stovepipe." Providing an invaluable visual metaphor, Hersh explains how ventures like the Office of Special Plans created a "stovepipe" through which raw intelligence from the field could bypass "customary procedures for vetting intelligence" and reach the highest levels of the executive branch without being "subjected to rigorous scrutiny." Hersh quotes Kenneth Pollack, a former National Security Council expert, to say that the Bush administration "dismantle[d] the existing filtering process that for fifty years had been preventing the policymakers from getting bad information. They created stovepipes to get the information they wanted directly to the top leadership."[33]

The power of the DoD to engineer pressure toward war is by no means limited to machinations such as these within the hallways of the

Pentagon. In the years since 1947, the DoD has become the gravitational epicenter of a vast system of recruitment centers, military bases, laboratories, testing grounds, command centers, defense-related corporations, and academic institutions. It was this constellation of institutions servicing the national defense that Dwight Eisenhower called the "military-industrial complex" and warned against in his legendary 1961 Farewell Address. These entities all revolve around the DoD, which, like the sun, both fuels them and exerts a gravitational pull on the trajectory of their activities.

Once the president makes a case for war—and even while that case is being mounted—this massive architecture of the military-industrial complex's interlocking parts can be marshaled to prepare and implement all aspects of a military enterprise. While troops are recruited at centers and then trained at bases, their equipment and weapons are developed, tested, and manufactured in laboratories, testing fields, and facilities administered through the cumulative efforts of military, academic, and corporate institutions.

Within a colossus like the DoD there will be a wide spectrum of views on war and peace, hard power vs. soft, but it can fairly be said that the DoD's primary "business" is war. Even on its own Web site, the DoD compares itself to several of the world's leading multinational corporations. The site boasts that "in terms of people and operations, we're busier than just about all of the nation's largest private sector companies," and goes on to claim that with "four hundred nineteen point three billion dollars" and "more than 3 million employees," the department has a larger budget and more employees than Wal-Mart, ExxonMobil, or General Motors.

With surprising temerity given the widely held view expressed by Major General Smedley Butler in 1935 that "war is a racket," the Web site takes the corporate metaphor further, calling the president "our CEO," the U.S. Congress our "Board of Directors," and the American people "our stockholders." Approaching near absurdity, the site goes on to stress that "our stockholders know us pretty well. Almost everyone has had a family member or friend who either works for us now, or used to. We exist to protect these citizen stockholders, for without their support we would be out of business."

As described so candidly, the DoD's acknowledged capacity to mobilize such private and public resources is indespensable in arming a president to overcome possible opposition to any war—in Congress, among the public, and even within his own administration. With the capacity to mobilize support from far-reaching constituencies of the military-industrial complex, the DoD has the capacity simply to dwarf the State Department.

Does this always happen? No. Under President Clinton, for example, Secretary of State Madeleine Albright was not marginalized by Secretary of Defense William Cohen. The dynamics at that time were actually reversed, with Secretary Albright famously arguing for military intervention in the Balkans. In her memoir *Madame Secretary* Albright recalls a now famous conversation with Colin Powell in which she asked the former chairman of the Joint Chiefs, "What are you saving this superb military for, Colin, if we can't use it?"[34]

This exchange is often cited as a demonstration of Albright's relative hawkishness, but it seems a rather healthy one inside any administration weighing the value of soft power against hard. The DoD had many of the same structural capacities under Clinton as under Bush, yet Clinton did not opt to marshal them as aggressively for war.

It thus does not necessarily follow that because the DoD is as vast as it is, the State Department will inevitably play a marginal role. What is the case, though, is that the National Security Act has created a structural imbalance in which, *should* an executive or those around him be inclined toward war, the DoD has the capacity to marshal a chorus of national support, while the State Department has no such structural capacity. With a budget roughly five percent that of Defense and no military-industrial complex to mobilize, it is hard to imagine a circumstance in which the State Department could ever outstrip the DoD.

A Private Army: The Transformation of the CIA

Just as pre-9/11 intelligence failures became grounds for the formation of the Department of Homeland Security in 2002, Pearl Harbor became in 1947 the basis for the formation of a new, improved, and more centralized instrument for managing "intelligence matters related to the national security." Yet, despite the desire of those in Congress for a system that would give them better and more accessible intelligence, the creation of the CIA instead produced the negative consequence of empowering the president to engage in covert national security activities with more limited involvement of Congress than ever before.

Indeed, so greatly did the CIA expand the president's power that Truman himself would be led in his twilight years to write a 1963 op-ed in *The Washington Post* decrying its shift of focus. "For some time," the former president wrote, "I have been disturbed by the way CIA has been diverted from its original assignment." Before identifying the danger of such mission creep, Truman confirmed Wilkerson's view that the original purpose of the CIA had been, in part, to remove departmental bias from the handling of intelligence, i.e., to reduce the State Department's intelligence-handling power. "At times," Truman wrote, "the intelligence reports tended to be slanted to conform to established positions of a given department. . . . Therefore, I decided to set up a special organization charged with the collection of all intelligence reports from every available source, and to have those reports reach me as President without department 'treatment' or interpretations."[35] At that time, the primary department performing such intelligence functions was the State Department, and Wilkerson believes that reducing the power of State was one of the goals of establishing the independent CIA.

"Before and up through World War II, most good strategic intelligence was coming out of the State Department," Wilkerson explains. "Truman didn't like this. He felt that when the State Department (or any other agency) gave him intelligence it came with that agency's bias and prejudice. So he wanted something that was responsible only to him. And so they created the CIA and the Director of Central Intelligence."

For Truman, though, this decision produced its own problems that emerged over time, as the CIA became what he came to call "an operational and at times a policy-making arm of the Government." Putting the finest point possible on his concern, Truman declared in 1963, "I never had any thought that when I set up the CIA that it would be injected into peacetime cloak and dagger operations. . . . I, therefore, would like to see the CIA be restored to its original assignment as the intelligence arm of the President. . . ."

So it was that the CIA, which was designed to give America an informational advantage over her adversaries, instead ended up giving the executive branch an informational advantage over the other branches. In the years before and after Truman's concerned editorial, the agency's activities have been far from purely informational. From early on, vaguely drafted elements of the act's mandate have been exploited to allow the agency to engage increasingly in covert operations.

Chalmers Johnson, who has served as a consultant to the CIA confirms Truman's view that the primary function of the agency has drifted over the decades since 1947 from an intelligence instrument to an operational one. "The original purpose of the CIA was to prevent surprise attack, to prevent the kinds of errors that had allowed us to be attacked by the Japanese on December 7, 1941. That's why it was called 'central' intelligence. It was the revelation that back in 1941, we had a lot of information but it was never coordinated."

Johnson recounts that the FBI had in fact "looked over the wall of the Japanese consulate in Honolulu a couple of days before December 7," saw documents being burned, and brought this fact to FBI director J. Edgar Hoover's attention. Hoover, though, never passed the information on, which at the time was perceived as a crucial severed link in the chain of events that led to the surprise attack. According to Johnson, "the idea of central intelligence was to coordinate intelligence processes to prevent a repetition of this." He makes the case, however, that beyond drifting into unanticipated functions as Truman noted, the agency has repeatedly failed in its original purpose.

A quick overview of the CIA's history reveals a disconnecting pattern of such failure.

When in a 1971 conversation with Henry Kissinger Chinese prime minister Chou En-lai alluded to the possibility of CIA involvement in Taiwanese affairs, Kissinger told him that he "vastly overestimates the competence of the CIA." Chou replied that "whenever something happens in the world they are always thought of." In response, Kissinger quipped, "That is true, and it flatters them, but they don't deserve it."[36]

Indeed, there is some truth to Kissinger's quip. Despite the widespread impression in Hollywood movies of an all-knowing and all-seeing agency, the CIA was never very effective at gathering useful intelligence on Communist China. It failed to predict the Soviet detonation of an atom bomb in 1949, the 1950 invasion of South Korea, popular uprisings in Eastern Europe during the 1950s, the placement of Soviet missiles in Cuba in 1962, the 1973 Arab-Israeli War, the 1979 Iranian revolution and Soviet invasion of Afghanistan, the 1989 collapse of the Soviet Union, Iraq's invasion of Kuwait in 1990, and the explosion of an atom bomb by India in 1998.

This list of shortcomings might give the impression that the agency has been largely ineffective, but this is not the case. It is only that it may have proved more effective in unanticipated ways than in anticipated ones. The National Security Act granted the agency and its director a broad mandate to "collect intelligence through human sources and by other appropriate means . . . in coordination with other agencies of the Government . . . [to] correlate and evaluate" as well as disseminate "such intelligence," and to perform additional services "of common concern" to the intelligence community that "can be more efficiently accomplished centrally." Harmless enough, but the act then went dangerously further, giving the agency the sweeping responsibility to "perform such other functions and duties related to intelligence affecting the national security as the President or the National Security Council may direct." Alongside this, though, provisions regarding the agency's obligation to account to Congress on its activities and intelligence it has gathered were left decidedly murky.

In its own language, the act stipulates that "under the direction of the National Security Council" (which reports to the president), the CIA is to provide national intelligence to the president, the heads of departments and agencies of the executive branch, and to the chairman of the Joint Chiefs of Staff and senior military commanders, all of whom once again ultimately report to the president. Only "where appropriate" is the CIA to provide such intelligence to "the Senate and House of Representatives and committees thereof." Congress has tried repeatedly through the years to assert its right to oversee the agency and gain access to its gathered intelligence. In 1971, for example, Kentucky senator John Sherman Cooper introduced a bill that would have expressly required the CIA to provide Congress with requested intelligence, but it died in committee. The history of such efforts has been a hopeless one, fraught with tension.[37]

If information is power, then giving the president such dominating authority over such an immense informational tool is another way that the National Security Act favors the executive over the other branches.

According to Chalmers Johnson, the CIA, almost from its inception, began to evolve into an instrument with a far more operational role than just providing unbiased information to the president. "Wild Bill" Donovan, Johnson explains, "who headed the Office of Strategic Services during World War II, once said that what he really wanted was a clandestine service—a private army, at the hands of the president, one that can be used secretly, and for which the president can deny he's responsible." Johnson contends that Donovan's vision of such an agency has been realized as the CIA has been "transformed over time into a private army, secret army, exclusively at the power of the presidency." For Johnson, America's involvement in the Middle East from 1953 to the present is a perfect case study in the unintended consequences of the CIA's role in U.S. foreign policy.

Beyond his work for the agency, Johnson is perhaps best known as the author of the 2000 book *Blowback*, published before 9/11, which warned of "the unintended consequences of covert operations," and was later given haunting resonance by the attacks. Johnson argues that there is a direct connection between actions taken by the CIA more than fifty years ago and the war in Iraq today. In 1953, the British government asked the United States for help in overthrowing Prime Minister Mohammed Mossadegh of Iran, whose intention to nationalize his country's oil resources had threatened British petroleum interests. In response, President Eisenhower declared Mossadegh to be a Communist and, with the three words, "Mossadegh must go,"[38] the CIA was authorized to support a coup against him. In its after-action report on Mossadegh's overthrow, the CIA recognized the possibility that "blowback," or unfortunate future consequences, could result.

And did they ever. The Shah of Iran replaced Mossadegh and ruled oppressively until he was deposed by the Islamic Revolution of 1979 and replaced with Ayatollah Khomeini. The perception that the Shah was a U.S. puppet made his overthrow an anti-American victory. And this spirit of anti-Americanism exploded further into a crisis on November 4, 1979, when a group of Iranian revolutionaries held sixty-six Americans hostage inside the U.S. Embassy in Tehran. This crisis in turn disgraced thirty-ninth president Jimmy Carter, who tried unsuccessfully to rescue the hostages. Carter's loss of face in this botched rescue operation helped his Republican challenger, Ronald Reagan, win the 1980 presidential election.

But the blowback didn't stop there. The conflict with Iran quickly gave birth to an unlikely alliance between the United States and the leader of Iran's southern neighbor, Iraq. Saddam Hussein waged a horrendously bloody war with Iran from 1980 to 1988, during which the United States provided him with support. In the infamous video of Donald Rumsfeld shaking hands with Saddam on December 20, 1983, the once and future secretary of defense has been sent by Ronald Reagan at the height of the Iran-Iraq War to assure Hussein of America's unwavering friendship.

In reality, U.S. support for Iraq lasted only until August 2, 1990, when Hussein's forces invaded Kuwait. America not only went to war with Saddam, but out of concern that he might go on to invade Saudi Arabia, the United States stationed troops in the desert kingdom.

This move outraged many Islamic fundamentalists, among them Osama Bin Laden, a wealthy Saudi national. Bin Laden's bona fides among Islamic radicals had been established during the 1980s through his support for Afghanistan's *mujahideen* or "freedom fighters" who fought against the Soviet Union from 1978 to 1989. This war, waged with CIA support, aligned Bin Laden for a time with American interests, yet when the war ended and Afghanistan spiraled into civil war, America was seen by Bin Laden and others as having abandoned its onetime *mujahideen* allies. Through this experience, Bin Laden became an outspoken and increasingly influential critic of the United States. Thus, even as they fueled his antipathy toward the United States, the CIA's covert activities in Afghanistan contributed to the rise of the very man who would ultimately emerge as America's most notorious contemporary adversary.

American support for the *mujahideen* in Afghanistan illustrates the extent to which the CIA has outdone Truman's worst possible "cloak and dagger" fears in becoming a proactively operational and policy-making instrument. Contrary to what he calls the "official version of history" that the U.S. armed the *mujahideen* in response to the Soviet invasion of Afghanistan, then-national security adviser Zbigniew Brzezinski has since startlingly claimed that the CIA's involvement in Afghanistan *preceded* and in many ways *precipitated* the Soviet invasion. "We didn't push the Russians to intervene," Brzezinski confessed to *Le Nouvel Observateur* in 1998, "but we knowingly increased the probability that they would."[39] In other words, he and President Carter sought strategically to lure the Soviets into invading Afghanistan. With the rise to power in Afghanistan of a pro-Soviet communist government under Noor Mohammed Taraki in 1978, the country was to become a staging ground for yet another satellite skirmish of the Cold War. The *mujahideen* were anticommunist by virtue of being opposed to Taraki's pro-Soviet government. They thus found themselves aligned almost by default with the United States, which, by supporting them, sought to undermine Soviet influence in the region. Brzezinski's astonishing revelation has been confirmed by then-CIA director and current secretary of defense Robert Gates in his 1996 memoir *From the Shadows*. Recounting a meeting on March 30, 1979, Gates recalls discussion of "sucking the Soviets into a Vietnamese quagmire," a reference to what Brzezinski calls "giving to the USSR its Vietnam War."[40]

Osama Bin Laden and the rise of al Qaeda represent a uniquely compounded case of blowback, in which long-term consequences of America's initial covert action in Iran came to fuel the anger separately produced by America's covert action in Afghanistan to produce a series of anti-American attacks culminating on 9/11. That this tragedy was in turn used by the Bush administration to beat a tortuous and highly secretive path to war in Iraq has created the prospect of longer-term blowback whose full scope is not yet known. What is clear, though, and ominously so, is that the Iraq War has already served to strengthen the recruitment of possible terror operatives by al Qaeda.

Taken together, this checkered legacy of increasingly secret activity and its chain reaction of unintended consequences illustrate how the National Security Act's introduction of a covert instrument of foreign policy has led not only to the gathering of increased intelligence on the affairs of other nations but, disconcertingly, to ever-increasing American entanglement in those affairs. In turn, the act has gravely undermined the transparency of government and balance of power between the branches so carefully crafted by the framers.

Jokers in the Deck: The National Security Council and National Security Adviser

In light of its significant expansion of the national security system, the National Security Act created a coordinating body within the executive branch, called the National Security Council (NSC), "to advise the President" on all matters affecting national security. The council reports to and is presided over by the president, and includes the vice president, secretary of state, secretary of defense, and other "Secretaries and Under Secretaries of other executive departments and the military departments." Though part of the motivation for the council had been to undo the secrecy with which FDR had made his national security decisions, notably absent were any officials from outside the executive branch, thus further tilting power toward the executive.

This tilt was only increased when Truman's successor, Dwight Eisenhower, sought an increased measure of control over national security matters when, upon his election in 1953, he created the position of national security adviser. Also known as the "assistant to the president for national security affairs," this cabinet official would become the de facto head of the NSC, appointed by and reporting to the president. Lawrence Wilkerson is a devoted student of Eisenhower, whom he describes as "iconic—one of the best presidents of the twentieth-century." Yet in the matter of the national security adviser, Wilkerson believes Eisenhower erred, creating a "nonstatutory position, contemplated neither by the original framers nor by the framers of the 1947 act." It may have been all well and good under Eisenhower—a man who had managed the most colossal military operation in history—but it did not account for how later, less prudent presidents could misuse such an adviser responsible to no one but him. If the Air Force, Defense Department, CIA, and National Security Council are four aces held by the president, Wilkerson views the seemingly innocuous national security adviser as an added joker that insuperably strengthens that hand. In this sense, to the extent members of Congress had hoped the National Security Council would democratize the executive's national security decision making by adding members of its own appointment, the addition of the adviser effectively produced the opposite result.

As Wilkerson sees it, rather than simply acting as a tool for improved "coordination," the adviser provides the executive with a covert asset in the decision-making process—a mystery player whose ostensible function is to mediate between various voices and provide the president with "objective analysis," but whose actual function is to serve as a presidential operative, making such objectivity unlikely.

The potential for abuse arising from this relationship was never more evident than in the vaulting power vested by Richard Nixon in his national security adviser, Henry Kissinger. Whatever one thinks of Kissinger's controversial career, it is defined by its secrecy and the extraordinary level of control that secrecy gave Nixon over the conduct of foreign policy—not only from the other branches of government but even from departments within the executive itself.

Nowhere did this secrecy manifest itself more ominously than in Kissinger's secret efforts to secure what Nixon called "peace with honor" in Vietnam. To be fair, it must be remembered that Vietnam was already a losing war by the time Henry Kissinger and Richard Nixon even entered the White House. The war they inherited was also already the product of significant executive overreach by previous administrations—from Eisenhower's earliest support in the 1950s for French anticommunist efforts in Vietnam, to Kennedy's tentative decision to commit "advisers" to aid the South Vietnamese, to Johnson's escalating effort to pursue American victory at great cost—all without any formal declaration of war by Congress and with a growing lack of transparency to Congress and the public. Yet, despite being heirs to the conflict, Kissinger and Nixon treated it as though it were their very own—intensifying its secrecy to an unprecedented new level of executive power.

"My worst memories of Henry Kissinger," recalls former National Security Council member Roger Morris, "are of him pandering to the president's worst instincts on Vietnam, misleading both Congress and the press, deliberately manipulating both his staff and the rest of the American government."[41] Morris had worked as chief of staff to Dean Acheson after earning his doctorate at Harvard, and he had joined the National Security Council under Lyndon Johnson. Initially asked by Kissinger to remain on the council after Nixon took office, Morris felt compelled to resign after Kissinger's decision in 1970 to begin bombing the neighboring country of Cambodia without the knowledge of Congress or the American people. Throughout the war, Cambodia had functioned as a kind of neutral neighbor to the unfolding conflict. Then, in 1970, Cambodia's king Norodom Sihanouk was overthrown in a CIA-supported coup. Irrationally, this event set off what Morris calls "a chain reaction inside the American government, in Richard Nixon, and in Henry Kissinger." Perceiving a challenge to American resolve and convinced that the events in Cambodia could jeopardize their desire to secure an honorable American exit from Vietnam, Nixon and Kissinger began secretly bombing Cambodia.

"I decided to resign . . . because I felt that the Cambodian invasion was a betrayal of the president's pledge to seek an honorable and just peace in Vietnam," recalls Morris. "The Cambodian invasion destroyed all of that, devastated it, for years to come and literally cost tens of thousands of American lives, hundreds of thousands of Vietnamese and Cambodian lives. I thought it was one of the great crimes of the century." From a constitutional perspective, the more one reads of the relentless secrecy and vigor with which Kissinger pursued his secret foreign policy activities, the more one sees a precursor to events of the Bush years. The more secret his and Nixon's activities became, the more paranoid the two men became toward those around them—not only in Congress but inside the executive branch itself.

"We used to joke," recalls Morris, "that the real hostile foreign powers were not Moscow or Beijing or any of our rivals in the world. The real hostile powers were the rest of the American government, the Department of State, the White House staff, the CIA, the Defense Department." Like the Bush White House, the overassertion of executive power by Kissinger and Nixon was accompanied before too long by acts of contempt for the Constitution. "Kissinger wiretapped at least a dozen—perhaps more—of his closest colleagues," Morris recalls. "We still don't know the whole story because many of those documents are classified. He wiretapped my closest friend and associate on the staff, Anthony Lake, who went on to become national security adviser under Clinton. He wiretapped aides and associates in the Pentagon. He wiretapped American journalists with whom he had supposedly friendly and close relations."

Before long, Kissinger's secret bombing campaign against Cambodia was leaked to the press, but by then it was too late. It had already cost countless Cambodian lives and destabilized the country. Given the chain-reactive nature of blowback, this facilitated the rise of the Khmer Rouge, who in turn launched a campaign of genocide and ethnic cleansing that led to the death and displacement of millions of Cambodians.[42]

And yet, Kissinger's expansion of executive power was limited neither to Indochina nor to the presidency of Richard Nixon. Under Nixon,

Kissinger lent support in Chile to internal efforts to overthrow the democratically elected government of Salvador Allende while, under Nixon's successor Gerald Ford, he authorized the sale of arms to Indonesian dictator Suharto that were used to massacre the people of East Timor. While Kissinger's activities in Chile resulted in a coup in which Salvador Allende was killed and which produced the brutal military dictatorship of Augusto Pinochet (under whom thousands of Chileans were killed, tortured, or otherwise "disappeared"), Kissinger's authorization of arms sales to Suharto was in direct violation of Congress's arms export control act that prevented the sale of arms to countries violating human rights.

Though Kissinger's years under Nixon and then Ford were by no means the country's first episode of expanded executive power, the extent of his secrecy and contempt for congressional oversight was revealed through the investigative efforts of the Church Committee, a congressional inquiry chaired by Idaho Senator Frank Church in 1975. Yet, even when called before the committee to answer charges that he had secretly and illegally supported efforts to overthrow democratically elected foreign governments and, therewith, had wittingly authorized the assassination of foreign leaders, Kissinger was not forthcoming; he provided the president with a layer of cover. What these hearings revealed, above all, was the way in which what Wilkerson calls the "nonstatutory" position of the national security adviser provides the executive wiggle room to engage in activities otherwise in violation of existing laws and restraints with the assurance that someone else will answer for them—someone whose position, not contemplated in the Constitution, is thus not legally accountable to Congress or, by extension, to the American people.

So great did Kissinger's power as national security adviser become during the Nixon years that it encroached upon the authority of the secretary of state. "When you hear the tapes that have been released in which Nixon calls the State Department a bunch of 'commie pinko dogs,' " Wilkerson laughs, "you realize that the secretary of state began to be marginalized very much under Richard Nixon." In keeping with his view that the National Security Act was in part designed to counterbalance the power of the State Department, Wilkerson perceives the introduction of the national security adviser as an outright assault on the power of the secretary of state. "It gives you the feeling that what's happening in the White House is really the essence of power in America—that the departments—particularly the State Department—are just appendages, not making any substantive contributions to the decision-making process."

To Wilkerson, Nixon showed commendable candor in 1973 when he dispensed with any pretense to the contrary and appointed Kissinger to serve simultaneously as national security adviser and secretary of state, underscoring the latter's redundancy. Since Kissinger, such national security advisers as Brent Scowcroft, Zbigniew Brzezinski, John Poindexter, Frank Carlucci, and Samuel R. Berger have at times visibly outranked their State Department counterparts in influence over and proximity to the president.

Though Kissinger's secret activities under Nixon and Ford would ultimately elude accountability, the same cannot be said for John Poindexter, Ronald Reagan's national security adviser, whose efforts to provide his boss camouflage to conduct the illegal activities of the Iran/Contra affair would make him a convicted felon. From the downing of an antiquated cargo plane over Nicaragua on October 5, 1986, through an investigation of illegal arms sales, money laundering, and negotiations with terrorists, the Iran/Contra affair unfolded like a John Le Carré novel, exploding in a media firestorm and a parade of official lies told under oath. Ultimately, what was revealed was a compound crime in which money illegally derived from the sale of arms to Iran in violation of Congress' Arms Export Control Act was diverted to provide support to the Contras, a loose array of political opponents of Nicaragua's communist government, in violation of a key amendment to a Congressional act. The Boland Amendment, as it was called, had been passed when evidence came to light that the CIA-trained Contras, without the knowledge of Congress, had engaged in atrocities against politicians and other civilians including murder, rape, torture, dismemberment, and summary executions. Despite this evidence, Reagan had maintained that the Contras were "the moral equivalent of our Founding Fathers," lauding them as heroes in the fight against communism and ultimately overseeing an administration that illegally supported them.

Ultimately, eleven members of the Reagan administration, including his secretary of defense, Caspar Weinberger, were convicted of crimes in connection with the activities of the Iran/Contra affair. Though these activities involved officials across the administration's various departments from CIA Deputy Director Robert Gates to Secretary of State George Shultz to senior State Department official Elliot Abrams to U.S. ambassador to Honduras John Negroponte and to Lieutenant Colonel Oliver North, the most sensitive and influential role was played by the president's National Security Council on which North served and which was led by John Poindexter. Ultimately, when the Iran/Contra scandal came to light, the National Security Council functioned much as it had during the congressional investigations of Frank Church. While Iran/Contra was more geographically limited than the full sweep of Kissinger's international activities, the affair was no less violative of domestic law and the constitutional separation of powers. Indeed, in violating both the Arms Export Control Act and the Boland Amendment, Iran/Contra was arguably a more brazen assault on Congress's authority than the more subtle workarounds engineered by Kissinger.

Nonetheless, however, the National Security Council and, in particular, the national security adviser, provided a buffer of safety for those at the highest levels of the administration.

"What began as a strategic opening to Iran deteriorated, in its implementation, into trading arms for hostages," Reagan ultimately concluded, confessing to error yet eluding any accountability for possible criminal involvement.[43]

While lower-level actors like Oliver North were convicted, fined, and indicted in limited ways, the executive himself maintained the privilege to admit error, preserve his deniability, and live on to become one of America's most revered presidents. In turn, those convicted under him ultimately enjoyed the executive's reciprocal protection from imprisonment or other penalties. Reagan's successor George H. W. Bush, who had been vice president during the affair, pardoned all eleven of those convicted.

Though Reagan emerged from the scandal legally unscathed, it represented the most brazen attack on the balance of power since the executive transgressions of the Vietnam era. In the context of America's longstanding debate over the balance of power between the branches, the Reagan administration's creation of a shadow government to circumvent the other branches was concentrated in the National Security

Council which in turn became a tool for obstructing efforts by Congress to exercise its checking authority and, through the ultimate presidential pardon of those found guilty, obstructing justice itself.

In keeping with the legacy of her predecessors, George W. Bush's national security adviser, Condoleezza Rice, has proven similarly useful in fostering wiggle room for the assertion of executive power. Wilkerson sees her as a figure who "sought to build intimacy with the president" not by providing him with "objective analyses" of a range of security viewpoints, but rather by allying herself with the views of influential cabinet members Dick Cheney and Don Rumsfeld, and actively shielding Bush from opposing viewpoints such as those offered by the Powell camp. To apply a crude sports metaphor, Rice was not the player who scored the slam-dunk but rather the one who set a pick for those who did. In effect, Rice provided cover under which Cheney and Rumsfeld could game the architecture of the decision-making process to their ends.

Wilkerson believes that Rice was instrumental in enabling Rumsfeld and Cheney essentially to engineer an internal administration putsch. Exploiting what he calls bureaucratic "sclerosis," Rice, Wilkerson believes, used the appearance of an intense debate to camouflage what was actually happening within a "secret decision-making process." Wilkerson says, "When you understand how Cheney operates—Rumsfeld too for that matter—you understand how they did it. They had a brilliant bureaucratic technique for thwarting the process in the National Security Council. Making decisions *off-line.* They would do that either by default—as in the case of Iran—by throwing a monkey wrench into the statutory process every time it looked like it might produce a national security document with regard to U.S.-Iran policy. That way they got by default the policy they wanted, which was no talks with Iran, period. No movement. No diplomacy. No nothing toward Iran.

"Other times, as in the case of detainee abuse, they allowed the statutory process to make a decision and then simply undermined that decision in the field. Since the principal executors of this policy were CIA and military, they didn't have much problem because Rumsfeld owned the military, and the CIA had Cheney's spies all over it."

The Big Cahuna: The Creation of the Air Force

A less obvious but no less significant way in which the National Security Act expanded the president's warmaking powers was by creating the Air Force as a separate branch of the military, with a command structure of its own. In the wake of World War II, expanded foreign air operations were anticipated, and the need for a more powerful independent air force became crucial. In turn, as the fear of nuclear war became America's primary security concern, the Air Force—charged with maintaining the nation's nuclear force and deterrence—fast became the lead service.

Between 1947 and 1953, World War II bombers were replaced with a long-range strike force capable of bombing anywhere on earth. Between 1951 and 1953, 329 B-47 Stratojets, which could fly over 3,000 miles without refueling, were added to the Air Force fleet. By 1955, the number of B-47s had risen to 1,086. That same year the Air Force also began to deploy B-52 bombers that could refuel in midair to reach targets in the USSR from the continental United States. By 1960, 539 B-52 bombers had been added, bringing the total number of strategic bombers capable of delivering nuclear weapons to 1,735.[44]

This explosion of aircraft required an equally massive diversion of defense dollars toward the Air Force and away from the other services. In its relatively short life, the Air Force has come to compete with, and, in some cases, outstrip the other services in its funding, accounting in 2009 for 14.4 billion dollars, which represents 28 cents of every dollar spent on American defense.

That concentration of economic power gave the Air Force vast influence in guiding national security priorities. As the world has become smaller and the United States has continued to exert itself overseas, airpower has increasingly become the centerpiece of U.S. military planning. The rise of the Air Force, whose high-altitude activities risk a small handful of pilots' lives compared to the vast losses risked in Army and Navy combat, has in turn led to the rise of a brand of "surgical" war for which it is easier to gain public and congressional support.

The framers designed the checks and balances in such a way as to require the president to seek a Declaration of War by Congress. The increased power of the U.S. Air Force has in this indirect but crucial fashion armed the executive branch with an immensely effective tool for engineering congressional support. The president is able to argue for a more limited engagement of troops, and a shorter war, with a war plan dominated by airpower. The Iraq War, for example, saw a war plan dominated by airpower, resisted by experienced army professionals like General Eric Shinseki, yet advocated by armchair generals promising an easy victory through surgical strikes. These strikes—and the impression of a quick, precise, and containable conflict—were instrumental in overcoming what limited opposition there was among members of Congress to the Iraq War.

Neoconservative Ken Adelman, a member of Rumsfeld's Defense Policy Board at the Pentagon, will long be remembered as the man who promised that the Iraq War would be a "cakewalk"—a lesson in choosing your words more advisedly in an age of sound bites. Yet a close reading of Adelman's argument for war reveals how central U.S. airpower was to the delusion of a quick and easy victory.

Adelman argued as early as February 2002 that "the advent of precision bombing and battlefield intelligence has dramatically spiked U.S. military prowess."[45] Opponents of the war naturally found it difficult to argue against the promise of a surgical strike intended to erase an overtly bellicose head of state while sparing the civilian population around him. While there is no way to know how the war might have been advocated in the absence of the elaborate capabilities and skillful marketing of American airpower, it is clear how these make the prospect of military action seem more viable and defensible and thus limit resistance—in Congress and among the public—to the executive's warmaking goals.

Though historically, critics of the Cold War have focused a great deal of attention on NSC-68—a seminal 1950 report written by an interagency committee of the executive branch led by Cold War strategist Paul Nitze—as a kind of blueprint for American conduct in the Cold War comparatively little attention has been paid to the sea change that took place in 1947.

Taken together, the innovations of the National Security Act—the DoD (and its secretary), the CIA, the NSC (and its adviser), and a separate Air Force—have massively influenced not only America's foreign affairs over the past half century but her domestic political dynamics as well. Above all, the act has given the executive branch in all aspects of planning and implementing foreign policy an advantage over the other branches and, within itself, an inclination toward the military rather than peaceful resolution of conflict. These implications have led to calls for a legislative course correction. Lawrence Wilkerson describes himself as part of "a very nascent movement in Washington, but a powerful one" to develop "a new National Security Act."

A HIGHER POWER

After his months of harrowing investigation into the Abu Ghraib atrocities, Wilkerson credits a higher power with his ultimate decision to go public. "My wife and I had some heavy conversations. And she said she thought I owed more to my country than I did to my boss and others." Still, the decision was a difficult one.

"It was very painful," he recalls. "For thirty-one years in the military I never spoke out politically as an officer. The tradition is, retired or active, you don't speak out. And personally, too. After sixteen years working for Colin Powell—and I have immense loyalty to Colin Powell—it has estranged me from one of my dearest friends in the world." Before going public, Wilkerson advised Powell that they would have to stop communicating lest it be misinterpreted that Wilkerson was speaking for his former boss. "A lot of people still think I'm speaking for him and I'm not."

To illustrate this, Wilkerson offers an extraordinary revelation. "Powell and I disagree fundamentally on a couple of substantive issues," he explains. "For example, I believe that in the decisions regarding detainee abuse, the president was unwitting and aloof from the details." After a pregnant pause, Wilkerson smiles, then drops a bombshell: "Secretary Powell and I disagree about that."

If this is so, it begs the question of why Powell has not spoken out more forcefully, as Wilkerson has, against the abuses. The answer, according to Wilkerson, lies in the fact that "Colin Powell is a creature of the executive branch." Throughout his White House Years, Powell became a study in military obedience, ever the soldier, supporting the mission undertaken by the president, and leaving the public to wonder just what it might take to make him speak critically about policies with which there was a strong sense he disagreed.[46]

In the end, Powell's abortive administration career would end as it began—in dutiful service to the executive. Wilkerson elaborates on this defining quality of his friend and mentor.

"He spent his entire career in the executive branch as a soldier, as deputy national security adviser, national security adviser, chairman of the Joint Chiefs of Staff, and then secretary of state. The most intense arguments we have had about governance in this country over the last sixteen years have been about such things as civil-military relations, the power of the executive, and the potential for military takeover of the country. In these arguments, he has almost always, unlike me, come down on the side of incredulity about any problems that might exist because it all boils down to needing a very powerful executive branch in order to survive in this very dangerous world and remain at the top of the pinnacle of power." According to Wilkerson, if loopholes in the National Security Act are what enabled the Cheney/Rumsfeld camp to dominate the administration's foreign policy, Powell's fundamental loyalty to his commander in chief was a further enabler.

In the wake of Abu Ghraib, Powell's decision to instruct Wilkerson and William Taft IV to "figure out how we got here" was a turning point, a notably mutinous act in his soldier's life and, in the end, one that would reveal his loyalty to the executive to be unrequited. On Powell's instructions in April 2004, Wilkerson and Taft spent the rest of the year investigating the path to Abu Ghraib, giving Powell several briefings on the results of their investigation. But by the time the awful truth of what had happened began to crystallize, Powell (and by association his team) had resigned from the administration.

Why? Why would a man who had devoted his career to upholding America's values in wartime choose to resign at a moment when these were so imperiled? A final revelation from Wilkerson explains: *Powell didn't resign. He was fired.*

Wilkerson recounts a story as astonishing for its larger implications about power in the executive branch as for Powell himself. "The president *asked* him to resign," Wilkerson smiles ironically. "It happened like this: First of all, Powell had told the president in the very beginning, as early as August or September before the 2000 elections, that if Bush won and asked him to be his secretary of state, he'd probably be there for only one term. There was an implicit understanding amongst the principals about this. But then reality took over as we marched through those first four years. And Powell became more or less the person whom the Europeans for example would call and beg not to leave, because they saw him as the only sober, sane member of the administration.

"So, by the time we got to the fall of '04, having to make some sort of decision about Bush's second term, Powell was saying things like, 'I serve at the discretion of the President.' I think it's fair to say he was planning on staying around through at least the Iraqi elections (because we had set them up) and possibly afterwards."

But it didn't turn out that way.

"When the election was over, the first thing that happened was Andy Card and Dina Powell and others from the White House called around to us and said, 'Hey, no one is going to have to submit his resignation' like some presidents do. You know, protocol is typically you submit your resignation, then the president tells you whether he's gonna keep you or not. But they went into a lot of detail about how they didn't want everybody leaving at one time. If you wanted a new job, let them know and they'd move you to that new job. If you were gonna leave, let them know so they could sequence the departures so it wouldn't be a whole lot of people leaving at once.

"Next thing we know, it was November 11—Veterans Day, of all days—Powell gets a telephone call telling him to submit his resignation. '*Now, that's interesting.*' " Wilkerson laughs bitterly, recalling Powell's amazement.

" 'I thought you said no one was gonna submit their resignations.'

" 'Well, no one is . . . *but you.*'

"Powell was so furious about it, he typed out his own resignation letter and sent it over there. But lo and behold if they didn't sent it back because there was a typo in it. He had to do it again!"

The story gets worse.

"When Powell was asked to come to the White House for his final call on the president, the president didn't even seem to know why he was there. That's very interesting, isn't it? *Did the president even know that he'd asked his secretary of state to submit a resignation?*

"I'll tell you what I think. I think Cheney had already decided before the election that Powell was gonna go. But he wasn't about to say anything before the election, because it would've impacted them. Might've even lost them the election. So they waited until after the election to slam the door on Powell."

Wilkerson sighs deeply before summing up the cumulative implications of the inside scoop he's provided. "I think it's fair to say that neither of us at the point when he was asked to submit his resignation in November '04 thought the system wasn't gonna work," Wilkerson says of the investigations into the Abu Ghraib abuses. "Powell had said publicly, *'Look, this was horrible. Unconscionable. But we're gonna show the world how a democracy takes care of problems like this. Heads are gonna roll.'* We thought the secretary of defense was probably on his last legs; two offers to resign, pretty soon the president was gonna accept one of 'em. We thought the system was going to work; not perfectly—it never does—but that it was gradually gonna find people at all levels and punish them."

Of course, Donald Rumsfeld did eventually resign, but not for many months to follow, and not due to Abu Ghraib, but rather to the disastrous course of the larger war and his primary role in its planning. The Justice Department has also launched its own investigation into the justifications of torture and repudiation of the Geneva Conventions. While this might suggest that the system retains some capacity to check executive abuses of power, these corrections have only come about as a consequence of the turn of public opinion so strongly against the war. They are only a tiny measure against a problem of Goliath proportions.

Though the Bush administration may be, as Wilkerson asserts, a worst-case scenario of how the executive branch has been empowered to undermine America's most time-honored democratic principles and guide the nation down a dangerous road toward militarism and imperialism, the cautionary tale of the National Security Act is that this imbalance of power has been institutionalized. In his portrayal of Powell's relative naïveté amid his discharge from the executive branch, to which he devoted his career, one sees the awful sweep of the national security state in its effect not only on the balance of power between the branches but within the executive branch itself. So overarching has the executive branch become—so insulated from external checks and so internally tilted toward war—that not even loyal soldiers like Powell and Wilkerson could slow its inexorable march to war.

Ultimately, the 1947 act, which promised to mitigate the dangers of an overgrown executive, has indeed only deepened its center of gravity under the weight of the kind of "overgrown military establishment" George Washington decried in his Farewell Address. Despite his support for the act in 1947 and even his feeling years later that it had provided the president invaluable tools for policy making, Dwight Eisenhower, like Washington before him, would come to see the dangers of militarism that had been unleashed by the National Security Act and undergo an extraordinary evolution in his understanding of how the American way of war, even with the best of intentions, can lose its way.[47]

4

Big White Men

The government of your country! I am the government of your country: I and Lazarus. Do you suppose that you and a half a dozen amateurs like you, sitting in a row in that foolish gabble shop, can govern Undershaft and Lazarus? No, my friend: you will do what pays us. You will make war when it pays us, and keep peace when it doesn't. You will find out that trade requires certain measures when we have decided on those measures. When I want anything to keep my dividend up, you will discover that my want is a national need. When other people want something to keep my dividends down, you will call out the police and the military. And in return you shall have the support and applause of my newspapers, and the delight of imagining you are a great statesman. Government of your country! Be off with you, my boy, and play with your caucuses and leading articles and historic parties and great leaders and burning questions and the rest of your toys. I am going back to my countinghouse to pay the piper and call the tune.

George Bernard Shaw
Major Barbara

The Buick hurtled down the gravel road, kicking up dust that made it hard to see the minivan desperately racing to follow. My driver, in his eighties, seemed to be squinting to make out the road ahead. I wondered about his eyesight. "I don't really know what you want with me," he half grumbled, gunning the pedal and shooting an annoyed glance in the rearview.

When John Eisenhower agreed to appear in my documentary film *Why We Fight*, it was a coup. For an independent film inspired by Dwight D. Eisenhower, scoring the former president's son was a double blessing. Not only was John the author of a just-published firsthand memoir of his father, *General Ike*; he was also an accomplished soldier and statesman himself. A West Point graduate, John served in World War II and Korea. Under his father, he served as assistant staff secretary in the White House and later, under Richard Nixon, as U.S. ambassador to Belgium.

My crew and I arrived early and excited. I'd expected some sort of Federal-style mansion, in which a butler would fuss over where to stow our arsenal of gear. Instead, we found ourselves scratching our heads at an office park along an interstate. It hardly seemed ambassadorial, but it was the right place. As I'd come to learn, it was pure Eisenhower—modest, functional, no bullshit.

I ordered lunch for my crew at a deli on the office park grounds, where I called John's office to announce our arrival and inquire "if Mr. Eisenhower would like us to bring him anything to eat." Dorothy Yentz, John Eisenhower's assistant of more than twenty years, advised me to order him "a BLT with mayo and an iced tea." I had just placed the same order for myself, so I asked the deli guy to double up.

Suddenly, the front door swung open, flooding the place with light. There, silhouetted in the doorway, was a tall man in a white linen suit. It was as if Dwight D. Eisenhower himself had entered the deli. John and I shook hands and ate lunch, during which he eyed me suspiciously. After a long life of his own political, military, and academic achievements (he is the author of more than nine books), John is weary of being asked to play the role of his father's son. Of course that's why I was there. So of course I lied. And of course John knew I was lying.

John grudgingly invited us to film at his home, which was when our back road adventure began. We sped off so quickly in the Buick that my film crew was left scrambling to reload the minivan and catch up. Glancing back to make sure they were in tow, I missed the first part of something John said.

". . . and now we got these idiots," he huffed.[1]

I couldn't reveal I hadn't been listening, so I let him continue without clarifying who "these idiots" were. It soon became clear that he meant the Bush administration. I framed my next question carefully.

"Correct me if I'm wrong, Mr. Eisenhower," I said, "but you're a *Republican*, right?"

"Lifelong." He tssked. "I voted for this guy."

I hadn't expected the son of arguably the most revered Republican of the twentieth century to express open discomfort with the administration of George W. Bush, let alone such unmitigated irritation. He sensed my confusion and did me the favor of explaining.

"I grew up in a Republican White House," he began, as if telling a story to a child. "And I always voted Republican. That's just how it was. Republicans are the party of big white men. I'm a big white man, so I vote Republican. When George W. Bush came along, he made clear he represented the party of big white men. So I voted for him."

He took a deep breath, considering his next comment.

"It has only been through the administration of George W. Bush that I've come to realize that big white men are the men *most to be feared in this world*."

Absorbing this, I knew three things: First, I would never forget what John had just said. Second, with my crew and equipment back in the chase car, I had failed to capture it on film. Third, the moment we started filming, I would never get him to say it again.

"IT AIN'T NOTHIN' TILL THE *BOSS* SAYS IT"

It was true. John never did repeat his startling revelation with the camera rolling. And all attempts to steer the conversation back there proved fruitless. A former brigadier general, John isn't one to be led anywhere he doesn't intend to go. And voicing his opinion of a sitting wartime president was more than he was prepared to do on camera. Nonetheless, his remarkable comment spoke volumes about the very subject of my visit.

Despite my protestations, I had indeed come to talk to him about his father. And not to discuss any old thing about his father but specifically his father's Farewell Address as president—arguably the most controversial moment of his career.

Along the timeline of the American way of war, the Eisenhower Farewell Address is a moment of hard truth, a blunt reckoning. Eisenhower delivered the address some fourteen years after the passage of Truman's National Security Act. Back then, he'd been a vocal supporter of the act. But by 1961, he had come to see its far-reaching consequences, and his words were a cry for help from the cockpit of a war machine barreling out of control.

Tracing Eisenhower's path from the unreserved glory of World War II to such deep reservations as those expressed in the Farewell Address, one begins to see how America itself underwent significant change during these years, reaching a point where even a revered general felt compelled to break ranks and voice concern. If World War II was a quantum multiplier of long-standing expansionist impulses in the republic, and the creation of the national security state formed an architecture for their permanent expression, Eisenhower's Farewell Address was an SOS on the dangers posed by this accumulation of events.

"We have been compelled to create a permanent armaments industry of vast proportions," Eisenhower declared on January 17, 1961. "We recognize the imperative need for this development, yet we must not fail to comprehend its grave implications."[2]

Unblinking behind thick lenses, Eisenhower's eyes peered thoughtfully into an ominous future. His next words would haunt America for decades to come and prove some of the most controversial ever spoken by an American president:

> In the councils of government, we must guard against the acquisition of unwarranted influence, whether sought or unsought, by the military-industrial complex. The potential for the disastrous rise of misplaced power exists and will persist. We should take nothing for granted.

The words were meticulously chosen and disarmingly candid. "Military-industrial complex," the phrase he introduced to the nation that January night, has in the years since become a hot button, praised by the left as prophecy and dismissed by the right as the work of some overzealous speechwriter. To left and right alike, the Farewell Address seemed a radical departure for such a central figure of the Cold War—like Al Capone denouncing organized crime.

Why did he do it? What did he mean? And what drove him to use his last few moments in office to make such an apparent about-face in the twilight of his life? By visiting with John and later with Eisenhower's granddaughter Susan (a noted Cold War scholar), I hoped Ike's progeny could help answer these questions. John's remarkable opening words—the confession of a recovering big white man—already began to demonstrate how his father could have undergone such a late-life reversal.

"He was complex," John explains. "He could sit in a meeting with his staff or Congress and talk about wiping out a third of the population of the country. Then go upstairs and talk about the Kentucky Derby on the second floor of the White House. Amazing. He was one hell of a poker player."

Before trying to divine Eisenhower's motivation in delivering the address, I wanted to settle a nagging question. Some weeks before visiting with John, I was disturbed to hear Richard Perle express contempt for the Farewell Address, echoing popular right-wing doubts over its authorship.[3] "I think the Eisenhower warning about the military-industrial complex was silly at the time," Perle scoffed. "It was the work of some speechwriter."

The history of the address disproves Perle's aspersion. Though Eisenhower employed speechwriters, he was known for taking a particularly active hand in the drafting of speeches, what presidential scholar Charles Griffin calls Eisenhower's " 'hidden hand' rhetorical style at work."[4] Eisenhower's feverish handwritten notes over countless drafts of the Farewell Address attest to his active role in its formulation. According to his chief speechwriter, Malcolm Moos, Eisenhower had first approached him about the speech some two years before leaving office. "The president," Moos recalled, "was in a philosophical mood one day, and turned to me and said, 'By the way, Malcolm, I want to say something when I leave here and I want you to be thinking about it.' "[5]

Though historians continue to debate who actually coined the phrase "military-industrial complex," there is no doubt among those directly involved that the concern it embodied and the decision to include it in the speech belongs to Eisenhower. Through at least seven drafts, he actively preserved it and fine-tuned its context, ensuring that the MIC formulation was the centerpiece of his final message.[6]

In any event, the simple history of presidential speechwriting renders

Perle's aspersion moot. Most presidential speeches—indeed, some of the most famous of our time—have included the work of speechwriters. If Perle would have us dismiss the Farewell Address because a speechwriter may have been involved, then we must likewise dismiss Roosevelt's "Nothing to fear but fear itself," Kennedy's "Ask not what your country can do for you," and Reagan's "Tear down this wall," to name a few.[7]

Susan Eisenhower bristles at Perle's suggestion that Eisenhower was aloof from the writing process. "Eisenhower was a great speechwriter," she declares. "He'd been Douglas MacArthur's speechwriter and was well known in the Army for being able to turn a phrase. The Farewell Address may have had more than one author, but it's pure Eisenhower from start to finish."[8] John is even more direct. "I do not believe in the habit some staff officers get into of saying, 'it's my idea,' " he scoffs. "It ain't nothin' till the *boss* says it."

MRS. IKE

To question Eisenhower's commitment to the ideas of the Farewell Address is to misunderstand him more broadly. Rather than representing a departure from his usual sensibilities, John and Susan see the address as the logical extension of them, one with roots that stretch far back in his life and career. In this sense the military-industrial complex warning takes on far-reaching significance as a watershed moment in Eisenhower's career and, by extension, in the story of the American way of war.

Eisenhower occupied the Oval Office for eight years, at a time when the implications of the nascent national security state were just beginning to crystallize. While previous presidents had felt the tightening grip of military-industrial influences, the demands of the Cold War had brought the military and industry into an unprecedented level of cooperation with one another, compounding their cumulative level of influence over policy. Eisenhower was also a different kind of president, one whose personal background and experiences uniquely conditioned him to perceive, analyze, and ultimately resist the machinations of the military-industrial elites.

"My grandfather's evolution as a thinker clearly underwent enormous change and was subject to great challenge when he made the transition from five-star general to American president," Susan explains. "But all the elements of this thinking were in place long before, owing to the contradictions in his background. Dwight Eisenhower was raised in a pacifist household." Then, with the knowing smile of a subtly powerful woman who has spent her life in a family dominated by men, she adds: "Dwight Eisenhower's mother was a huge influence on her seven boys. And she had a life-changing experience during the Civil War."

Long before John ever grew conflicted over his membership in the party of "big white men," he brought Susan into the world, a serious but gentle woman with enormous reserves of intellect and compassion. "I can't take credit for her"—John shrugs lovingly—"she's an independent thinker. And she's made herself her own way."

A renowned expert on U.S.-Soviet relations, Susan is the author of several books, including *Mrs. Ike,* the untold story of her powerful grandmother Mamie, and the wonderfully titled *Breaking Free*, in which she recounts her own courageous decision to marry a Russian nuclear physicist in the wake of the Cold War. Between John's about-face on the subject of big white men, his father's epiphanous Farewell Address, and Susan's decision to "break free," fearless self-determination would seem to be an Eisenhower family trait.

John supports Susan's view that Ike's mother is to be credited for his more peaceable impulses.

"I don't recall Dad ever being called a peacenik," John chuckles, "but my grandmother was a Mennonite. She was born in Shenandoah Valley, Virginia. And she was three years old before the Civil War was over. And she remembered the Confederate soldiers coming through the house looking for her brothers. She told me she'd been a pacifist ever since."

Susan recounts that her great-grandmother found it devastating when Eisenhower chose to go into the military. "But still," she explains, "he took much of his mother's strong impulses with him into his adult life." After being turned down by the Naval Academy at Annapolis, Eisenhower was accepted to West Point when a prior applicant failed his physical. "It's one of the great what-if's of history," Susan muses. "What if he hadn't gotten in there?"

BAPTISM BY FIRE

In his definitive biography, *Eisenhower,* the late Stephen Ambrose describes Eisenhower's military career before World War II as an uneventful one, giving him little hands-on preparation for his extraordinary responsibilities in the war. What one rather sees in these early years are qualities of statesmanship first emerging and being influenced by key experiences. It is these qualities that will ultimately shape Eisenhower's unique perspective on the Cold War as a pivotal chapter in the American story.

After graduating from West Point in 1915, Eisenhower served stateside but did not see combat in World War I. When the war was over, many of his friends moved to lucrative jobs in American industry as he climbed slowly but persistently through the ranks. He was executive officer during the early 1920s to General Fox Conner, from whom he learned much about military history and strategy. From 1933 to 1935, he was chief military aide to Douglas MacArthur, in whose service Eisenhower not only sharpened his speechwriting skills but experienced firsthand the difficult tensions between the military and the political.[9]

"My duties were beginning to verge on the political, even to the edge of partisan politics," Eisenhower would later write. Indeed, during his sixteen years as a major, Ambrose reports, much of Eisenhower's time was spent lobbying congressmen for appropriations.[10]

Promoted to lieutenant colonel in 1936 and to brigadier general in 1941, Eisenhower was already fifty-one by the time of Pearl Harbor. He had never seen combat and was far from any short list of candidates for major command posts. After the attack, like much of America's armed forces, he had to hit the ground running. Assigned to the General Staff in Washington to prepare war plans against Germany and Japan, he became assistant to Chief of Staff General George Marshall, who quickly recognized his organizational and administrative talents. Marshall promoted Eisenhower to Commanding General, European Theater of Operations in 1942, and then to Supreme Allied Commander in Europe in 1943. It was in this capacity that he would command "Operation Overlord" and the victorious D-Day invasion of Germany in 1944.

Given his relative unpreparedness before the war and his meteoric rise through the ranks during it, Eisenhower's experience of World War II was a baptism by fire. "We cannot underestimate the extraordinary impact that World War II had on everybody who participated in it, no matter at what level," Susan notes. "It was a very brutal war. Very up close and personal, unlike our wars today." Being a relative stranger to combat and suddenly thrust into a position of such tremendous responsibility gave Eisenhower a great sensitivity to the human cost of war.

"During the war," Susan points out, "General Eisenhower made it his business to set aside a certain number of notices to family to write himself about his sorrow at the passing of their son. He forced himself to do that because he never wanted to lose touch with the consequences of his decision making." Speaking at a time when sitting president George W. Bush shows little desire to recognize U.S. military losses, let alone attend military funerals or communicate with grieving families, Susan pauses to let the pregnant contrast speak for itself.

Following Germany's defeat, Eisenhower toured the concentration camp at Ohrdurf on April 12, 1945, to which he invited cameras to bear witness to the atrocities.[11] The newsreel images offer a defining portrait: the commanding general in his starched uniform reacting to what he sees not as a hardened soldier but as a heartbroken human. The depth of feeling beneath the medals is quintessential Eisenhower—an unmistakable preview of the curious mix of authority and humanity in the Farewell Address.

"My grandfather believed deeply in the necessity for World War II and felt that Nazism was a terrible tyranny," Susan explains, "and he brought this conviction and drive to defeating Nazi Germany. But he never lost his understanding of the costs of war."

According to Ambrose, Eisenhower's return to America was marked by unexpected and jarring fame. His words as he stepped off his plane back to Washington became headlines a day later.[12] He spoke to a joint session of Congress, earning him "a standing ovation that was the longest in the history of Congress."[13]

Two weeks later, John Eisenhower traveled with his father to Potsdam to attend the conference at which Truman learned of the successful atomic test in the New Mexico desert. John recalls the moment his father told him about the bomb:

> One night in July of '45, we returned from Potsdam to Frankfurt. That day, the Secretary of War Henry Stimson had told my father about the development of the atomic bomb. We were sitting in his bedroom. And he said his own first impression, his own emotion, had been to be feeling down low. He wished we hadn't invented it. He just thought war was terrible enough as it was. You could have all the thermonuclear weapons in the world but that doesn't solve human problems. We live on earth.

Less than a month after this extraordinary moment between father and son, Eisenhower learned of the bombings of Hiroshima and Nagasaki.[14] Given the extent to which the bombing was a pre–Cold War check on the rise of Stalin, it's illustrative of his distance from Truman's decision that Eisenhower was actually visiting with the Russian leader in Moscow when he heard the news. Like several other military leaders discussed in Chapter Two, Eisenhower would later write in his memoirs that he had expressed "grave misgivings" on the basis of his belief "that Japan was already defeated and that dropping the bomb was completely unnecessary." He believed that America "should avoid shocking world opinion by the use of a weapon whose employment was, I thought, no longer mandatory as a measure to save American lives."[15]

As a military historian and one who was there, John is quick to qualify that though his father shared with him his discomfort over the development of the atom bomb, it is unclear how much he knew of or protested in advance of the actual bombings. Like many noted figures from the time, John believes his father's memory of vocal opposition grew as the years went on. "When you're older," John laughs knowingly, "memories sometimes get a little more vivid in our favor. Dad got more and more convinced about thinking it was the wrong thing to do as time went on. And I think maybe he came to picture himself as having protested more loudly than he originally had."

To whatever extent Eisenhower did or did not make his feelings known at the time, John's candor only deepens the impression that the bombings of Hiroshima and Nagasaki left Eisenhower with a profound sense of regret—based either on having been vocal in his concerns but ignored, or having been less vocal than he wished. Either way, Eisenhower's growing discomfort with the bombings helps to explain the caution with which he approached matters of security in the Cold War.

Susan describes how, as her grandfather transitioned into civilian life, "the shattering reality of what mankind had done to itself" stayed with him. "There was a strong feeling that war is a terrible, terrible business." She shakes her head. "And he wanted to make sure after the war was over that things would be set up to make this much harder to ever happen again."

AS ONE WAR ENDS . . .

For all the ticker tape, Eisenhower's homecoming was a conflicted one. He had left for Europe three years earlier a little known staff general and returned a national hero. Within minutes of his return, speculation swirled about his political ambitions. But he demurred, declaring in 1945: "I intend to have nothing whatsoever to do with partisan politics. I will never seek political office."[16]

Setting an example emulated by future soldiers like Colonel Wilkerson, Eisenhower kept mum when it came to his personal political leanings. As the election of 1948 approached, both parties saw his peerless popularity as the stuff of a candidate—a pattern repeated in the 1990s with General Colin Powell and again in 2004 with General Wesley Clark—and sought to curry favor with him.

With his own popularity waning in 1946, President Truman made Ike the surprising offer of the 1948 Democratic nomination, with Truman demoting himself to run as Eisenhower's vice president. But even to so generous an offer Ike flatly said no.[17]

He did spend two years as Truman's chief of staff, though the relationship between them, unlike that between Roosevelt and his chief George Marshall, was distant. Truman is reported never to have consulted Eisenhower on key decisions of his presidency, even those with significant military implications like the Truman Doctrine. Unlike many of Truman's advisers, Eisenhower was initially a reluctant cold warrior. As Ambrose describes, Eisenhower was skeptical of the hysteria toward the Soviet Union that gripped many in Truman's inner circle over the course of 1946. By mid-1947, he had begun to regard the Soviet Union with concern, but was decidedly "soft" on the Soviets compared to many others around Truman.[18]

Again, John Eisenhower is quick to qualify that, however measured, his father remained first and foremost a soldier, with a few basic principles. "The first is *keep your powder dry*," John explains, which in peacetime means being prepared for war. Like many who had been involved in the planning of World War II, Eisenhower credited America's victory to her military-industrial strength. "The lessons of the last war are clear," he wrote in an April 1946 memo to the War Department. "The armed forces could not have won the war alone. Scientists and businessmen contributed techniques and weapons which enabled us to outwit and overwhelm the enemy."[19]

Eisenhower took this lesson to the logical extension that military-industrial collaboration should figure centrally in future U.S. planning:

> It is of the utmost importance that the lessons of this experience be not forgotten in the peacetime planning and training of the Army. The future security of the nation demands that all those civilian resources which by conversion or redirection constitute our main support in time of emergency be associated closely with the activities of the Army in time of peace.[20]

A witness to the human cost of America's unreadiness in World War II, Eisenhower favored the sanity of confident preparedness to the trigger-happy hysteria of an arms race. For this reason, he supported Truman's National Security Act and its reliance on military-industrial development. Ironically, just fifteen years later he would become outspoken in his view that through such reliance on military-industrial cooperation, he and other postwar planners had—intentionally or not—created a monster.

Eisenhower's resistance to entreaties that he run for office did not stop the efforts of elites to lure him into either the private sector or national politics. According to Ambrose, Eisenhower in 1947 faced an uncertain future. He had left his post as chief of staff with a modest but guaranteed $15,000 annual salary and was to some extent at loose ends. To make matters more confusing, his high profile had placed him in the company of America's richest powerbrokers. As Ambrose explains, "the elite of the Eastern establishment moved in on him," lavishing him with "gifts, services, free trips, etc."[21]

"The gang," as an almost bewildered Eisenhower called these rich new friends, was a totally different circle from the obscure Army men and their wives who had been his and Mamie's principal acquaintances before the war. "When they played bridge in the thirties," Ambrose writes, "it was with other majors and their wives; in the late forties, it was with the president of CBS, or the chairman of the board of U.S. Steel, or the president of Standard Oil."

"The gang" loved the heroic general, and through them, his interaction with the top tier of Americans expanded exponentially. "Every member of the gang had his own circle of rich and powerful friends," Ambrose explains. "Eisenhower met on a social and private basis innumerable members of the American business, financial, publishing and legal elite, near every one of whom, after a few minutes with the general, became an Eisenhower-for-president booster, putting their time, money, energy, experience, and contacts into the cause."

As Ambrose goes on to report, Eisenhower's relations with wealthy men only grew through the years, "until his friends were almost exclusively millionaires." Invariably, these millionaires would approach Eisenhower to perform some innocuous function for a public institution or cultural organization—a museum or university—with more involved designs to follow.

While in the long term these movers and shakers lobbied for an Eisenhower presidency, in the short term they offered him the presidencies and board chairmanships of countless major corporations with "fantastic sums" attached. He declined every one.[22] Yet, though he refused to take money or jobs, Eisenhower was not above accepting the offer of a fishing or hunting cottage in the Deep South or the use of any number of golf courses where he could indulge his love of the game.

Historians debate the effect of these new relations of power on Eisenhower. Did they change him? Did they make him more at ease with economic power? Do they account for the fervor with which he advocated industrialization in his 1946 memo to the War Department? Or was it this new milieu that gave him the wisdom, as reflected in the Farewell Address, to know that "the power of money is ever present and is gravely to be regarded"?

In the end, the only mogul who successfully penetrated Eisenhower's defenses was IBM founder Thomas Watson. A trustee of Columbia University, Watson had visited Eisenhower at the Pentagon in 1946 when he was still chief of staff to invite him to speak at New York's Metropolitan Museum of Art. Eisenhower accepted, and while he was staying as Watson's guest at the Waldorf-Astoria, Watson asked him if he would consider serving as Columbia's president. At first, Eisenhower declined. But over the months that followed, Watson found the perfect way to persuade him. He advised Eisenhower that joining Columbia was not a move into the national spotlight; rather, it would provide him a kind of refuge from the whirlwind of speculation over his political ambitions. Eisenhower accepted.

Though he had left his post as chief of staff, Eisenhower continued while at Columbia to commute unofficially to Washington to help implement Truman's National Security Act. Before long, America's Cold War expansion would draw Eisenhower back into official public service. Yet the Columbia years proved to be a fateful period of transition and self-reflection. As he took refuge from the gathering storm of the Cold War, Eisenhower's concerns expanded from those of a wartime general to those of an American statesman.

"THE FOUNTAINHEAD OF FREE IDEAS"

In his inaugural address to the Columbia student body, Dwight Eisenhower displayed the analytical and speechwriting skills that are hallmarks of his career. The Columbia inaugural is an indication that, thirteen years before the Farewell Address, its themes had already begun to crystallize:

> It is not enough merely to realize how freedom has been won. Essential also is it that we be ever alert to all threats to that freedom. Easy to recognize is the threat from without. Easy too is it to see the threat of those who advocate its destruction from within. Less easy is it to see the dangers that arise from our own failure to analyze and understand the implications of various economic, social and political movements among ourselves.

Eisenhower's belief that members of society must "analyze and understand" the forces moving amongst themselves is echoed in the Farewell Address, in which he declares that "only an alert and knowledgeable citizenry" can act as a check on the "unwarranted influence" of the military-industrial complex.

"The total influence—economic, political, even spiritual," he warned in 1961, "is felt in every city, every state house, every office of the Federal government." But the spirit of the two speeches tracks even more closely when Eisenhower cautions his 1948 Columbia audience thus:

> One danger arises from too great a concentration of power in the hands of any individual or group: The power of concentrated finance, the power of selfish pressure groups, the power of any class organized in opposition to the whole—any one of these, when allowed to dominate, is fully capable of destroying individual freedom, as is excessive power concentrated in the political head of the state.[23]

The threat to "individual freedom" posed by "the power of selfish pressure groups" is echoed in Ike's farewell caution that "we must never let the weight" of the military-industrial complex "endanger our liberties or democratic processes." Likewise, the danger of what Eisenhower in 1948 called "the power of concentrated finance" finds its 1961 analogue in his pointed phrase "the power of money."

The radical tone of the Columbia address notwithstanding, Eisenhower's years at the university were by most accounts unremarkable. According to Ambrose, the presidency of Columbia was an experience for Eisenhower in exasperating bureaucracy, what he called "mountainous white piles" of paperwork.[24] Though Watson had won Eisenhower over with the assurance that he would have little responsibility for purely academic matters and no involvement in fund-raising, both seemed to demand a disproportionate share of his time.[25] In *Eisenhower at Columbia*, Travis Beal Jacobs describes a relationship of mutual dismay between Ike and the university. Despite the percieved prestige of this appointment by the outside world, inside the university he was seen as coarse and anti-intellectual—woefully out of touch with Ivy League pedagogical values. "And so the story goes," Ambrose writes, "Columbia suffered as much as the General did."[26]

Years later, in the Farewell Address, Eisenhower would offer a penetrating analysis of the university system—one that suggests (contrary to the impression of his being disconnected) a profound vision of the precious societal role of the university. In an alarming corollary to his warning about the danger of the military-industrial complex to American democracy, Eisenhower's Farewell Address also cautions that this same conjunction of forces threatens the purity of curriculum development at America's institutions of higher learning.

"Today," he warns, "the free university, historically the fountainhead of free ideas and scientific discovery, has experienced a revolution in the conduct of research. Partly because of the huge costs involved . . . the prospect of domination of the nation's scholars by Federal employment, project allocations, and the power of money is ever present—and is gravely to be regarded."

A week after Eisenhower delivered his 1961 Farewell Address, *The New York Times* published a collection of alarming statistics revealing the extent of federal investment in scientific research. "Four-fifths of planned Federal expenditures for research and development next year will be directed to national security needs," the *Times* reported, adding that more than 60 percent of all research in the United States was being funded by the federal government.[27]

That was in 1961. But according to Jacobs, federal funding was actually at a relatively low point during Eisenhower's stay on campus. Seven years before that, however, Columbia had been the birthplace of the Manhattan Project (hence the name), a case study in the explosive potential of federally guided research. By 1943, most atomic coordination and development had moved to the national laboratories at Oak Ridge, Tennessee, and Los Alamos, New Mexico. But in late 1942, early development work was still taking place at Columbia, with vast quantities of uranium stored in warehouses all over Manhattan. In a haunting (if overdrawn) metaphor for the impact of federal science on the welfare of the student, the Manhattan Project at one time enlisted the Columbia University football team to move uranium from one storage area to another. (Recalling Eisenhower's discomfort with the atom bomb and his proud memories of having been a running back on the West Point football team, one can only wonder how he would have felt about the use of the student body to develop a weapon of mass destruction.)

Propelled by the postwar industrial boom and the emphasis placed by Eisenhower and others on military-scientific cooperation, federally funded research returned with a vengeance during the 1950s.[28] With this resurgence, many in academia would come to share Eisenhower's concern for the disfiguring effects of money on the university. But during his own time at the university—a brief period of perceived peace between World War II and the renewed tensions of the Cold War—the issue was less pressing.

Still, Eisenhower developed a sense for the sanctity of academia. This may in part have come from watching his brother serve as president of Johns Hopkins amid the pressures of the Cold War. It may also have stemmed from the singular position Eisenhower occupied during his Columbia years, a time of strangely conflicting influences on his thinking. While in his developing relations with the wealthiest of Americans he was surely gaining an appreciation of the power of money, his time at Columbia also exposed him to a range of left-wing voices, shaping his understanding of pedagogy and the imperative that the expansion of young minds be the highest priority.

Between these opposing values, Eisenhower forged his own pedagogic vision, one that often caused friction within the university faculty. It prized the notion of citizenship. In a conversation with a faculty member, Eisenhower posed a question that demonstrated the gulf between himself and the institution. "What good are exceptional physicists," he asked, "unless they are exceptional Americans?" The idea of citizenship as a goal of pedagogy (as opposed to academic achievement) was seen as naive and simplistic by the faculty, to when Eisenhower made the university "sound like a high school civics class." Eisenhower's effort to found a Citizenship Education Project at Columbia Teacher's College only furthered this impression.[29] How could he have been so looked down on by the faculty? Beyond Eisenhower's folksy demeanor, there is nothing about his life that would suggest a lack of intellectual processing power. Yet, somehow Columbia's intelligentsia saw his vision as doltish and jingoistic.

In the context of his broader career, Eisenhower's emphasis on citizenship makes perfect sense; it is part of a far-reaching vision of the individual's role in national and global affairs. In his Columbia inaugural address, Eisenhower cautioned that "we be ever alert to all threats" to freedom and that "a definite task for the teacher" is to help the student "analyze and understand the implications of various economic, social and political movements among ourselves." In the Farewell Address, he echoed this argument, declaring that "only an alert and knowledgeable citizenry" could compel the military-industrial complex to function in accord with America's democratic values.

Columbia had gone from refuge to purgatory, but world events would soon offer a clean exit. Despite his frustrations, Eisenhower had written in his diary in 1949 that he would "never seek political office," unless there were "a series of events that crush all my arguments, that there appears to me to be such compelling reasons to enter the political field that refusal to do so would always thereafter mean to me that I'd failed to do my duty."[30]

On June 25, 1950, North Korea invaded South Korea. Truman responded, committing U.S. forces to the South's defense. America was once again at war. A year before, Truman had joined other European nations in the formation of NATO (the North Atlantic Treaty Organization), an alliance providing for the military cooperation of its member countries. As America assumed a posture of increased internationalism under the Cold War, the former Supreme Allied Commander was drawn out of his Ivy League reclusion and back into uniform. In November 1950, Truman invited Eisenhower to serve as NATO's first Supreme Commander. Ever the soldier (and at loose ends in academia), Eisenhower accepted.

IS COLLECTIVE SECURITY A EUPHEMISM FOR FOREIGN ENTANGLEMENT?

Truman's decision to send Eisenhower overseas was a blurring of the military and the political—a military decision, but one with direct and indirect political effects. Undeniably, Eisenhower was a natural choice, having been Supreme Allied Commander in Europe. Who better to preserve the peace in Europe than one who had been so instrumental in securing it? Yet it was surely not lost on Truman (or Eisenhower) that sending the general abroad was a good way to get him (and his political power) off the domestic stage. For Eisenhower, too, command of NATO provided a respite from pressure by "the gang" and others that he run for president. Yet, as might have been expected, the Supreme Command of NATO would have the exact opposite effect—providing "the perfect platform" to enhance his image as a world leader and viable presidential prospect.[31]

Command of NATO was thus both another step toward the presidency and, significantly, one toward an internationalist vision of America's role in the world. In 1950 and 1951, in what was called "The Great Debate" over the role the country should play on the world stage, conservatives vigorously opposed what was seen as the "liberal interventionism" of Truman and his supporters.[32] They were opposed both to the commitment of troops to NATO and to the appointment of Eisenhower, who found himself in a delicate political position.

Though Eisenhower was more measured in his concerns about Stalin than Truman and other liberal interventionists, he shared Truman's sense of the need for a fortified international system, one in which, as Susan Eisenhower explains, America would act as "a first among equals." While Eisenhower was inclined toward a Republican vision of domestic politics, he felt that the isolationism of conservative Republicans, such as presidential candidate Senator Robert A. Taft, risked allowing the spread of communism to undo all that he had fought for in Europe.

In addition to supporting Truman's National Security Act and accepting his appointment to NATO, Eisenhower supported Truman's signing of the UN Charter in 1949. "We all have to recognize," Truman declared at the signing, "no matter how great our strength, that we must deny ourselves the license to do always as we please."[33] According to his granddaughter, Eisenhower saw in the United Nations the opportunity "to bring the Soviets into a framework based on an international rule of law. He deeply believed that one of the tremendous advantages of the UN was that it gave the international community a set of rules that make it possible to weigh in on the good or bad behavior of nations and isolate the bad actors." With the triumphant Allied experience of World War II fresh in their minds, Truman and those around him reversed both America's past isolationism and her capacity to act unilaterally.

This interweaving of America's interests with those of other nations—a concept so foreign to the framers and yet so fundamental to the United

Nations and NATO—expressed itself in the notion of "collective security." NATO members would be bound by the North Atlantic Treaty, which states that "an armed attack against one or more of them in Europe or North America shall be considered an attack against them all." Under the treaty, each signatory country would be responsible to take military action in the event of an attack on any other. Never before had American interests been as closely interwoven with those of Europe in such official defiance of George Washington's Farewell Address caution against "permanent alliances with any portion of the foreign world."

Despite the parallels between Washington and Eisenhower on the topic of excessive militarism, it's clear that Eisenhower saw the need for some level of American international expansion. Washington's caution against "permanent alliances" was, for the moment, outmoded by the perception of crises of a scale unimagined by the framers. Thus, as the perceived security imperatives of the time drew the country away from its founding principles toward a new self-concept—one in which the American way of war was changing in its assumptions and aspirations—Eisenhower's own career and perspective were shifting with it.

As discussed in Chapter Three, Truman's National Security Act set the stage for the defense sector to acquire the "unwarranted influence" over policy making that Eisenhower would later decry in his Farewell Address. Yet at the time, Eisenhower's primary focus was on the need for America to establish the most effective instruments necessary to play an expanded international role in preventing a recurrence of yesterday's horrors.

It is important to note that, at a time when a sense of inevitability was building among Republicans that Eisenhower would be their next presidential candidate, he was actively departing from the traditional Republican isolationism. As the 1952 presidential election approached, disillusionment with Truman and the Korean War produced another "Draft Eisenhower" campaign from within the Republican Party. After a film reel of 33,000 supporters singing Ike's name was flown to him in France and he won the New Hampshire Republican primary without even declaring himself a candidate,[34] Eisenhower finally accepted the invitation. Buoyed by the slogan "I like Ike," he defeated the isolationist Senator Taft to secure the Republican nomination. Then, campaigning on a platform critical of Truman's handling of "Korea, Communism and

Corruption," Eisenhower handily defeated Democrat Adlai Stevenson to become the thirty-fourth president of the United States.

A CHANCE FOR PEACE?

On January 20, 1953, Eisenhower took the oath of office with his hand on two Bibles—one used by George Washington at the nation's first inauguration and the other given to Eisenhower by his mother upon his graduation from West Point. The symbolism was significant. In Washington, Eisenhower found a model predecessor—a fellow general-turned-president and a paragon of military and political virtues. In his mother lay the humanism of his pacifist roots—a lifelong counterweight to his military training, indoctrination, and experience.

Eisenhower echoed in his first inaugural address his familiar theme that human beings often realize too late the implications of certain systemic developments unfolding around them. "In the swift rush of great events," he began, "we find ourselves groping to know the full sense and meaning of these times in which we live. How far have we come in man's long pilgrimage from darkness toward light? Or are the shadows of another night closing in upon us?"

Underscoring the double-edged power of atomic technology, Eisenhower declared that "the promise of this life is imperiled by the very genius that has made it possible" and that "science has conferred upon us, as its final gift, the power to erase human life from this planet."

"It was a very dangerous period of time," Susan Eisenhower explains. "And Eisenhower was the first to acknowledge that a permanent military establishment would be required during this period. But that unless we could find some kind of breakthrough, it would end up creating a terrible cost."

Eisenhower's measured approach to the nuclear age is summarized elegantly in his Farewell Address. "Crises there will continue to be," he declared in 1961. "In meeting them, whether foreign or domestic, great or small, there is a recurring temptation to feel that some spectacular and costly action could become the miraculous solution to all current difficulties." Instead, he contends, "each proposal" for such action "must be weighed in light of a broader consideration; the need to maintain balance in and among national programs." This notion of balance in the Farewell Address was evident in Eisenhower's thinking from his first days in the White House as he sought a middle ground between the challenges of a dangerous world and the need to meet them with reason and farsightedness.

Less than three months into office and just one month after Stalin's death, Eisenhower delivered his "Chance for Peace" speech, in which he underscored the senseless tragedy of the Cold War. Speaking to the American Society of Newspaper Editors on April 16, 1953, he accused the Soviet Union of spending vast sums to develop weapons and thus compelling the United States to follow suit. He also asserted that, whatever its purpose, the arms race was diverting America's resources and energy disproportionately toward defense at the cost of other aspects of her national life. "Every gun that is made," he declared, "every warship launched, every rocket fired, signifies, in the final sense, a theft from those who hunger and are not fed, those who are cold and are not clothed. This world in arms is not spending money alone. It is spending the sweat of its laborers, the genius of its scientists, the hopes of its children."

The Chance for Peace speech, Susan explains, "was a very prophetic speech. It was the president's first major foreign policy address after taking office. And it was an opportunity for him to set out what he saw then and anticipated in the future to be the costs of a Cold War, where societies were spending unconscionable amounts of money on armaments instead of on human betterment."

The economic data from this period underscores Eisenhower's fear, demonstrating how, in a determined effort to outproduce the Soviet Union, the United States had begun to spend a disproportionate amount on defense in comparison with other areas of its national life. According to the Office of Management and Budget, postwar defense expenditures, which had shrunk to $9 billion by 1948, suddenly more than quadrupled, to $46 billion by 1952. By contrast during this same period, federal outlays on "Human Resources" such as education, health, and environment held steady at around $10 billion. By 1952, Human Resources represented only 17.4 percent of federal outlays and 3.4 percent of GDP.[35]

As a fiscal conservative and a meticulous military planner, Eisenhower was repulsed by profligate spending on defense. But as his pacifist mother's son, he was particularly saddened by the way in which such money spent on national defense was taken from other areas of national need. In "A Chance for Peace," he outlines a stark vision of these trade-offs:

> The cost of one modern heavy bomber is this: a modern brick school in more than 30 cities.
> It is two electric power plants, each serving a town of 60,000 population.
> It is two fine, fully equipped hospitals.
> It is some 50 miles of concrete highway.
> We pay for a single fighter with a half million bushels of wheat.
> We pay for a single destroyer with new homes that could have housed more than 8,000 people.
> This, I repeat, is the best way of life to be found on the road the world has been taking.
> This is not a way of life at all, in any true sense. Under the cloud of threatening war, it is humanity hanging from a cross of iron.

With the country at war in Korea and the "Red Scare" gripping the country, it was a courageous position for a new president to take. Eisenhower took office at the height of Joseph McCarthy's anti-Communist crusade. McCarthy openly opposed a number of Eisenhower's early appointees and opened eleven investigations into possible Communist sympathy among members of Eisenhower's State Department.

Critics have fairly charged over the years that Eisenhower never openly denounced McCarthy. Privately, Eisenhower confessed to hating the Wisconsin senator, but he offered various reasons for not openly opposing him, such as that engaging with McCarthy would only further the senator's desire for publicity and simultaneously degrade the presidency. Though Eisenhower's own anticommunism had deepened since the end of World War II, he abhorred the kind of national division wrought by McCarthy's methods. Still, he feared the consequences of alienating the senator's constituency, many of whom had voted for him. "I really believe," Eisenhower said privately, "that nothing will be so effective in combating his particular kind of troublemaking as to ignore him. This he cannot stand."[36]

In contrast to the courage of the Chance for Peace speech, this nonconfrontational approach to the McCarthy issue casts a shadow over Eisenhower's career. As a moment in his path to the Farewell Address, it reveals how soon into his White House years Eisenhower felt the pressure of private groups politicizing matters of national security.

In his unofficial role helping to implement Truman's National Security Act, Eisenhower had watched the various service branches exert formidable pressure on defense policy. He had watched Truman make concessions to the Navy in order to get it to support the unification of the armed services under the Department of Defense. Among these compromises was the proviso that the first secretary of defense would be then-secretary of the Navy, Admiral James Forrestal. He had watched Truman navigate between the Air Force's desire for the development of the B-36 bomber and the Navy's desire for more and bigger aircraft carriers. He had seen the efforts by the newly established Air Force to consolidate all airplanes—including those on naval carriers—under its control. For a time, the Air Force was almost successful, until the Navy rallied with what has come to be called "the revolt of the admirals."

As Eisenhower entered the White House, these defense sector power dynamics had only grown in depth and complexity. Even as one who knew the armed forces so intimately, he was unprepared for the kind of internecine turf wars he would have to wage. "When my dad first became president," John recalls, "the situation facing the country was changing. And he came in at the real beginning of the thermonuclear age. They'd had the atomic weapon before. But the hydrogen weapon of course is so much bigger. So that resulted in a considerable cutting back of the Army. But ground force is relatively inexpensive in wartime compared to the building of planes and missiles. And that was really the birth of the military-industrial complex." After just six months in office, Eisenhower fulfilled his campaign promise to end the war in Korea. That same year, he initiated a policy called the "New Look," which sought to reduce wasted expenditure on conventional arms by placing greater emphasis on nuclear weapons. In the context of America's standoff with the Soviet Union, these weapons promised the threat of mutually assured destruction, or MAD, and thus acted as a deterrent to conflict. This became the guiding doctrine of Eisenhower's use of the nuclear threat throughout his presidency and was the basis for the New Look program. The logic, according to Stephen Ambrose, was simple: "Fewer conventional forces, more atomic firepower, less cost."[37] The threat of "massive retaliation" with nuclear weapons was both a deterrent and, in the worst case, a form of devastating but cost-effective warfare.

In a contemporary context, this reliance on nuclear weapons might seem a bit dangerous. Yet at the time, one message of the bombings of Hiroshima and Nagasaki (even for Eisenhower, who opposed them) was that if the destructive potential of nuclear action could work as a deterrent, it would prove a cost-effective substitute to maintaining massive conventional forces. If the mushroom cloud had any silver lining, it should have been the prospect of deterring the threat of future conflict and reducing wasteful conventional defense spending.

Ever willing to recognize his father's strengths and weaknesses, John Eisenhower concurs. "It might be a bit debatable," John reflects, "whether the policy of massive retaliation was really ideal. Because it would admit terrible damage to the United States too if we ever commanded our weapons." As Ambrose further explains, the "massive retaliation" doctrine drew wide criticism in Congress as a threat to the balance of power. In January 1954, Eisenhower's secretary of state John Foster Dulles stirred up controversy when he declared that the president had made a "basic decision" that the United States would respond to any Soviet attack with "a great capacity to retaliate instantly."[38] The comment lacked any mention of Congress' right to declare war. Dulles put a finer point on the matter in March, declaring that "if the Russians attacked one of America's allies, there was no need for the President to go to Congress for a declaration of war."

In addition to congressional objections, the New Look policy met resistance from among the Joint Chiefs, who not surprisingly objected to Eisenhower's cuts to their conventional forces. "What I need to make the Chiefs realize," an exasperated president declared, "is that they are men of sufficient stature, training, and intelligence to think of this balance—the balance between minimum requirements in the costly implements of war and the health of our economy."[39]

Far too much, it turned out, was at stake, and the resistance Eisenhower experienced from both the Pentagon and those in Congress to his New Look reforms was certainly a formative one in shaping his ultimate concerns about the military-industrial complex. "My dad had pretty strong guiding principles that today would be considered simplistic, perhaps," John sighs. "Modern weapons take food from the hungry and shelter from the homeless. So he was fighting with the Pentagon all the time for asking for too much and with Congress for giving it to them."

Increasingly, Eisenhower's political adversaries seized upon his effort to reduce conventional forces as a way of more broadly impugning his stewardship of America's national security. The Joint Chiefs fueled these critiques, arming members of Congress with alarmist facts and figures concerning U.S. prepardness in a joint effort that only strengthened the growing alliance between them.

Eisenhower forged ahead, undeterred. Matching his actions to the words of his Chance for Peace speech, the New Look program succeeded in reducing conventional defenses. From 1953 to 1955, U.S. Army manpower shrank from 1.5 million to 1 million, the Navy and Marines from 1 million to 870,000. Budgetarily, too, the Army, Navy, and Marines shrank, while Air Force appropriations, already the highest at $15.6 billion, grew to $16.4 billion.[40] Eisenhower's goal to seek a greater level of balance between military and nonmilitary federal expenditure was mitigated by the reality that airpower was taking an increasingly central role in the picture of America's defense.

"WAR IS A RACKET"

Though his withdrawal from Korea and introduction of the New Look policy showed a measure of restraint in the president's approach to foreign policy, it was on his watch that the United States entered the era of covert activity. Using the newly established Central Intelligence Agency and the State Department (run respectively by Allen Dulles and his brother John Foster Dulles), the Eisenhower administration conducted several covert operations in foreign countries. Between 1953 and 1954, the CIA orchestrated the overthrows of two democratically elected leaders, President Jacobo Arbenz Guzmán of Guatemala and Prime Minister Mohammed Mossadegh of Iran. These overthrows heralded the dawn of a new era of secret international engagement conducted by the executive without the knowledge of members of Congress or the American people.

For Eisenhower and John Foster Dulles, these CIA actions were an effort to gain geostrategic ground in the larger struggle against communism. But with increasingly frequency, the economic interests of corporations were also involved. The idea that corporations wield influence over foreign policy in Washington was not new. In 1935, Major General Smedley Butler, two-time Medal of Honor recipient and the most decorated Marine in U.S. history, had published his *War Is a Racket*, exposing his own participation in profit-driven U.S. military action around the globe. As Butler put it:

> I spent 33 years and four months in active military service and during that period I spent most of my time as a high class muscle man for Big Business, for Wall Street and the bankers. In short, I was a racketeer, a gangster for capitalism. I helped make Mexico and especially Tampico safe for American oil interests in 1914. I helped make Haiti and Cuba a decent place for the National City Bank boys to collect revenues in. I helped in the raping of half a dozen Central American republics for the benefit of Wall Street. I helped purify Nicaragua for the International Banking House of Brown Brothers in 1902–1912. I brought light to the Dominican Republic for the American sugar interests in 1916. I helped make Honduras right for the American fruit companies in 1903. In China in 1927 I helped see to it that Standard Oil went on its way unmolested. Looking back on it, I might have given Al Capone a few hints. The best he could do was to operate his racket in three districts. I operated on three continents.[41]

Six years after the book's publication, in 1941, then-senator Harry Truman established a congressional committee to investigate fraud and corruption in the defense sector. The Truman Committee held more than four hundred hearings on the corrupt activities of war profiteers, whom Truman himself called "treasonous." The hearings led to hundreds of firings, and in one investigation of corrupt practices by the aerospace firm Curtiss-Wright, an American general was jailed. At the time, Wisconsin senator Robert M. LaFollette, Jr., called these profiteers "enemies of democracy in the homeland." Truman's hearings catapulted him into the national spotlight and were responsible for his selection as Roosevelt's running mate in the 1944 election.

War profiteering was thus nothing new. What was new in the era of covert activity was the use of the CIA to implement invisibly the plans hatched in private consultation between the executive, select advocates in Congress, and their cronies in industry. In this way, the establishment of the CIA helped to create a new layer of secrecy and reduced accountability, blurring the line between America's national interest and the private interests of corporations friendly to the U.S. government.

In Iran, the corporation in question was the Anglo-Iranian Oil Company, a British-owned company (later to become British Petroleum) whose interests were threatened when Mossadegh nationalized Iran's oil resources on May 1, 1951.[42] In an echo of the British government's request to Truman to intervene to safeguard British interests in Greece and Turkey, the British appealed to Eisenhower for help. He quickly labeled Mossadegh a Communist and, in an operation called "Ajax," the CIA worked to overthrow him.[43] Reflecting the continuum of America's expanding international posture, the CIA operative in charge of the coup operation was Kermit Roosevelt, grandson of Theodore, and the brigadier general working with internal security forces to depose Mossadegh and replace him with the Shah was H. Norman Schwarzkopf, father and namesake of General Norman Schwarzkopf, who would lead U.S. efforts against Saddam nearly forty years later.[44]

Beyond being an expression of solidarity with Britain, U.S. petroleum interests may have also motivated the coup. When Mossadegh first took power from the Shah in 1951, American oil executives had expected to receive 40 percent of Iranian oil output from him. To their disappointment, this never came to pass.[45] Prior to joining the CIA, Allen Dulles had been a lawyer for Standard Oil and the Anglo-American Oil Company, both companies with antipathies toward Iran.

According to Stephen Kinzer, author of *All the Shah's Men*, when the coup was over and Shah Mohammad Reza Pahlavi had been reinstated in power, he signed agreements that set up an international consortium to manage Iran's oil industry. U.S. companies owned 40 percent of the shares. Although the consortium was run by foreigners, it retained the name Mossadegh gave it—National Iranian Oil Company—to preserve the facade of nationalization. The consortium shared profits with Iran on a fifty-fifty basis yet did not open its books to Iranian auditors or allow Iranians on its board of directors.[46]

In Guatemala, the company was United Fruit, the same produce giant for whom Smedley Butler had "helped make Honduras right" in 1903, which had strong ties to the Eisenhower administration.[47] Before becoming secretary of state, John Foster Dulles had served on the company's board, and his brother Allen had served as president while the law firm both men had worked for, Sullivan & Cromwell, represented the company. Assistant secretary of state for Inter-American affairs John Moors Cabot was also a major shareholder.[48] In 1954, United Fruit's vast land ownership in Guatemala was threatened by an initiative pushed by President Arbenz to redistribute land more equitably among the country's poor.[49] In response, the CIA sponsored a coup d'état. The operation behind it was code-named "Operation PB SUCCESS." It led Arbenz to resign and flee the country. Nationalization of industries and wealth redistribution were populist aspirations that had arisen during the Spanish-American War and have ever since become hallmarks for leftist revolutionary influence. Thus, while the Anglo-Iranian Oil Company and United Fruit had profit motives for seeking to disrupt Mossadegh's and Arbenz's nationalization initiatives, U.S. officials authorized covert actions against them in the name of fighting communism.[50]

If Eisenhower had any misgivings about corporate influence on his policy making, there is no indication of it at the time. In his diaries, he offers only the most passing references to the CIA's increasing role in America's foreign affairs. After the coup in Iran, for example, he wrote: "The things we did [in Iran] were covert," and then, referring to the agent who engineered the coup, "I listened to his report and it seemed more like a dime novel than an historical fact."[51]

As Ambrose attests, Eisenhower was certainly in charge of these operations, yet his diaries suggest a great distance from and impunity regarding them. "Establishing a pattern he would hold to throughout his Presidency," Ambrose writes, "he kept his distance and left no documents behind that could implicate the President in any projected coup. But in the privacy of the Oval Office, over cocktails, he was kept informed by Foster Dulles, and he maintained a tight control over the activities of the CIA. . . . The methods used were immoral, if not illegal," Ambrose continues, "and a dangerous precedent had been set. The CIA offered the President a quick fix for his foreign problems. It was there to do his bidding; it freed him from having to persuade Congress, or the parties, or the public."[52]

The CIA's capacity to help a president short-circuit the usual checks and balances of a decision to engage in foreign conflict was indeed a "quick fix," with lasting, far-reaching implications. Despite Eisenhower's hesitance to join the national hysteria over overt conflict with the Soviet Union, these methods reflect his willingness nonetheless to put national and corporate economic interests ahead of respect for democratic processes at home and abroad. As such, they also reflect Eisenhower's contribution to the ever-growing trend toward international entanglement at the expense of the framers' carefully crafted separation of powers.

What happened? Just five years earlier, Eisenhower had warned the faculty and students of Columbia of the threat posed to freedom by "private pressure groups" and "the power of concentrated finance." Did he not see that these very forces were guiding America's actions in Iran and Guatemala? Had a blind spot emerged in his thinking? Worst of all, was Eisenhower seduced by the power afforded him by the newly formed CIA? Was he willing to overempower the executive branch in relation to the other branches?

Despite his relative reluctance to join the domestic chorus of Red Scare panic, the covert activity undertaken on his watch is a dark underside of his presidency. Given the widespread fears of the time and the formidable influence of McCarthy on the domestic landscape, one can fairly see how any president—even one as disinclined toward reactionary foreign policy as Eisenhower—could have been drawn into the vortex of runaway anticommunism. Yet Eisenhower's covert activity reveals that despite his vigilant concern for the delicate balance between security and liberty even he was susceptible to the temptation to engage in covert activities, thus undermining a genuine commitment to the nation's founding principles.

UNDER THE CLOUD OF THREATENING WAR

Eisenhower's White House years were a period of conflicting extremes for America. Beneath the smiling veneer of a postwar boom lay the stress fractures of a society under strain. Much as policy makers decades later would fail to reap a "peace dividend" in the wake of the Cold War, Eisenhower's America would forgo the fruits of victory from World War II as she pursued the arms race with the Soviets. Eisenhower's own measured pulse notwithstanding, the years between 1953 and 1961 saw increasing tension between the superpowers abroad and the disfiguring impact of this tension at home.

U.S. foreign policy in these years was a mix of controlled aggression, in the form of covert action and proxy wars, and halting diplomacy, in the form of several efforts at cautious conciliation with Moscow. As predicted in George Orwell's 1945 essay, "You and the Atomic Bomb," the proxy conflicts between the United States and the USSR in such places as Korea, Iran, Guatemala, Indonesia, Laos, and Vietnam, employed conventional arms and covert activity to engage in satellite skirmishes that averted what might have otherwise been a conflict of nuclear annihilation. To those experiencing these conflicts firsthand—from Guatemala to Iran to Indonesia and Laos—they were destructive enough; but for the superpowers they were a lesser evil.

Eisenhower was the oldest serving president of his time and suffered both a heart attack and a stroke while in office. His opponents were quick to paint a portrait of him as a war-weary old soldier, struggling to keep his wits about him as those around him were losing theirs. Much as Republicans during the Bush years have sought political advantage by portraying the opposing Democrats as being soft on terror, in Eisenhower's day Democrats accused him of being soft on the Soviets, and of allowing the United States to fall behind Moscow in the arms race. These accusations took shape in two successive lines of negative propaganda: the "bomber gap," which plagued the president's first term, and the "missile gap," which plagued his second. Both were reflections of the insidious intertwining of the interests of the military, Congress, and the defense-industrial sector that Eisenhower would so gravely come to warn the country about.

The Bomber Gap

The so-called bomber gap was a political canard promoted by an alliance of Air Force brass and defense contractors seeking money to build more bombers. The claim, which spanned the years 1954 to 1957, was that the

Soviet Union was surpassing the United States in its production of jet-powered strategic bombers, and that these bombers were capable of delivering a nuclear attack on the United States.

In *Perils of Dominance*, Gareth Porter provides vital statistics that refute this claim.[53] Soviet airpower, Porter argues, was primarily deterrent in nature. Not only did the Soviets possess far fewer aircraft than proponents of the bomber gap claimed, none of these planes was able to cover the vast distance to the continental United States, deliver an attack, and return. Even from Arctic bases, their lumbering planes would have taken thirteen hours to reach their targets, giving the United States ample time to bring them down. Prior to the 1960s, Porter argues, the Russians could not project power much farther than their own territory.[54]

Despite evidence refuting the bomber gap, it was popularized by members of Congress, including Missouri Democratic senator Stuart Symington, who before entering the Senate had served as the first secretary of the Air Force. An ardent Eisenhower opponent with his own presidential aspirations, he was a tireless promoter of increased defense appropriations.

"It is now clear," Symington declared from the Senate floor in May 1956, "that the United States, along with the rest of the free world, may have lost control of the air." Symington would haunt the entirety of Eisenhower's White House years, accusing the administration of putting the country's national security at risk by enacting the New Look defense cuts. In many ways Symington is the prototype of the role played by many members of Congress today in lobbying—and fear-mongering—for the desires of the military-industrial complex.

"Each community in which a manufacturing plant or a military installation is located," Eisenhower would later write in his memoirs, "profits from the money spent and the jobs created in the area. This fact, of course, constantly presses on the community's political representatives—congressmen, senators, and others—to maintain the facility at maximum strength."[55] Eisenhower correctly suspected the bomber gap claim to be false. To dispel it conclusively and avert wasteful defense expenditure, he authorized the top-secret U-2 spy program to conduct flights over the Soviet Union to assess its actual bomber strength.

Eisenhower's use of the U-2 was itself a case study in the blurring of the military and political. The U-2 had only been in development for one year when the charge of a gap arose. Lockheed had been experimenting for some years with the top-secret idea of a lightweight high-altitude espionage aircraft, but it was not until 1954 that Eisenhower authorized its production. The decision was tricky because of the political implications and dangers of a military aircraft entering another country's airspace. As a result, though the U-2 would ultimately be flown by the Air Force and even the Navy, it originated as a secret CIA program. Accordingly, U-2 pilots resigned their military commissions before joining the CIA and flying as civilians. As this bureaucratic sleight of hand betrays, the U-2 was part of the growing concealment of executive power implied more broadly by the rise of the CIA.

By mid-1955, the U-2 was being test-flown, and a year later, on July 4, 1956, the first U-2 Soviet overflight was conducted. Though the U-2 confirmed Eisenhower's suspicions, it did not prevent the bomber gap claim from achieving its desired effect, contributing to the expansion of the Air Force while the New Look policy was shrinking the other services. In 1953, the U.S. Air Force had 329 B-47 Stratojets capable of bombing targets inside the Soviet Union from U.S. bases in Europe and Japan. By 1955, the number of B-47s had risen to 1,086. That same year, the United States also introduced the B-52 bomber that could, by refueling in midair, reach Soviet targets from the continental United States. By 1960, there were 539 such B-52s in the U.S. Strategic Air Command, bringing the total number of strategic bombers able to deliver a nuclear attack on the USSR to 1,735.[56]

The Missile Gap

The missile gap claim, a second fearmongering propaganda device, emerged in 1957 following the Soviets' surprise launch of Sputnik 1, a robotic spacecraft capable of orbiting the earth. Earlier that summer, the Soviets had successfully tested their first intercontinental ballistic missile. The launch of Sputnik struck fear in Americans that the Soviets were achieving technological superiority in missile development. Two months later, the spectacular televised failure of America's Vanguard TV3 rocket compounded this fear of Soviet advantage, generating the claim that Eisenhower had allowed a "missile gap" to emerge between the United States and the Soviets.

As with the bomber gap, Eisenhower rejected the missile charge. But he was reluctant to authorize additional U-2 espionage for fear that the Soviets would discover the program. Under intense pressure from the CIA, he relented, but not without stipulating that he personally approve each mission. Once again, U-2 reconnaissance confirmed his suspicions: There was no missile gap. Yet this knowledge failed to stem the tide of public fear since Eisenhower could not publicly divulge the information obtained by the spy planes.

In fact, the Soviets were comparatively more focused on the building of intercontinental ballistic missiles (ICBMs) than the Americans. But this was only because the U.S., with its extensive forward basing in Europe and Turkey, could attack the Soviets with shorter-range missiles and therefore didn't need to work as hard to develop the intercontinental variety. The Soviets had no such forward basing from which to attack the United States and thus their focus had to be on ICBMs. So, while the notion that the Soviets were more focused on the ICBM may technically have been accurate, it was misused by proponents of the missile gap to suggest that the USSR was better able to deliver a destructive nuclear attack on America.

The myth of the missile gap became very much the blueprint for the tangled web of interlocking public and private interests that Eisenhower would ultimately call the military-industrial complex. In *Eisenhower and the Missile Gap*, Peter Roman traces the missile gap episode to Senator Stuart Symington, a defense contractor executive, and the dangerous interplay of partisan politics and corporate gain. The defense contractor was Convair, a division of General Dynamics, and its executive was Thomas G. Lanphier, a decorated fighter pilot from World War II who had shot down numerous Japanese fighter planes, sank a destroyer, and downed a plane believed to be carrying the Japanese admiral Isoroku Yamamoto, mastermind of the Pearl Harbor attack. When Symington was the secretary of the Air Force, Lanphier had been his special assistant.

In 1946, Convair had been awarded a contract to explore the development of an intercontinental ballistic missile system, funding what would become the Atlas program. After the Soviets successfully exploded an H-bomb in 1953, new emphasis was placed on the development of an ICBM. Lanphier was instrumental in working with his former boss to push the Eisenhower administration to adopt a crash program under which Convair would complete development of the Atlas and produce missiles at a cost of $1.5 million each.

"By early 1955 [the Air Force's] Atlas project was mushrooming: from the fiscal year 1953 figure of $3 million, in 1954 it went to $14 million and in 1955 to $161 million," Eisenhower writes in the second volume of his memoirs.[57] In 1956, Eisenhower enacted substantial cuts in defense spending, which involved cutbacks in the funding of the Atlas program, and further cuts were made the following year. Lanphier and Symington went on the offensive, criticizing the president for being too complacent about America's need for greater operational missile capability. With the 1957 launch of Sputnik, the growing friction with Eisenhower over the Atlas program became the basis of Symington's missile gap charge.

From late 1957 to mid-1958, the CIA released a series of conflicting reports on the Soviet Union's missile production. Eisenhower disagreed with their estimates, which were far higher than anything reported by his secret U-2 program. In mid-1958, when the agency revised its estimate to bring it more in line with Eisenhower's, Symington seized on this shift to intensify his critique of the president. He even met with Eisenhower to share new evidence that by 1960 or 1961 the Soviets "will have 500 ICBM's," more than triple what the United States planned to produce. Much of Symington's new information had been provided to him by Lanphier.[58]

Symington's strident posture reflected a combination of factors: his personal bias toward airpower, his closeness to Lanphier and thus to the Atlas program and—of growing importance in the 1957–59 timeframe—his presidential ambitions. As the missile gap charge became the rallying cry for Symington's bid for the Democratic presidential nomination of 1960, his partisan political ambitions became increasingly interwoven with Lanphier and Convair's private goals. Lamphier ardently pressed the public case for increased missile development. In 1960, Lanphier suddenly resigned from Convair in a highly public fashion, citing his "right and privilege as an American citizen to criticize my government . . . without being factored as a 'missile salesman.' "[59] Some reports indicated he had been forced out by General Dynamics chairman Frank Pace, who objected to Lanphier's criticism of the Eisenhower defense cuts. Just one day after this dramatic resignation, *The New York Times* speculated that "the decision to quit may also have some connection with the unavowed Presidential candidacy of Senator Stuart Symington." Thereafter, Lanphier actively campaigned for Symington.[60]

For Eisenhower, however, the problem ran far deeper than any one politician or contractor. When a conflict with the Soviets over the city of Berlin emerged in 1958, defense contractors Boeing and Douglas issued advertisements fanning the "missile gap" flames. An exasperated Eisenhower told Republican leaders he was "getting awfully sick of the lobbies by the munitions. . . . You begin to see this thing isn't wholly the defense of the country, but only more money for some who are already fat cats."[61]

Though Symington would lose the Democratic nomination, his charge would live on for his Democratic rival, John F. Kennedy. A month after Sputnik, Kennedy had joined the ranks of those declaring that the nation was losing the satellite-missile race with the Soviets. Kennedy's first recorded use of the actual term "missile gap" was on August 14, 1958. "Our Nation," he declared during a heated debate on the floor of the Senate, "could have afforded, and can afford now, the steps necessary to close the missile gap."[62]

Kennedy blamed "complacent miscalculations, penny-pinching, budget cutbacks, incredibly confused mismanagements, and wasteful rivalries and jealousies."[63] He had been preparing for a Senate reelection campaign when the news of Sputnik broke. Over the next few years, he repeated the missile gap claim loudly and often, despite a lack of evidence to support it. As the 1960 election approached, the claim became as much a partisan political platform for him as it was for Symington.

After winning the nomination to face Vice President Richard Nixon in the presidential election of 1960, Kennedy continued to echo the charge as a tool to embarrass Eisenhower and, by association, Nixon. Later, as president, Kennedy would concede that the missile gap had been a myth. In a December 1962 conversation with his secretary of defense Robert McNamara, Kennedy admitted with some self-irony that he had been a "patriotic and misguided man" in the late 1950s, who had been "one of those who put that myth around."[64]

A candid enough confession; but by then it was too late. America's foreign policy had been disfigured by the fearmongering, even bringing the two superpowers to an international incident.

Though the U-2 program had successfully demonstrated the claims of a gap in bombers and missiles to be fatuous, this demonstration came at a tremendous cost. On May 1, 1960, a U-2 deployed to photograph ICBM development facilities in the Soviet Union was shot down by a Soviet surface-to-air missile. Soviet premier Nikita Khrushchev announced the downing of the aircraft but deliberately omitted the fact that pilot Francis Gary Powers had been captured alive. The Eisenhower administration, assuming Powers was dead, pretended publicly that the plane was a NASA "weather research aircraft" and that Powers may have fallen unconscious due to oxygen failure. After the Eisenhower administration went through many contortions to prove this, including grounding the entire U-2 fleet to pretend to check the oxygen issue in all the planes, Khrushchev produced Powers publicly, revealing that the downed U-2 had indeed been on a spy mission.

An international summit between Eisenhower and Khrushchev scheduled to begin in Paris on May 15, 1960, collapsed, because Eisenhower would not apologize. The U-2 incident became the greatest embarrassment of Eisenhower's White House years and was an unintended foreign policy consequence of the domestic pressures of the missile and bomber gap campaigns. In this sense, Eisenhower associated the greatest mistake of his presidency with his effort to navigate the treacherous domestic pressures of the MIC.

The mind-set with which Eisenhower approached his Farewell Address was clearly deeply influenced by the impact of the missile gap charge on the 1960 election. Peter Roman maintains that "Eisenhower called Symington, Johnson and Kennedy demagogues who attempted to manipulate national security for personal political gain—but he did so in the Oval Office, rarely in public."[65] Eisenhower's staff secretary Andrew Goodpaster confirms this, noting that Eisenhower privately "expressed his deep concern over what men like Senator Symington or Senator Kennedy might do as President."[66]

Stephen Ambrose recounts an episode that was perhaps the last straw for Eisenhower—an experience with the Kennedy camp over the missile gap. Though Eisenhower knew conclusively from the U-2 program that the charge of a missile gap was untrue, he still could not publicly divulge the proof without compromising the program's secrecy. Yet he became so frustrated by Kennedy's accusations that he went to the length of authorizing CIA director Allen Dulles to share the U-2's intelligence quietly with Kennedy, seeking to dissuade him from continuing to spread an untruth that, among other things, would give comfort to America's enemies.[67] After meeting privately with Kennedy and his running mate, Lyndon Johnson, at their Massachusetts and Texas residences, Dulles reported to Eisenhower on the briefings in a letter on August 3, 1960. He had provided "both candidates," he told Eisenhower, with "an analysis of Soviet strategic attack capabilities in missiles and long-range bombers."[68]

Even after this briefing, Kennedy pressed on with the charges undeterred, angering Eisenhower, who saw how recklessly a matter of national security could be exploited for political gain. Given his experience with Symington and Lanphier, and countless other examples of the intertwined interests of the Pentagon, its manufacturers, and Congress, Eisenhower saw in Kennedy's conduct a fulfillment of George Washington's fears of an "overgrown military establishment." "God help this country," the general-turned-president was overheard to say in the Oval Office, "when someone sits at this desk who doesn't know as much about the military as I do."[69] Even Eisenhower's vice president, Richard Nixon, joined the chorus during his own presidential campaign, declaring that "there must be no price ceiling on American security."[70]

WAGING PEACE

The Farewell Address represents the sum wisdom of Eisenhower's experience as much on foreign battlefields as in the turf wars of Washington. Certainly, Stuart Symington, as well as John F. Kennedy's fearmongering on the campaign trail, were much on the president's mind as his administration drew to a close. Yet the farewell warning clearly represents the convergence of a much larger set of formative forces in Eisenhower's career.

From his pacifist childhood he cultivated a lifelong unease with war, which was given unforgettable intensify by the trauma of his experience in World War II. While the devastating horrors of the concentration camps underscored the need to fight for freedom, the gratuitous mass destruction of Hiroshima instilled in him an equal and opposite awareness that the fight for freedom, conducted without reason and a steady moral compass, could itself lead to atrocities. From his postwar flirtation with America's power set, Eisenhower seems to have developed a simultaneous respect for the power of money and a healthy skepticism of it. From his early political education under MacArthur, he had acquired a discomfort with the politicization of issues of security, which would take on urgency in the political minefield of his White House years.

Taken together, the forces shaping Eisenhower's warning mirror America's own evolution over the half century from World War I to Vietnam. World War I engaged the country in foreign affairs more broadly than ever before. It was followed by a demobilization consistent with the framers' hesitance toward foreign entanglement, but the evils of fascism produced a moral imperative for America to enter World War II and thereby greatly expand its international role. Though the impulse of her people was again to demobilize and seek a state of relative isolation, for policy makers "the lessons of the last war," as Eisenhower called them, made such a retreat seem dangerously naive.

With the dawn of Truman's national security state and the era of covert action, unprecedented power shifted to the executive branch, but not without strings attached. The newly empowered executive was to find his decision-making power hamstrung, not by the proper constitutional checks and balances of the legislative and judicial branches but by unholy new alliances of actors in the national security landscape. "This conjunction of an immense military establishment and a large arms industry is new in the American experience," Eisenhower declared in the Farewell Address. "The total influence—economic, political, even spiritual—is felt in every city, every Statehouse, every office of the Federal government. We recognize the imperative need for this development. Yet we must not fail to comprehend its grave implications."

With atomic fear in the air, Eisenhower saw the increasing difficulty for any public servant to ignore the call for ever-increasing defense expenditure. Yet, given the unique combination of personal, military, and political perspectives he brought to the Oval Office, the dangerous machinations of those in Congress, the armed forces, and the defense sector were clearer to him than they might have been to another president. "It's not by accident," says his granddaughter Susan, "that he called his second body of memoirs *Waging Peace*. He never lost his understanding of the cost of war. He had that so much from his mother and from the religious community in which he was raised. I think at the end of the day, he wanted to be thought of as a man of peace. And he was a man of peace—understanding full well that sometimes in order to have peace, war must be waged."

Whether it was his experience on the battlefield, his Mennonite roots, or plain old Kansas common sense, Eisenhower ultimately understood that a nation's defense is about more than just bombs. He saw firsthand that a country that allocates a disproportionate share of its wealth toward defense and away from other aspects of its national life is a country driven by an incomplete vision of national security. In the final analysis, Eisenhower understood that an uneducated country is an undefended country; that a country without adequate health care is an undefended country; that a country in debt is an undefended country; that a country that acts without regard for the international community is an undefended country; and above all, that a country whose people have lost faith in their leaders is a country they will not die for.

A FEW FINAL WORDS

While Eisenhower's warning would come to seem prophetic, it was greeted in its day with a mix of surprise and unease. In his essay "New Light on Eisenhower's Farewell Address," Charles J. G. Griffin suggests that many at the time were surprised to hear "a professional military man bracket the military with big business as potential enemies of the national interest."[71] Others, as demonstrated by the next day's front-page headline in *The New York Times*, expected a more sentimental leavetaking from the general-turned-president and "were surprised by the jeremiadic cast of his final message."

In his farewell, it's clear that Eisenhower took his cue from George Washington. In his memoir *At Ease*, Eisenhower calls Washington "my hero" and writes that Washington's Farewell Address "exemplified the human qualities I frankly idolized."[72] Griffin contends that what Eisenhower most sought to emulate from Washington's farewell was the capacity "to convey his legitimate concerns about an expanding defense establishment and score a tactical blow against his political adversaries, even as it enhanced his ethos as a statesman 'above politics.' "As Eisenhower himself later explained: "The idea, then, of making a final address as President to the nation seemed to call on me to warn the nation, again, of the danger in these developments. I could think of no better way to emphasize this than to include a sobering message in what might otherwise have been a farewell of pleasantries." It was, Eisenhower recognized, "the most challenging message I could leave with the people of this country."[73]

Yet overall, the speech went largely unnoticed, overshadowed as it was by the celebration of Kennedy's inauguration and the dawn of what felt like a new era. Compared to the tanned and youthful new president, the aging general, however radical his words, seemed yesterday's man.

Still, as if on cue, Kennedy immediately began to fulfill Eisenhower's prophecy. Having run on a platform accusing Eisenhower of being soft on the Soviets, Kennedy moved quickly to assume a more hawkish global posture. Declaring at his inauguration that America "would pay any price, bear any burden . . . to assure the survival and the success of liberty," he proceeded to oversee what he himself would call "the most far-reaching defense improvements in the peacetime history of this country."[74]

Indeed, these improvements accounted for a 14 percent increase in defense spending between 1961 and 1962—the largest single peacetime increase in U.S. history. Beyond the economic impact of the appropriations, they would exact a significant human cost as well. In a further fulfillment of Eisenhower's fears, Kennedy would soon involve America in the budding conflict in Vietnam. By the time of his death, Kennedy had committed 16,300 "advisers" to the conflict, with 118 American lives lost in the first year alone. The war would continue for another decade, costing more than 58,000 American and 3 million Vietnamese lives.[75]

As Vietnam wore on, Eisenhower's words came back to haunt America, seized upon by critics of the war. But by then, of course, the damage had been done.

Four months after John Eisenhower shared with me his frustration at George Bush and the party of big white men, he went public. In late September, during the 2004 presidential race between George W. Bush and his challenger John Kerry, Eisenhower's son made known his decision to leave the Republican Party. Publishing an editorial in the *New Hampshire Union Leader*, he surely sought to influence the referendum on the Bush administration that November.

In the presidential debate just a few days later, Kerry alluded somewhat obscurely to John Eisenhower's decision to leave the Republican Party and vote for him instead, including John's name among a list of military supporters. The comment was lost, however, in the insipid blur of Kerry's generally hapless candidacy.

Despite Kerry's inability to derive meaningful political capital from John Eisenhower's decision, the message was unmistakably resonant. Forty years after his father issued his farewell warning, the Bush administration had become a case study for John in just the sort of misplaced national priorities Ike feared. "Today's 'Republican' Party," John wrote, "is one with which I am totally unfamiliar. To me, the word 'Republican' has always been synonymous with the word 'responsibility,' which has meant limiting our governmental obligations to those we can afford in human and financial terms. Today's whopping budget deficit of some $440 billion does not meet that criterion." He went on to accuse the administration of isolating America through "hubris and arrogance."

By breaking ranks so publicly, John took a page from his father's playbook, offering a much needed dose of nonpartisanship and, ultimately, nonmembership in the club of big white men. "I celebrate, along with other Americans," he wrote, "the diversity of opinion in this country. But let it be based on careful thought. I urge everyone, Republicans and Democrats alike, to avoid voting for a ticket merely because it carries the label of the party of one's parents or of our own ingrained habits."[76]

Forty years earlier, watching the world become one with which he could no longer march in lockstep, Ike couldn't have said it better himself.

5

John Boyd, Donald Rumsfeld, and the Meaning of Transformation

Our scientific powers have outrun our spiritual powers; we have guided missiles and mis-guided men.

Martin Luther King, Jr.
Strength to Love, 1963

When the four 2,000-pound bombs dropped by Fuji and Tooms in the opening moments of Operation Iraqi Freedom struck a suburban Baghdad compound called Dora Farms, the attack missed its targets—Saddam Hussein and his sons Uday and Qusay. Though only time will reveal the attack's larger repercussions, the war the strike launched was a fulfillment of Eisenhower's fears of runaway American militarism. Yet, to its planners, the opening strike seemed a natural extension of America's expanding foreign role since World War II and of the technological advances made possible by the American way of war.

Whereas for the neoconservatives the strike fulfilled long-standing foreign policy aspirations for a "New American Century," it seems to have meant something different, though not incompatible, to Donald Rumsfeld. Despite the defense secretary's apparent collaboration, Fukuyama points out that there is no evidence from Rumsfeld's history that he was inclined toward the kind of Pax Americana the neocons advocate. To him, Fuji and Tooms' strike (which he personally authorized) more narrowly represented the fulfillment of a technological military ideal, one that had emerged over the decades of his military-industrial career. "Transformation," as this concept is called, is a catchall for a wide array of technological advances that comprise a twenty-first-century vision of American war fighting.

The transformation ideal is commonly associated with the late maverick Air Force colonel, John Boyd, a household name among military brass, who is all but unknown to the mainstream. Yet a close analysis of Boyd's career by those who knew him reveals that while Rumsfeld's war plan for Iraq may have emphasized the kind of high-tech airpower commonly associated with Boyd, it fundamentally violated John Boyd's larger vision of American war strategy. To those who knew Boyd, Rumsfeld's plan—and notably its failure—is a case study in how the military-industrial forces Eisenhower feared may not only prove disfiguring to the nation's balance of power and its spending priorities but even distort U.S. military strategy in the field. As such, they fuel a self-perpetuating cycle of overzealous militarism and gross miscalculation, with spiraling consequences.

THE TOOTH-TO-TAIL RATIO

Colonel Richard Treadway is an Air Force commander out of central casting. Disarmingly handsome, with piercing blue eyes and immaculate salt-and-pepper hair, he has the unflappable poise one hopes to find in a pilot, surgeon, or ship captain. Fuji and Tooms' commanding officer in their strike against Dora Farms, Treadway is an experienced pilot himself and a scholar of military history. He sees the opening strike—whatever its outcome—as a triumph of both American policy and know-how since World War II.

"It was a bold move," Treadway declares, betraying obvious pride not only in his men but in their mission. "The decision to attack Iraqi leadership at the opening salvo was a courageous political decision. It was a new way of making war, and technology was able to provide our leadership that opportunity."[1]

Though the particular technologies involved—four GPS- and laser-guided bunker-busters launched by arguably the most advanced aircraft in the U.S. arsenal—were indeed state of the art, the capacity for such a surgical strike was long in the making. If one could freeze on the moment of impact and push rewind, one could travel back in time to see the capacity for such a surgical strike take shape over a half century of American warmaking. Along the path of Fuji and Tooms' bombs—not just from the plane to the target but from farther back in time—one would discover how the ambitious notion of a push-button war, launched from high altitudes, is a direct extension of the rise of the military-industrial complex and its influence on the very concept of American war.

Treadway sees the MIC as the engine of all that is great about the American way of war. "The military-industrial complex," he glowingly explains, "was a creation during the Eisenhower years when it was understood that the way to address the overwhelming military might of the Soviet Union was to create an industrial capacity in the United States to produce the weaponry, the ammunition, to carry out the American way of war." Though America is by no means the first country to develop a military industry, Treadway argues that it has done so on an unprecedented scale and in its own unique way.

"The American way of war," Treadway declares, "has historically been described as 'overwhelming firepower supported by overwhelming logistics.' *The tooth-to-tail ratio.* The fact that for every shooter out there—every man with a gun—there are hundreds behind, supporting, providing the food, the ammunition, the boots, the fresh water, the gas for the tanks, the oil. The great logistic tail that goes into the biting tooth up front." Treadway argues that such military industrialization has shaped not only America's warmaking but its civilian life as well. "The great industries that have become some of the foundations of modern America—General Dynamics, Lockheed-Martin, McDonnell Douglas, Bell Aerospace, and Boeing—many of these companies have also in the intervening years created much of what is great about American industry for civilian uses."

Beyond the Keynesian principle that weapons R&D yields ancillary civilian benefits, Treadway sees the military-industrial complex as a force that can liberate people through the power of its weapons while winning their trust through the care that surgical strikes imply. "That's one of the premises of modern airpower," he says. "The minimization of collateral damage, the risk to innocent life. We have made huge leaps in that direction. And this is extremely important to those whose hearts and minds we're trying to win."

Above all else, Treadway sees the opening strike—in its use of Stealth aircraft and precision weapons—as a major advance over the barbarism of past wars. "It's a remarkable leap," he explains, "not only in technology but in the ability to wage war and risk fewer lives. Not only the lives of the pilots delivering the weaponry, but the lives of everyone else on the ground."

Perhaps not surprising, Treadway sees the military-industrial complex that produces such life-saving innovations as a force for good. His idealism is genuine; he believes in the goal of minimizing war's ravages. Yet, if the broader mission of Fuji and Tooms' operation was to win Iraqi hearts and minds by using surgical technology to effect regime change, the fact that the strike failed to eliminate Saddam and his sons, and that a full-scale and indefinite U.S. military occupation of Iraq was instead required, suggests that, at minimum, the operation failed. No one bears greater responsibility for this failure than Donald Rumsfeld.

"THE ENEMY"

For Rumsfeld, the opening strike was a watershed moment in a meteoric career in the public and corporate sectors. After serving as a naval aviator in the 1950s and then an investment banker in the early 1960s, Rumsfeld was elected to Congress in 1962, where he remained until 1969. He joined the Nixon administration as assistant to the president and became ambassador to NATO in 1973. After Nixon's resignation, Rumsfeld was appointed by Gerald Ford to serve first as White House chief of staff and then as the youngest secretary of defense in U.S. history. He returned to the corporate sector in 1977 as CEO of G. D. Searle & Co., a pharmaceutical giant responsible for, among other things, the patenting of the artificial sweetener aspartame. From 1990 to 1993, he was CEO of the technology firm General Instrument Corporation.

By the time he was appointed by George W. Bush to serve as the twenty-first secretary of defense, Donald Rumsfeld had reason to see himself as a person of destiny. Both the youngest and oldest person ever to serve as defense secretary, and the only one to have held the position twice, he knew the halls of Congress intimately and had been a CEO with a Midas touch. He was, by all accounts, a walking military-industrial complex.

Yet, from the start of his second tour as defense secretary, Rumsfeld revealed himself to be anything other than a defender of the status quo. He made no secret of his uncompromising intention to overhaul what he saw as an American military apparatus in a state of arrested development, tangled in the cross-purposes of its own bureaucracy, and armed only to fight yesterday's battles.

Peter J. Boyer, who covered the war extensively for *The New Yorker*, recounts that "by the time he undertook this second tenure at the Pentagon, Rumsfeld was a guy entering his eighth decade, a man who knew what he knew, and basically wasn't going to brook any nonsense. He knew that he was coming in to deal with a bureaucracy he thought was inefficient, that didn't serve the nation's interests well, that wasted money, and as it happens, wasn't as good as it could be at warfighting. Rumsfeld meant to come in and change it from top to bottom, and not necessarily to make friends."[2]

Rumsfeld was on a mission. And the opening strike on Baghdad was the apotheosis of that mission. Though "transformation" was a term that long preceded him, with his return it became a catchall for his promised overhaul of the Pentagon—a shift to the wars of the future, driven by airpower, precision, and a deemphasis of ground conflict.

Joseph Cirincione, a defense expert who has spent more than twenty years monitoring the growth of the military-industrial complex, remembers the optimism that attended Rumsfeld's return to the Pentagon. "There was tremendous hope when Secretary Rumsfeld came in with the Bush administration, that we would finally see this transformation in military affairs, transformation in military thinking. The idea was that we were going to scrap the Cold War weapons that had been designed for set-piece battle across the Fulda Gap (tanks, carrier battle groups, attack submarines) and replace them with something that emphasized the information superiority of the United States (quick maneuverability, precision-guided munitions, lighter, faster, smaller)."[3]

Seeking to bring his vast experience from the corporate sector to bear on a Pentagon Rumsfeld saw as frozen in time, "transformation" was where the mind of a military technocrat met those of the neoconservatives so influential with the president and vice president. In their now infamous 2000 policy paper *Rebuilding America's Defenses*, William Kristol, Paul Wolfowitz, and others had endorsed the notion that America must undergo a "revolution in military affairs."[4] This revolution was required "to change today's force into tomorrow's force," replacing brute power with maneuverability, speed, and flexibility.[5] Referenced throughout the paper, "precision-guided munitions" like those dropped in the opening strike were to be the vanguard of this revolution. Though Rumsfeld appears to have had misgivings about some aspects of neoconservative ideology, the technocrat in him found common ground with the neocons in this futuristic vision of a push-button war.

From the start, Rumsfeld's transformational crusade met with resistance at various levels across the services. Nowhere was this resistance stronger than in the Army. Rumsfeld's early move to kill the Army's $11 billion Crusader artillery system seemed to take a page right from the neoconservative playbook and signaled the Army that dark days lay ahead. As General Norman Schwarzkopf would tell *The Washington Post*: "When he makes his comments, it appears that he disregards the Army." This sense of Rumsfeld's neglect for the "boots on the ground" was shared by many Pentagon Army officers, who began referring to him as "the enemy."[6]

Rumsfeld was a shrewd turf warrior, who co-opted the idea of "transformation," made it his own, and brought it to a level that alienated even its former proponents. Nowhere did this tension erupt more pointedly than in one episode in the lead-up to the Iraq War.

At a February 2003 press conference, Rumsfeld derided Army Chief of Staff Eric Shinseki—a "Clinton general" who had been an outspoken advocate of transformation—for claiming that to conquer Iraq would require "something on the order of several hundred thousand soldiers" rather than the 80,000 Rumsfeld had claimed. Though the fullness of time has vindicated Shinseki, both Under Secretary Wolfowitz and Vice President Cheney wasted no time in joining Rumsfeld to publicly denigrate him.[7] In short order, Shinseki was marginalized and ultimately replaced by Commander Peter Schoomaker, a former Special Ops commander more amenable to Rumsfeld's approach.

Given Rumsfeld's demonstrated disdain for "Clinton generals" and for the value of the Army, Tommy Franks—a Clinton general *and* an old

Army man—might have seemed an unlikely partner in the war on terror. As Peter Boyer would later report, Franks addressed this point-blank with Rumsfeld at one of their first meetings: " 'If you can't work with anybody who Bill Clinton promoted, you need to get a whole new team. But if you want to work with me I'll work my heart out for you.' "[8] The strategic wisdom of Franks' candor wasn't lost on the savvy Rumsfeld, who saw that a "good ol' boy" from the Army was just the front man he needed to sell his transformational ideas to a skeptical brass.

Whatever their differences, Rumsfeld and Franks were thrust together by the events of 9/11, when neoconservative goals for a New American Century took center stage in American foreign policy. The next day, President Bush called on Rumsfeld and Franks to produce a plan for war in Afghanistan.

True to form, Rumsfeld wanted a transformational campaign, involving airpower and specialized ground forces to achieve maximum maneuverability against an elusive, nonstate enemy. Franks saw practical limitations to an overly technological approach that ignored the need for heavy ground forces. "You have to have somebody for the enemy to give their guns to," he would later tell Peter Boyer. As Stephen Robinette, an Army colonel who has followed Franks's career, told a reporter for *The Washington Post*, "He's not the kind of guy who is convinced that some number of laser-guided munitions at a standoff distance is going to do the job every time."[9]

But when Franks and Rumsfeld began to work closely, the Army man proved surprisingly flexible in his capacity to put the technocrat's transformational ideas into action. Central to the Afghan campaign was the Guided Bomb Unit-24 (GBU-24), a precursor to the bombs later dropped at Dora Farms and a case study in transformational warfare. Specially redesigned to attack al Qaeda's network of underground tunnel complexes, the "24" was a precision-guided bunker-buster, fitted with a special state-of-the-art "thermobaric" warhead, which on impact creates a heat vortex that incinerates anything (even weapons of mass destruction) in its path.

Shortly after 9/11, Rumsfeld had called on the Pentagon's Defense Threat Reduction Agency (DTRA) to produce such a weapon almost overnight. The speed with which the DTRA organized a quick response team of military, energy, and industry experts to meet this challenge and custom-tailor such a specialized precision weapon was transformation at work. In just a month, the new warhead was developed, tested, and commissioned for the Afghan campaign.

"This revolution in our military is only beginning," President Bush declared in December 2001, echoing the language of the 2000 PNAC report. "Afghanistan has been a proving ground for this new approach. These past two months have shown that an innovative doctrine and high-tech weaponry can shape and then dominate an unconventional conflict." Though America's apparent victory in Afghanistan would in time prove illusory, it was initially perceived as a success and thus galvanized the working relationship between Franks and Rumsfeld. As Army brass grew more adversarial to Rumsfeld's approach, a kind of mutual respect emerged between the secretary and General Franks. This respect would be tested over the months that followed as the two men prepared their plan for war against Iraq.

The plan would be a compromise between a technocrat and an Army man. Rumsfeld initially wanted an innovative campaign taken straight from the transformation handbook. Combining precision munitions with a light commitment of ground forces, he sought to take the Afghanistan model to the next level. Franks's original plan—first submitted to the president just two and a half months after 9/11—also called for significant airpower and precision-strike capability, but with a much larger force of 200,000 troops and three divisions of tanks and armored vehicles.[10] Over the next fourteen months, secretary and general hammered out their differences over countless iterations. The tension between them was essentially an age-old one between the Air Force innovations of the military-industrial sector and the more Army-oriented common sense that war is a dirty business that must be won with blood and guts.

The result was lauded as a triumph of transformational thinking—a dazzling array of twenty-first-century airpower combined with conventional and unconventional forces on the ground to provide unprecedented flexibility and destructive capacity. Settling the original dispute with the Army over troop needs, Rumsfeld and Franks agreed that the campaign would start with the 80,000 troops Rumsfeld thought sufficient, but that Franks would have additional men "in the pipeline" (more like the number Shinseki had foreseen) to call upon if push came to shove. It was an elegant denouement to months of struggle between

Army man and technocrat. At a March 22, 2003, CENTCOM press briefing, Franks summarized the war plan as though it were his own:

> This will be a campaign unlike any other in history, a campaign characterized by shock, by surprise, by flexibility, by the employment of precise munitions on a scale never before seen, and by the application of overwhelming force.

Though secretary and general had managed to bridge their differences, Rumsfeld seemed to have swayed Franks more than vice versa, with tragic results.

While the Iraq War might seem a test case for "transformation," a closer look at transformation's roots reveals that, though Rumsfeld's emphasis on airpower *appears* transformational (and though he may have adopted some of the language of those long advocating transformation), his crusade was undermined not only by resistance from military-industrial forces but also by his own failure to understand the larger vision of transformation's guru, John Boyd.

THE ROOTS OF TRANSFORMATION

Like many observers of the Iraq War, Peter Boyer sees John Boyd as the "intellectual patron" of the transformation movement. Boyd's "themes of maneuver warfare—speed, agility, flexibility—became the language of the military-reform movement," Boyer writes. "The idea of maneuver warfare is to defeat the enemy by disrupting his capacity to fight rather than by overcoming him in a head-on contest of firepower."[11] According to Boyer, when espousing transformation, Rumsfeld was tapping into the contemporary expression of longstanding efforts to reform America's military establishment from within. "Transformation broadly speaking is the belief that the military system, the military-industrial complex needs to change," Boyer notes. "There was a reform movement anticipating the end of the Cold War. Some, like Newt Gingrich, tended to be Republicans. Some were Democrats, who called themselves the Military Reform Caucus. These were guys within the military who were sort of underground reformers. People who thought that the army was antiquated, slow, self-serving, and in everything from its personnel systems to its doctrinal modes, outdated. They fought, and in some cases published books to get the institution to change."[12]

The original idea of transformation was born amid this effort at reform, and by all accounts this movement drew its inspiration from the thinking of John Boyd. In his book *Boyd: The Fighter Pilot Who Changed the Art of War*, Robert Coram describes Boyd as "one of the most important unknown men of his time." Indeed, ask around military circles and Boyd turns out to be one of the most admired and controversial figures in U.S. military history. A self-made genius, he served in the Army Air Corps during World War II, flew in Korea and Vietnam, and earned a reputation as a leading fighter pilot of his day. He is most famous, though, as a thinker who made historic contributions to American aircraft design and military strategy.

Imperious, inscrutable, and contemptuous of authority, Boyd was a lightning rod for controversy, whose contributions to the art of war are as far-reaching as they are misquoted and misapplied. According to those who worked with Boyd, Rumsfeld and his fellow proponents of transformation may appear to be operating in Boyd's spirit when they pursue a high-tech push-button war. But a look at the full evolution of his remarkable career through the eyes of those who knew him reveals a very different vision of the American way of war—one in which Boyd actually came to challenge many of the premises on which Rumsfeld and company have operated.

Boyd was just a lowly Air Force captain in 1960 when out of nowhere he authored the *Aerial Attack Study,* a groundbreaking innovation in the history of air combat. With the U.S. Air Force little more than a decade old, it was the first time anyone had codified dogfighting maneuvers in such an organized fashion. Within months, this 150-page tour-de-force of charts, descriptions, and diagrams was adopted and classified by the Air Force as an official tactics manual. In the ensuing years, the study was declassified and went on to influence the aerial combat tactics of countries the world over. At age thirty-two, Boyd had already changed the way the world's air forces plan and conduct operations.

It was, of course, just at this time that the missile gap controversy was shaping Eisenhower's understanding of military-industrial forces in the society. Though Boyd's focus had been largely limited to air combat tactics, his insatiable intellect would now unwittingly embark on a collision course with the very forces Eisenhower had identified.

In 1962, with a mere bachelor's degree in industrial engineering, Boyd introduced his second earth-shattering innovation in aerial combat. While recounting his dogfighting experiences in Korea, he arrived at a concept he called the Energy-Maneuverability Theory, a scientific formula for optimizing aircraft performance. By placing the various characteristics of an aircraft—thrust, drag, wingspan, and speed—into an equation with one another, Boyd made it possible for engineers to understand the effect on an aircraft's capabilities of trade-offs made in the design process. The more maneuverability you wanted, the less speed you might be able to have. The more weight, the less maneuverability. And so on.

So intense was Boyd in pursuing his ideas during this period that he earned the nickname "the Mad Major." Some questioned his sanity and others accused him simply of overstepping his rank. Still, his ideas would rise to the top, significantly shaping America's military evolution over the subsequent decade. The Energy-Maneuverability Theory, in particular, fit perfectly the new direction in U.S. military policy initiated by Eisenhower's successor.

John F. Kennedy had campaigned for the presidency in part on the platform that Eisenhower had relied too heavily on nuclear deterrence for America's security and thus let its conventional forces founder. Kennedy felt that the "massive retaliation" doctrine, while possibly deterring nuclear conflict, at once made conventional war more likely and America less prepared for it. America needed to reinvigorate its conventional capabilities, he argued, and develop a more credible approach to warfighting. Along with his secretary of defense, Robert McNamara, Kennedy undertook to replace the "massive retaliation" doctrine with what they called "flexible response."

Boyd's Energy-Maneuverability Theory, explicitly designed to improve U.S. conventional air-fighting capabilities, perfectly fit the Kennedy Zeitgeist. Like Rumsfeld, McNamara made enemies from early on by canceling systems, such as the F-105 program—an aircraft chiefly designed to carry out Eisenhower's nuclear deterrence doctrine—which were ill-suited to Kennedy's reemphasis on conventional forces. But not all of McNamara's decisions were in step with Boyd's analysis.

When McNamara elected to procure the massive F-111 fighter aircraft for the Air Force and the Navy, Boyd used his Energy-Maneuverability Theory to demonstrate that the F-111 was inferior to any Soviet aircraft at any speed or altitude,[13] and so should not be commissioned. If Kennedy wanted to walk the walk and not just talk the talk of reinvigorating America's conventional capabilities vis-à-vis the Soviets, then not just America's tactics but her aircraft themselves needed to be brought up to competitive speed. The idea that the United States needed a new, faster, lightweight kind of fighter aircraft was an unwelcome message both to certain Air Force brass, who still clung to the principle of massive retaliation, and to those in the corporate sector like General Dynamics, who produced the F-111.

Military hierarchy being what it is, there would be a lot of briefings and tilting at windmills before Boyd's ideas were heard by top generals in the Pentagon. All the while, America was using an outclassed aircraft in Vietnam and losing pilots. A wave of increased U.S. air losses between 1965 and 1967 gave new currency to Boyd's conviction that the air fleet needed serious improvement.

In 1966, after he received orders to transfer to Thailand to fly support missions in the F-4 Phantom, Boyd's orders were suddenly withdrawn. He was sent instead to the Pentagon to help work on a new Air Force fighter. At that time, Navy admirals had successfully duped McNamara into believing that they would accept the Air Force's F-111 as long as they could continue to develop their own new jet engine (the TF30) and missile (the Phoenix). Secretly, though, they planned not to accept the F-111 and instead convince Congress to fund a dedicated Navy fighter using the TF30 and Phoenix. This plane would be the F-14 Tomcat (made famous in the movie *Top Gun*). During this time, Boyd and a group of like-minded engineers and officers came to be known as the "Fighter Mafia," and this "Mafia" soon got a sobering firsthand glimpse at what Eisenhower had warned against five years earlier.

Thomas Christie, a mathematician and computer scientist who worked closely with Boyd, first at Eglin Air Force Base and later at the Pentagon, recalls how the various corporations and their allies in Congress sought to game the system for their own purposes rather than enhance aircraft performance, pilot safety, or national security. "General Dynamics was making the F-111, McDonnell Douglas was building the F-4, and Grumman was making the F-14," he recalls. "Back then, you had about five or six companies that were in the game, compared to just one or two today. There were several fighter attack aircraft programs underway. So most of these companies could look out to the future and think that they had an opportunity for the next fighter. And these companies would cut each other's throats to get there."[14] Watching these military-industrial dynamics unfold, Boyd and company increasingly perceived a threat to America's best defense not only from across the sea but from inside the system as well.

AN UPRISING OF ACOLYTES

A lightening rod for adrenaline as much as for controversy, Boyd attracted followers, who became known as "acolytes." Boyd launched a crusade against several deficient but sacred aircraft programs, and under his leadership the acolytes developed and promoted his radical ideas. In addition to Tom Christie, Pierre Sprey and Franklin "Chuck" Spinney joined Boyd in a loose association that grew over time into the "Military Reform Movement"—a far-reaching campaign by the Pentagon's best and brightest to reform the seemingly immutable Goliath from within. It is from this movement that the modern-day notion of "transformation"—however far it has strayed from its original intent—was born.

There is special poetry in any uprising of insiders against institutional corruption, but the story of the reformers is a remarkable one. Here is a group of dedicated soldiers seeking to give America the best defense possible, to reduce the number of her pilots lost in combat, to provide taxpayer value for hard-earned money, and, not least, to contribute to the eternal human quest to build a better mousetrap. Yet these worthy aspirations put the reformers on a collision course with the corruption of the Complex.

As resistance mounted, Boyd and his acolytes became an ever closer band of brothers. The classic story of this conflict took place in 1975 during the development of the F-16 and F-17 fighters. The F-15 that preceded them had been the first plane inspired by Boyd's Energy-Maneuverability Theory. Boyd was dissatisfied, though, with the way the Air Force made compromises in its ultimate design, which hindered its performance. In the late 1960s, he began to think about a better, more lightweight fighter, and it was from these thoughts that the F-16 and F-17 were born.

Pushing for a new, lightweight fighter was sure to prove highly unpopular to an Air Force leadership deeply invested in the F-15. Boyd had to be clever. "It was one of the most audacious plots ever hatched against a military service," writes Robert Coram, "and it was done under the noses of men who, if they had the slightest idea of what it was about, not only would have stopped it instantly, but would have cut orders reassigning Boyd to the other side of the globe."[15]

Once Boyd had generated some support for his lightweight concept, he initiated a contest, from which two designs would be selected and developed into prototypes. The contest was portrayed in the spirit of vigorous intellectual competition. A competition, or "fly-off," between prototypes would be conducted to let the best plane win, and the winning plane would be put widely into production. As Franklin Spinney recalls, "It was an exciting time. You could cut the excitement with a knife. Guys were saying *Now this is the right way to do it!* You know? 'Cause guys like to build good things."[16]

But there were forces at work that made building "good things" a naive aspiration. During the fly-off, Boyd learned from the test pilots that there was unanimous preference among them for the F-16 over the 17. Both were excellent aircraft, but the 16 was more agile in transitions between maneuvers. Accordingly, it should have won the fly-off, and its designer General Dynamics, been awarded the contract to produce it. Instead, the corruption within the MIC took its toll. Spinney, whose corruption-busting activities would later land him on the cover of *Time* magazine (more on this in Chapter Six) recalls that General Dynamics had a less powerful corporate lobby than that behind the F-17, designed by Northrop, whose advocates had stronger ties both in Congress and to the White House.

Christie puts an even finer point on the corporate-political dynamics at work. "Tom Jones was CEO of Northrop and very close to Nixon. Though Nixon resigned in the middle of this, Northrop's corporate lobby was also far stronger than General Dynamics'. Inside the Pentagon, I was deluged by both companies during this time. But Northrop just had far more people beating the bushes and paid a lot more to lobby the Pentagon, lobby the Hill. They pulled some real underhanded things to try to stop the F-16 from winning."

Christie recounts how on a particular weekend in January 1975 the situation reached a point of critical urgency. That week, a U.S. senator with close ties to Northrop exerted pressure on the Office of Secretary of Defense James Schlesinger to refrain from announcing the F-16's victory in the fly-off. Basing his argument on a technicality in the Pentagon's reporting procedures, Arkansas Democratic senator John McClellan called Schlesinger on a weekend to advise him that he was not authorized to announce the results. His stated reason for this was that the report by Boyd and company on the fly-off had not yet been submitted to Schlesinger. In cahoots with both executives at Northrop and Air Force brass who opposed the F-16, McClellan spearheaded an effort to override the outcome of the fly-off and secure authorization for the F-17. "Clearly," Christie recalls, "Northrop's lobby was playing into this."

Behind McClellan's maneuver, though, was a combination of motives reflective of the larger, tangled interests of the military-industrial complex. Personally, McClellan felt antipathy toward General Dynamics, which dated back to his days as chair of the Senate Permanent Subcommittee on Investigations. With Robert F. Kennedy as his chief counsel, McClellan had overseen a sweeping investigation of organized crime in which General Dynamics had been implicated. For its part, Northrop wanted to win and felt that the fly-off put its F-17 at a disadvantage since the F-16 had been in operation longer, giving General Dynamics more time to ready it for the test. Finally, from the Air Force's perspective, the whole idea of a lightweight flyer remained anathema. The Air Force and its corporate allies were heavily invested in the F-15 program, in particular the plane's producer, McDonnell Douglas. Since there was a statutory cap on the number of aircraft the Air Force could have overall, the number of F-16s foisted upon it would mean cutting back on F-15s.

Defense Secretary Schlesinger saw the benefit of the lower-cost F-16, however, and on that January weekend called upon Boyd's acolytes to arm him with the information needed to push the F-16 through. "Schlesinger didn't like the pressure he was getting," Christie recalls. "He was reaching out to us as allies. So I spent the whole day Sunday out there crunching numbers so he could go to McClellan and get that turned off, which he did."

In the end, Christie explains, Schlesinger struck a compromise that overcame the Air Force's resistance to the F-16, one that shows the perverse power of the military-industrial alliance. By lifting the "cap" on the total number of "wings" the Air Force could have in its force structure, Schlesinger incentivized the Air Force to buy the F-16, without forcing cutbacks on the F-15 program.

"Schlesinger calls in Air Force chief George Brown and he says, 'Okay, here's what I'm offering you—I'll take the cap off, you can grow your forces, in exchange for signing up for this cheaper airplane, the lightweight fighter,' " Christie recounts. Spinney sees this outcome as a triumph for Boyd and the Military Reform Movement. "The Air Force was basically forced to buy the better plane over their own dead bodies!" He laughs. "And they ended up building thousands of them!"

Yet while Boyd and his group may have won this particular battle with the bureaucracy to honor the result of the fly-off, the victory was a frustrated one, actually resulting in increased overall expenditure. Boyd and company then watched as the F-16 was retrofitted by the Air Force with superfluous technologies—like excessive radar technology and tactical nuclear delivery capability—whose price tag benefited defense interests but whose weight added drag to the plane and hindered its performance. This kind of opportunism had taken its toll on the F-15 a decade earlier. Boyd was forced to watch history repeat itself.

Boyd retired from the Pentagon in 1975. He had seen the best and worst of the military-industrial era. As a pilot, engineer, and strategist, Boyd had contributed to the growth of the MIC, only to become disaffected as its corrupting forces undermined the very defenses he sought to perfect. For all his brilliance, he had been able to achieve only limited and mixed results with his efforts at transformation. Here, one can already see how the military-industrial complex, which began as an engine for the American way of war, had already evolved into a force driven by its own imperatives at the cost of a dedicated soldier like Boyd, unable to abide its contradictions and deficiencies. A quarter-century later, these shortcomings would demonstrate themselves more worryingly than ever before in the abortive and misguided second Pentagon career of Donald Rumsfeld.

THE TYRANNY OF FIXED NUMBERS

November 26, 2006, was a haunting milestone for the Iraq War. On that day, far from being the overnight sensation the neoconservatives had predicted and Rumsfeld had planned for, Operation Iraqi Freedom quietly surpassed the length of U.S. involvement in World War II. For Rumsfeld, who once told a congressional committee inquiring about the war's costs that "to me, numbers almost are distracting," the numbers—in dollars and death tolls—just wouldn't go away. Rumsfeld had been successful in bullying Franks into accepting his transformational notions of arm's-length warfare; yet time would prove him less able to bully reality. That reality took its toll in what his own Pentagon came to call "the tyranny of fixed numbers."[17]

Ultimately, the Iraq War's descent from a technocrat's fantasy of transformational war into a quagmire of mud and blood on the ground has vindicated those who opposed Rumsfeld's approach in the first place: General Shinseki, General Shwarzkopf, and others, including, early on, General Franks. By November 26, 2006, however, Rumsfeld was not around for anyone to tell him, "I told ya so." Three weeks earlier, on November 8, he had resigned. Ever inscrutable before his critics, he bid farewell with a quip from Winston Churchill. "I have benefited greatly from criticism," he joked, "and at no time have I suffered a lack thereof."

Despite his effort at levity, Rumsfeld's body language acknowledged what his words would not—that his tenure as secretary of defense had been defined by a misbegotten, poorly planned, and dismally executed conflict, which had undermined the very strategic precepts it was meant to demonstrate.

TACTICS AND STRATEGY: WHERE RUMSFELD LOST SIGHT OF BOYD

To Spinney, Christie, and others from Boyd's Military Reform movement, Rumsfeld's failed war plan for Iraq reveals a schism between the real John Boyd and the understanding of him among those who profess to carry his strategic torch. Spinney fears that the tendency by Rumsfeld and company to associate their flawed ideas with Boyd might lead to the equation, long term, of the war's failure with weakness in Boyd's thinking. "What these guys have done here," Spinney exclaims, "has nothing to do with Boyd. He'd be rolling in his grave right now if he heard that."

Though in theory Boyd is lionized, policy makers tend to evoke his legacy simply when they want to promote high-tech air combat technology. Spinney sees this use of Boyd as a cheap travesty of his ideas and historical significance. While Rumsfeld's crusade to overhaul the Pentagon may initially have seemed to echo Boyd's spirit, his vision of American war fighting diverged dramatically from Boyd's. Rumsfeld's fundamental failure was to think that Boyd's focus on airpower could be implemented in isolation from the larger context of his strategic vision. Boyd was very far from the neoconservatives in his worldview, and the kind of air superiority he emphasized was only part of a highly complex vision of U.S. military strategy.

Two major aspects of Boyd's thinking would have greatly broadened Rumsfeld's understanding of the role of air superiority. The first is a tactical one, weighing the interplay and relative priority of manpower and machines in the tactics of war. The second is a strategic one, called the OODA loop, reflecting Boyd's ultimate revolutionary vision of grand strategy in warmaking.

Boyd's Tactics: People First, Ideas Second, Hardware Third

"What Boyd figured out," Spinney declares, "was that we were becoming prisoners of our technology. But technology is just the application of scientific principles to human needs. What you have to do is find out how humans behave in this unique environment called war. And that means you gotta keep things in order. It's people first, ideas second, hardware third."

So zealously had the planners of the Iraq War bought into the idea that America could launch a push-button attack, eliminate the head of state, and then, as the vice president himself promised, "be greeted as liberators," that they had failed to do the homework required to devise a strategy appropriate to their adversary. As the unfortunate unfolding of events has shown—from the myth of Saddam's WMDs to the illusion that Iraqis would greet invaders as liberators to the mirage of "Mission Accomplished"—the Iraq War has been a tragedy of woeful unpreparedness, cultural ignorance, and primitive military strategy, all disguised by the dazzle of the high-tech weapons used to implement it.

"Unfortunately," Spinney explains, "technology shapes our perception of war. You can see this in Rumsfeld's transformation jargon. It's all technology-driven, when in fact war is an intensely human experience. And human activity is governed by the nature of information and the environment that must be processed." America's war planners needed, in other words, to understand the situation inside Iraq much better than they did.

The underlying tragic flaw in the war plan lay in its misguided premise—that Saddam was hiding weapons of mass destruction and that once America eliminated him, the Iraqi people would welcome American troops as liberators. This suggested that Saddam was a serious adversary and that only he, and not the country, would need to be overcome. As events have demonstrated, the war plan was cursed by a grave blind spot as to both Saddam's thinking and the complex texture of Iraqi culture.

Had the war planners been more interested in understanding their adversary, they might have heeded the warnings of weapons experts who argued that Saddam was simply keeping up the appearance of having WMDs to instill fear in his neighbors. As for understanding Iraqi society, if the war planners had been more attentive to knowledgeable experts, they would have understood that after the first Gulf War and a decade of UN sanctions, though a majority of Iraqis did not support Saddam they would also not see a U.S. invasion as a welcome alternative. Or they might have availed themselves of experts in Iraqi culture, who could have predicted the Pandora's box of ethnic antipathies that would be unleashed by Saddam's ouster.

In contrast to Spinney, Christie, and their fellow reformers, Fuji and Tooms' commander Colonel Treadway believes that Rumsfeld's campaign of "shock and awe" took John Boyd's ideas to a new level. "Colonel Boyd espoused the idea of parallel warfare," he explains, "being able to attack all levels of an enemy's ability to make war." The concept of "parallel warfare" is a doctrine developed in part out of Boyd's thinking, in which the object is to attack a set of vital strategic targets so rapidly and simultaneously—i.e., in parallel—that the enemy has no time to mount a response. Precision air strikes are the primary means of attack. The goal is to disorient the enemy by isolating the leader from his troops and thus disabling the leadership so that governmental collapse and widespread troop capitulation results. "During Iraqi Freedom," Treadway explains, "we immediately tried to influence the leadership in the most powerful way possible. We got inside the enemy's decision loop, his decision-making capability, by threatening the very basis of it. It was a great move to bring the war home without having to wade through the civilian population to get there."

All of this sounds terribly sleek, catchy, and athletic, and Treadway didn't get to be an Air Force commander without having a way with words. But on second glance, the words take on haunting resonance for a conflict that did not go according to plan: *without having to wade through the civilian population to get there.* These words gloss over a glaring reality that has come to haunt U.S. forces. If the war has shown anything, it's that if you don't "wade" into a country through the civilian population, then you'd better hope the population welcomes you, or you may have to "wade out" if and when you ever want to leave. Herein lies the catch and the exact spot where the war plan—in its high-tech zeal—lost sight of Boyd's strategic wisdom. The lesson may be as simple as "Know your enemy," but the fullness of Boyd's evolution and career puts a finer point on it.

The OODA Loop: Boyd's Last Hurrah

After leaving the Pentagon, Boyd entered a period of self-imposed exile that lasted from 1975 to 1982. During this period, he delved deeper into the nature of war and military strategy than ever before, becoming a character of infamous eccentricity. Since a man with no needs has no needs that can be met by those currying favor, Boyd reduced the cost of his creature comforts to a bare minimum, putting himself beyond the corrupting reach of money. He stopped buying clothes and let his personal effects fall into decay. Having used his mind to discover so much that was of benefit to the U.S. military, Boyd now turned his formidable mental energies inward upon themselves, charting the mechanics of his own thinking. He withdrew into his mind, immersing himself in a sweeping study of philosophy, physics, and military strategy, from Sun Tzu to Hegel to Heisenberg and Clausewitz.

"Boyd spent seven years working on a thirteen-page paper called 'Destruction and Creation,' " Spinney recalls, "a monumental study of the art of war through history, how technology affected it, and how people and not machines fight wars." Spinney recalls his mentor's bouts of agony and ecstasy, like the roiling seas of a tempest. During this period, Boyd would disappear for months at a time, barely sleeping. He would reemerge only to give briefings that were "windows into madness—presentation slides crammed with ideas, questions, contradictions. He was searching for something deeper than anything he had found before, and he wasn't there yet."

If this process might seem self-indulgent, its result would prove the most lasting contribution Boyd would make to the world. By analyzing the workings of his own mind, he began to dissect the process by which human beings come to the understandings upon which they base their actions.

He broke this process down into four phases that would come to be called the OODA loop, a behavioral pattern in which a person

> **Observes** elements in his (or her) environment;
> **Orients** his observation into a context familiar to him;
> **Decides** based upon such oriented observation; and finally
> **Acts** upon such decision.

Given his background, the military applications of this formulation quickly became clear. During the Korean War, the U.S. Marines had developed a strategic model comprised of just three phases: See, Decide,

Act. What Boyd discovered may seem minute, but it has vast implications. By breaking the "see" phase into the two discrete phases of "observation" and "orientation," Boyd highlighted a vital opportunity for confounding an enemy. If one could determine in advance the process by which an enemy would make sense out of what he was observing—an attack under way against him, for example—then one could influence his thinking and, by so doing, undermine his decision-making process. Or, as the case might be, by more rapidly observing the circumstances of a heated battle and evaluating one's position and strategic advantages or disadvantages more quickly than one's enemy, one could get a jump on the enemy's thinking and disorient him. A historical example Boyd used to illustrate the OODA loop was the German invention of the lightning-fast tank assault they called *Blitzkrieg*, used in the attack on France in World War II, which utterly befuddled the French by circumventing the Maginot line.

Boyd's strategic ideal of getting inside and undermining an adversary's thinking has come to be referred to as "penetrating" the enemy's OODA loop. In battle, this essentially comes down to focusing certain operations specifically on disrupting either what the enemy observes or how he processes that observation. As Boyd wrote, the intention is to "enmesh [the] adversary in a world of uncertainty, doubt, mistrust, confusion, disorder, fear, panic, chaos . . . and/or fold [him] back inside himself so that he cannot cope with events/efforts as they unfold."[18]

The OODA loop became a fixture in U.S. military planning. For years, Boyd continued to expand on his ideas in "Destruction and Creation," evolving them into what became, by 1986, a 196-page briefing called *Patterns of Conflict*. This briefing took the form of a series of overhead slides crammed with battle diagrams, bullet points, and strategic analyses of the thoughts and actions of history's leading generals. Among these, Boyd examined the military genius of Sun Tzu, whose *Art of War*, written around 400 BC, became a standard against which Boyd judged all other notions of war strategy. Sun Tzu's "desired outcome," Boyd argues, is to "subdue [the] enemy without fighting" and to "avoid protracted war." The goal is to acquire and exploit such awareness of one's adversary that one causes him "to unravel before the fight."

The legendary military success of the first Gulf War has been widely attributed to the skillful penetration of Saddam's OODA loop, compelling just such a collapse of his military and his withdrawal from Kuwait, in a dizzyingly brief period. In 1991, Secretary of Defense Dick Cheney actually consulted with John Boyd prior to the Gulf War, and is reported to have been greatly influenced by his thinking. As Robert Coram writes, "Cheney threw out Gen. Norman Schwarzkopf's plans for prosecuting the war and developed his own: a Marine Corps diversionary feint at Kuwait while the Army raced far to the west in the now-famous 'left hook.' Everything about the plan was out of Boyd's *Patterns of Conflict*—the multiple thrusts and deception operations created such rampant confusion among enemy forces that they surrendered by the thousands. America picked when and where it would fight and when and where it would not fight—and won without a prolonged ground war."[19]

After 9/11, Cheney even betrayed a measure of regret that Boyd was no longer around to advise them. "We could use him again now," he said of Boyd. "I wish he was around. . . . I'd love to turn him loose on our current defense establishment and see what he could come up with."[20]

"SHOCK AND AWE": WHAT WENT WRONG

The opening strike of the Iraq War indeed unleashed the forty-eight hours of "shock and awe" that Rumsfeld and Franks had promised. It made for dazzling television as explosion after explosion lit the Baghdad sky, followed by belated booms traveling at the speed of sound. Crowding the airwaves were pundits praising the attack as a transformational military event, and the language they used was borrowed from Boyd's lexicon.

In advance of the assault, Special Operations troops infiltrated Iraq, under cover of night, to disrupt its infrastructure. Psychological operations were undertaken, in which Iraqi radio signals were jammed, preventing leadership from communicating with the people. High-ranking members of Saddam's infamous Republican Guard had allegedly been directly contracted by e-mail and incentivized to break ranks. Leaflets had been dropped over Iraq to undermine Saddam's popular support, citing America's good intentions in seeking his ouster. Finally, battle plans were designed to defy Saddam's expectations and jam his ability to mount a timely resistance, such as the rapid assault that came to be called the "Baghdad 500," in which ground forces were sent on a breakneck rush to the capital, bypassing numerous strategic strongholds. All of these indirect and nonfrontal assault tactics were proudly cited as examples of transformation in the Boyd mold. In a March 21 Pentagon briefing while "shock and awe" was taking place, Rumsfeld himself borrowed phrases directly from Boyd: "The regime is starting to lose control of their country," he declared ominously. "The confusion of Iraqi officials is growing. Their ability to see what is happening on the battlefield, to communicate with their forces, and to control their country is slipping away."[21]

"Shock and awe" successfully led to the collapse of Saddam's regime. Yet for all the hype, it failed to secure decisive victory over the country. The war plan may, in some discrete tactical ways, have succeeded in penetrating aspects of Saddam's decision-making process, but it failed gravely to have taken any real measure of Boyd's thinking. In particular this overlooked the deeper implications of Boyd's insights on how the "orientation" phase works. As Boyd wrote: "The second O, orientation—as the repository of our genetic heritage, cultural tradition, and previous experiences—is the most important part of the OODA loop since it shapes the way we observe, the way we decide, the way we act."[22] Boyd had originally developed his insights about an enemy's orientation out of his experience as a fighter pilot, considering the tit-for-tat between two planes in a dogfight. But he went on to consider the implications for war of the vital role played by culture, reflecting on how an invaded population's cultural heritage and ways of thinking would come into play in responding to invasion. In this, he stressed the importance of breaking the resolve of those resisting as the primary goal of a short war.

In *Patterns of Conflict,* Boyd specifically addresses a number of lessons from guerilla warfare—such as the tactics used by the Russians in the Bolshevik Revolution—that he argues should be incorporated into an optimal military strategy. Particularly relevant to the Iraq war, he asserts that in order to win over a population, it is vital to " 'arrange the minds' of friend, foe and neutral alike. Must 'get inside their minds.' " He also highlights that a hallmark of success of guerilla campaigns in winning over the mass population is that guerillas must "exhibit moral authority, offer competence, and provide desired benefits in order to further erode government influence, gain more recruits . . . hence expand guerilla influence/control over population and countryside."[23]

If the Iraq war plan had taken the fullness of Boyd's insights into account, it might have taken much more seriously the need to understand the perspectives of the Iraqi people, the cultural issues at play in the country, and also quickly to begin providing persuasive benefits to the mass population, such as clear signs of infrastructure improvement, for example. The war plan might have involved evaluating the key grievances of the Iraqis, the hardships they suffered under Saddam's reign—and under U.S.-led UN sanctions—and their own aspirations for themselves and their country. It might also have stressed that U.S. troops must at all times exhibit moral authority, a million behavioral miles from the sort of humiliation and outright abuse of Iraqis authorized at the highest levels and revealed in the Abu Ghraib scandal.

Simply put, in their zeal to launch a transformational war that would look and sound like Boyd, the war planners overlooked the crowning message of his life.

In this light, "shock and awe" becomes a high-tech fireworks show based on a deficient strategy. Despite its precision weaponry, transformational tactics, and the hype about penetrating "decision cycles," the war plan was fundamentally undermined by its planners' failure to account for the necessity of understanding their adversary and winning him over to their cause.

How did this happen? How did Rumsfeld, a seasoned executive and two-time defense secretary, seek to realize the transformational vision of John Boyd, and end up instead with a clumsy, unwinnable, and tragic set-piece battle of old ideas delivered with the hollow sound and fury of high-tech weaponry?

A glimpse at the answer may lie in Rumsfeld's own words spoken on January 31, 2002, just a few months after 9/11, to a military audience at the National Defense University. "The notion that we could transform while cutting the defense budget over the past decade," Rumsfeld confessed, "was seductive, but false." With this simple sentence, the secretary of defense who had made "transformation" his operational mantra conceded that some part of that agenda might have to be reined in. In other words, the events of 9/11 produced a level of fear and paranoia that made the canceling of outdated defense systems and a wholesale rethinking of Pentagon priorities politically infeasible.

Into the post-9/11 vacuum stepped the neoconservatives, for whom 9/11 provided a once-in-a-lifetime moment. By their own recognition, their vision of a "New American Century" needed just such a "new Pearl Harbor" to be launched. The adoption by the administration of neoconservative foreign policies post-9/11 brought with it their vision of a "revolution in military affairs" in which precision air war figured centrally, with no corresponding emphasis on the challenges of attempting "regime change."

Rumsfeld, meanwhile, had staked this latter chapter of his career—and made early enemies—on transformation. Rather than lose face by retreating from so bold a commitment, he simply allowed its meaning to blur. Rather than the total overhaul of strategy, tactics, and technology that Boyd had proposed, Rumsfeld used the concept of transformation as a catchall for the simple use of any number of high-tech defense systems and unconventional battle strategies for this new kind of war, the "war on terror." Under this oversimplified notion of transformation, he failed to address the cultural and practical realities of his adversary—precisely what a deeper reading of Boyd's analysis would have emphasized.

Perhaps no statement that Rumsfeld made during the war expresses this failure quite so starkly as his comment, in the wake of the widespread looting that broke out in Iraq, including of the cherished antiquities from the National Museum, that, during war, "stuff happens."

"A lot of people thought when the attack on September 11 occurred," Rumsfeld told an August 14, 2003, Pentagon Town Hall meeting, "that we had to set the transformation issues aside and forget it because you can't walk and chew gum at the same time. Just quite the contrary is the truth. The global war on terrorism has provided an impetus for the transformation."[24] Franklin Spinney disagrees. "Transformation," he says, throwing up his hands, "is a bureaucratic buzzword put together by a bunch of people in the Pentagon who are trying to protect the status quo. Rumsfeld may think it's transformation. But it's not. The ideas being promoted are business as usual that's been pumped out by the high-tech community—which means big bucks—forever. It's phony transformation when real transformation is required."

Defense expert Joseph Cirincione concurs. "After September 11, every single weapons program that should have been cancelled was just relabeled," he says. "Instead of trimming the military, instead of reorganizing the military, we just threw money at it. Everything was funded. Even though we're talking about fighting a war against terrorists in caves, we're buying weapons designed to pulverize an advanced industrial nation. So suddenly things like the B-2 bomber—a bomber that costs $2 billion a copy and was designed to penetrate Soviet radar—was being justified as an antiterror weapon. You re-label an F-22 fighter aircraft from something that would kill Soviet aircraft to something that will kill terrorists. You just repackage it as the 'new military thinking' weapon. Wrap the flag around it. Keep the program going."

Despite its devolution in the years since, the successful military campaign to overthrow the Taliban in Afghanistan was at the time perceived to have been an overnight success. Images on TV of precision bunker-busters destroying Afghan caves served to fortify the impression of the war on terror as a kind of high-tech bazaar. And indeed, 9/11 compelled a massive upsurge in defense contracts.

But beyond providing grounds for a renewed flurry of weapons sales, September 11, 2001, also sent a message of weakness in U.S. intelligence gathering. "Why do they hate us?" was the question that came to characterize America's relative ignorance both of the cultures of foreign countries and of their way of seeing America. Statistics proliferated on how ineffective U.S. intelligence gathering had been and about how few Americans travel abroad. Even the president it was said had visited less than five foreign countries prior to his election.[25] While vast new sums of money were appropriated for expensive new weapons, the value of cultural understanding—the lowest cost weapon possible and the one Boyd's analysis shows is most essential was overlooked.

"Transformation," which may at one time have meant a real "revolution in military affairs," became an excuse for more of the same weapons and systems used in past conflicts, repackaged to seem appropriate to the new war on terror, dressed in the language of John Boyd and the military reformers, but tragically lacking adherence to their spirit.

6

The Missing "C": An Insider's Guide to the Complex

How is it possible for this small clique to bend the will of the majority, who stand to lose and suffer by a state of war, to the service of their ambitions? An obvious answer to this question would seem to be that the minority, the ruling class at present, has the schools and press, usually the Church as well, under its thumb. This enables it to organize and sway the emotions of the masses and makes its tool of them.

Albert Einstein,
Letter to Sigmund Freud
July 1932

If the Iraq War has produced anything of value, it is to have brought the term "military-industrial complex" back into focus for an American public largely unaware of how and why their country is led to war. A simple Google search of the phrase conducted on August 3 yielded more than three hundred entries of which two hundred were written since Fuji and Tooms dropped their bombs on March 19, 2003. Still, for all the renewed attention on the MIC, coverage has focused on a handful of isolated war-profiteering scandals rather than on a deeper analysis of what these more broadly reveal about our political and economic system.

Countless scandals have quickly come and gone, all treated in relative isolation:

- In December 2003, the Pentagon confirmed that a program under which one hundred Boeing KC-767 tankers that were to be leased to the U.S. Air Force had been corruptly negotiated, resulting in a vastly higher cost than an outright purchase of the same fleet of aircraft would have entailed. In response to criticism, the Pentagon opted to purchase eighty of the one hundred, leaving twenty to be leased, but even this modified deal was later frozen altogether by the Pentagon. Concurrently, an investigation was launched into the conduct of Darleen Druyun, a former Air Force procurement official turned Boeing executive. Druyun pled guilty to conspiracy in having inflated the contract price to benefit her future employer and to passing secret information to Boeing about its competitor, European defense contractor EADS. Several other government officials, including Air Force Secretary James Roche, were investigated for their involvement in the scandal.
- In 2004, reports revealed that a five-year, $7 billion "no-bid" contract had been awarded by the Department of Defense to Halliburton, raising concerns about cronyism. Pentagon auditors later determined that $1.8 billion of Halliburton's charges to the government had not been adequately documented. The Defense Contract Audit Agency has "strongly" requested that the Army withhold approximately $60 million a month from its payments to Halliburton until proper documentation is provided.
- In June 2005, news broke that California congressman Randall "Duke" Cunningham, a member of the House Defense Appropriations Subcommittee, had received more than $1 million in payments from defense contractors for whom he had secured favorable treatment from the Pentagon. Cunningham resigned from Congress and pled guilty to federal charges of conspiracy to commit bribery and fraud. In March 2006, he was sentenced to eight years and four months in prison.

As is so often the case with issues that might shake fundamental public confidence in the righteousness of America's mission, these scandals have been particularized by the media rather than interpreted for their deeper implications. They are covered in minute personal detail, and portray the individuals involved as singularly corrupt characters rather than as manifestations of a larger systemic phenomenon. We learned, for example, that, in addition to carousing with prostitutes, Duke Cunningham would invite women onto the private yacht provided to him by his defense contractor benefactor and, wearing just pajama pants and a turtleneck sweater, serve them champagne "by the light of a lava lamp."[1] Yet we learned virtually nothing about whether Cunningham's abuse of office is the exception in Congress or the rule, and nothing about why the system is vulnerable to such conduct. If anything, the implication is that the exception proves the rule—that beyond a few "bad apples" like Cunningham and Air Force Secretary James Roche, the world of congressional defense contracting is no more or less worrisome than other areas of American business.

In some cases, the perpetrators have been held accountable. Beyond Cunningham's 2003 sentence, Darleen Druyun was found guilty in October 2004 for her role in the Boeing tanker scandal and sentenced to nine months in jail for corruption. These results are significant, but they also have the perverse effect of suggesting that the system is somehow self-correcting, successfully weeding out its bad apples and prosecuting them to the full extent of the law. Absent in the coverage of these cases is any mention of the vast number of scandals that do not result in prosecution. Penny-ante hucksters like Cunningham and Roche thus make the system safer for the more systematized types of legal corruption that take place in the ordinary course of events. For all the individual scandals that have arisen in connection with the Iraq War, the public has gained little understanding of the depth, nature, and scope of the military-industrial complex as a driving force of corruption in the American way of war and, more broad, in American society.

THE IRON TRIANGLE

The fact that Americans remain largely unaware of how the Complex works allows it to flourish. And this growth is further enabled by the collusion of Congress. Eisenhower recognized this while drafting his parting words. "Few people realize this," his granddaughter Susan reveals, "but in the earlier drafts of the Farewell Address, the original configuration had not been 'military-industrial complex,' but rather 'military-industrial-*congressional* complex.' "

Before Eisenhower gave the speech, Susan explains, he removed the word "congressional" because he prided himself on the strength of his relations with a Congress of the opposing party. "He was afraid it might be misconstrued as a direct criticism against the sitting Congress, and he prized the spirit of bipartisanship higher than making the specific point," she notes.

Susan's revealing anecdote illustrates that, however radically speech is perceived, even it fell victim to a measure of political pressure. Eisenhower's knockout punch turns out to have been a pulled one—softened just before the moment of impact to be less challenging to the system as a whole. Susan feels confident nonetheless in her grandfather's political calculation. "I think he felt the point could be made through the sheer articulation of 'military-industrial complex.' And really this idea has entered the English language through his words, which are understood pretty instinctively by people. Clearly Congress is part of a triangle here."

The "iron triangle," says Joseph Cirincione, who served for many years as a staffer to politicians from Republican Tom Ridge to Democrat John Conyers, is a term that emerged over the years to compensate for Eisenhower's omission of the word "congressional" from the farewell. "When you look at what keeps the contracts going and the policies in place," says Cirincione, "It's not two links, it's three. It's the military, and industry, and Congress. And these together form the basis for the national security policy of the United States."

To be sure, "military-industrial complex" makes for a catchier phrase, and certainly less unwieldy than "military-industrial-congressional complex," but the loss of attention to the role of Congress is consequential. Without pointing the finger at congressional collusion, a less accurate understanding of the problem is perpetuated, providing the public no practical target for its concerns. Representatives of the military and of industry are not elected by the people and are thus beyond the public's reach.

While recognizing Eisenhower's courage in having said what he said, returning the missing "C" to MIC is a necessary step in understanding how the more aptly named "MICC" acquires its "unwarranted influence." If the lesson of Boyd's OODA loop is to know your enemy, appreciating Congress' place in the iron triangle is vital to mapping the full shape of the complex and understanding where to apply efforts at reform.

For this, one must go where the headlines do not—into the tangled undergrowth of the complex itself.

BOYD'S BULLDOG

Among those who recognize the existence and influence of the Complex, there is a division similar to that between advocates of the theory of evolution and those who subscribe to creationism. Much as the mystery of life on earth has inspired some to believe in an intelligent designer while others subscribe to the idea of natural selection, the military-industrial-congressional complex has produced two schools of thought. The first sees the system as the intelligent design of a cohort of individuals who knowingly conspire to seek profit through war. The second sees a godless system of individual components each pursuing its own interest, irrespective of the others. This second version posits that, as in a natural system, whether these components compete or collaborate, they cumulatively evolve toward a state of heightened voracity that fattens the system as a whole.

The MICC is ultimately composed of human beings. And human nature being what it is, avaricious individuals surely exist and will seek to gain private benefit at public cost. But the idea that any such person or group of people could knowingly conspire to mastermind so intricate a system is harder—and unnecessary—to prove. It is more likely—and indeed more troubling—that corruption among defense contractors, representatives in Congress, and military brass is "standard operating procedure," in which these actors simply exploit the thick camouflage that an incestuously overtangled system provides. However challenging, untangling systemwide corruption is a far more useful task than holding any particular corrupt actor to account.

Just as it took a five-star general and brilliant systems analyst like Eisenhower to identify and name the Complex in its infancy, so, too, it would take soldiers and analysts in the Eisenhower mold to uncover the particulars of its more recent machinations as they evolved, and to reverse-engineer the system to mount serious efforts at reform.

Among those who led such efforts were several of John Boyd's acolytes at the Pentagon. Though Boyd is famous for his contributions to air tactics and the strategic principles of the OODA loop, his most lasting legacy may indeed prove to be the work carried on by his compatriots in the Military Reform Movement. As engineers seeking to optimize America's defenses, the reformers had discovered firsthand how the economic interests of the complex take their toll on product quality. They had won short-term battles against the entrenched bureaucracy but had come to see these victories as Pyrrhic, undermined by the steady and inexorable pressure of vested interests in the Complex.

Among these reformers, the most outspoken was Boyd's protégé Franklin Spinney. If you ask around military circles, no one knows the Complex better than Spinney, who spent thirty-five years at its cutting edge—first as an Air Force officer, then working alongside Boyd to improve America's defenses, and then for twenty years as his own self-styled watchdog toiling in the bowels of the Pentagon.

Spinney in many ways became to Boyd what Thomas Huxley was to Charles Darwin. Within days of Darwin's publication in 1859 of his controversial *Origin of Species*, Huxley wrote a letter in which he thanked Darwin for "the great store of new views you have given me," and vowed that he was "prepared to go to the stake if requisite" to defend them.[2] Huxley's passion to take up Darwin's cause earned him the nickname "Darwin's Bulldog."

Just before Boyd's death in 1997, Spinney wrote his mentor a good-bye letter in which he likewise promised to "continue the good work you taught me to do." By all accounts, Spinney became Boyd's "Bulldog" in the years that followed, taking his mentor's efforts further than the program-specific turf wars fought by the reformers, into a far more penetrating analysis of the system's deepest levels of dysfunction and corruption. "When Chuck Spinney talks about defense cost overruns," Dan Rather reported in a 1983 *CBS Evening News* segment, "Congress listens. And so do his Pentagon bosses."[3]

By the time Spinney retired on May 30, 2003, he had become arguably the most effective watchdog ever to make his voice heard from inside America's defense establishment. He had produced a vast body of work explaining how the Pentagon operates that was even used to bring about a measure of real reform. Though much of his reporting consisted of facts and figures that might seem mind-numbing to the average person, his impact was felt throughout Washington and even landed him on the cover of *Time* magazine under the heading "Pentagon Maverick." If you want to know how the Complex works and how to pursue meaningful reform, Spinney's the man to talk to. That is, if you can track him down.

WHY ARE WE MEETING ON A BOAT?

After much effort, I find Spinney a couple hundred miles off the coast of Florida. Flying in a puddle jumper to a remote tropical airstrip, I caught up with him aboard his 40-foot cutter. He is on the first leg of an open-ended sea voyage that will take him and his wife Alison halfway around the world.

"Why are we meeting on a boat?" He laughs mischievously while trimming a sail, his boyish hair blowing in the wind. It all seems very cloak and dagger, but the voyage is really just an overdue vacation, a lifelong dream of setting sail and leaving decades of Pentagon infighting behind.

"I guess whistle-blowers end up having to live offshore," I joke, finding a spot on board beside his dog. "I am not a whistle-blower!" Spinney snaps. "In fact, I despise the term. I'm a military reformer." The distinction, according to Spinney, is that a reformer tries to make change from the inside, while a whistle-blower is someone who has stopped believing internal reform is possible or likely and thus takes his concerns public, hoping increased outside attention will bring about change. It's clear Spinney's made it his life's work not to become the latter.

I apologize for having mischaracterized him, but before long I'm back at it, only to be schooled again. Spinney's pleasant, but a stickler for accuracy. I learn, for example, not to call him "a voice in the wilderness" because, as he says, "I was by no means alone. There were a lot of us reformers working to improve the system." He was not a "systems analyst" either, because what he did was not simply to analyze data but to synthesize that data in a creative process through which new and previously unseen perspectives emerge. He is not a "genius," he corrects me, because that is a term he reserves for John Boyd.

As we speak, America is sinking deeper into a preemptive war against Iraq; the appearance of its victory over Afghanistan's Taliban government is crumbling; the U.S. defense budget has spiraled to $400 billion; and Beltway profiteering scandals dominate the news. But from the way Spinney talks, you'd barely know it. Not because he lacks concern for the situation America faces—on the contrary, he's greatly concerned—but more because it's nothing new. The corruption he sees today is an extension of corruption he's been fighting for thirty-five years, and his concern runs deeper than any one administration, conflict, scandal, or rising budget.

While it's clear that, like many in the Military Reform Movement, Spinney sees the Iraq War as a misguided departure from the strategic wisdom of John Boyd, he also sees it as an inevitable outgrowth of a broader problem—one with roots far deeper in America's history. As he explains with the clarity of one who has devoted his entire career to fighting the military-industrial-congressional complex, its influence has become a force that corrodes U.S. policy making, leading not just to misbegotten defense expenditures, but, ultimately, to war.

Spinney joined the Air Force in 1967, at the height of the Vietnam War. A mechanical engineer by training, his father had served in the Air Force before him. Spinney was first assigned to Ohio's Wright-Patterson Air Force Base, where he worked in the same building his father had worked in during World War II. He quickly earned a reputation for being a smart-ass, irreverent to authority. Spinney's first formative brush with the complex came in 1968 when, as a young second lieutenant, he decided that the defense contractor Booz Allen Applied Research was failing to meet its obligations under a consulting contract with his department at Wright-Patterson.

"I literally didn't have any authority." He laughs now. "But they were basically raking in the money for the contract and not performing. So I decided, *to hell with these bastards. I'm gonna cancel this fuckin' thing.*" If Spinney had any illusions about what he was getting himself into when he took steps to cancel the contract, they were shattered when he was invited for lunch by William Sommers, president of Booz Allen Applied Research.

"He calls me and says, 'I'm coming out there and I'm going to take you down to the King Cole restaurant.' " The King Cole, Spinney explains, was the swanky French restaurant in Dayton where all the contractors would take government employees to "wine and dine 'em." Spinney had a better idea.

"I said, 'We're not goin' to the King Cole. We're goin' to the Officer's Club and it's on me.' "

Over roast beef sandwiches, the young Spinney bluntly explained his reasons for canceling Booz Allen's contract. Sommers smiled confidently before responding. " 'Let me explain to you the facts of life,' " Spinney recalls him saying. " 'You do this, and I'm gonna destroy your career.' "

Looking back, Spinney guffaws with genuine amusement. "I remember thinkin', *Christ, I'm a second lieutenant. I can't go any lower!* So I told him, 'Well, you gotta do what you gotta do.' "

So what happened?

"We canceled it." Spinney grins, enjoying the memory. "I wrote a nineteen-page memo on all the problems. My superiors were impressed and went ahead with the cancellation. But then the people at Booz Allen put pressure on those in charge of the funding. And the next think I knew, the project was back on. There was a small consolation, though. They replaced the deadbeats who weren't performing with new people."

The episode would prove to be classic Spinney, whose ensuing years of service involved countless such battles.

In 1972, at age twenty-seven, after five years in the Air Force, Spinney was transferred to the Pentagon, where he worked as a glorified mailman, moving communications traffic to all corners of the building. Today, he credits this somewhat demeaning experience with giving him an indispensable sense of the building's bureaucratic geography. He became a walking organizational chart of an organism whose complexity might otherwise not have become second nature to him.

When John Boyd arrived at the Pentagon a year later, Spinney jumped at the chance to work with him. Long fascinated by Boyd's pioneering work, the decision would change Spinney's life. Spinney was baptized by fire in the infamous controversy over the 1975 F-16/F-17 fly-off. Though Boyd and his reformers won that battle, it girded Boyd's team for a war of permanent vigilance against the MICC. The ingenuity and rigor the reformers had brought to optimizing aircraft performance now suddenly turned inward on the defense bureaucracy itself—it became another underperforming machine requiring their special brand of problem solving to re-engineer it.

THE PLANS/REALITY MISMATCH

Fed up with its corruption, Boyd and Spinney both retired from the Pentagon in 1975. Or at least they tried to. "I swore I'd never go back to the Pentagon," Spinney recalls. "I went to work for a 'Beltway bandit,' making money to support myself while I did my Ph.D." Spinney recalls that it wasn't long before he missed fighting the good fight at the Pentagon. Then one day Tom Christie called to say they wanted him to come back. "To sweeten the deal," Spinney laughs, "they told me Boyd was coming back, too." Spinney decided he'd rather have fun with Boyd while working on his Ph.D. than selling his soul at a defense contractor. So back he went. "Of course, then I got sucked in and never did finish the Ph.D."

Does he regret it?

His simple answer: "No."

Although the American people and many soldiers entered a period of soul-searching after Vietnam, this spirit did not infect the upper ranks of the Complex, whose growth, contrary to the general perception, continued largely unabated. Yes, there were some token reductions in certain defense programs, but they were minor, and their significance was exaggerated to form the basis of the rearmament campaign of Ronald Reagan. The "decade of neglect," as this period came to be called, was in fact a period much like any other in the life of the Complex.

What did diminish during this time was troop morale. By the late 1970s, officers and enlisted personnel were leaving the military in alarming numbers. Disillusionment over America's defeat in Vietnam was aggravated by the reluctance of the military brass to face that defeat and heed its implicit call for reform. Fueled by this exodus of disenchanted officers and enlisted soldiers, the Pentagon's decision makers simply concluded that the military could make do with fewer men so long as it could buy more weapons to replace them. From this deranged notion, the catchy but delusional concept of the "electronic battlefield" was born.

An intervention was required.

In their war with the corruption of the Complex, it was as though

Boyd and Spinney had retreated for just long enough to let the enemy forget about them, only to return with a vengeance. Inside the Pentagon, using Spinney's peerless knowledge of the inner workings of the building, the reformers started investigating waste and pushing solutions through the same arteries and back channels through which the poison of corruption otherwise flowed. Outside the Pentagon, Spinney would quickly become, for Republican and Democratic members of Congress alike, the go-to guy for straight talk about defense matters.

During the latter part of Carter's administration, Spinney published the first in a series of controversial reports. *Defense Facts of Life*, as it was titled, was Spinney's baby, but like all the reformers' work it went through a rigorous Socratic process of refinement by Boyd and the others to make it airtight.

Owing to the disproportionate power accorded to the Air Force by the National Security Act of 1947, it had become the most influential of the services in its military-industrial-congressional activities. *Defense Facts of Life* thus focused attention primarily on the Air Force as a case study in military profligacy. The report marshaled a vast array of data into a simple, undeniable message: Like an addict destroying his life, the Air Force had spent so much on its addiction to expensive and technologically overcomplicated systems that it had cannibalized its ability to maintain those systems. As a result, though on paper the Air Force could boast all kinds of fancy new technologies, its readiness, or its actual capacity to implement those technologies in a wartime situation, was at an all-time low.

"Don't misunderstand," Spinney recalls. "I actually believed we needed more money, not less. I didn't see how we could fix it without more money in the budget. But I also wanted to bring about change that would make our military more effective by getting control of this technology tail that was wagging the dog."

Spinney was meticulous in keeping his criticisms to a statement of the facts, free from subjective interpretation. He left conclusions about corruption to be drawn by others, simply revealing how a propensity toward expensive, high-tech product development and acquisition was weakening America's defenses from within.

Defense Facts of Life was perceived by some, like Air Force Generals Bob Mathis and Wilbur Creech, commander of the U.S. Tactical Air

Command, as a declaration of war by the reformers against the Air Force. Others, like Air Force Generals Bryce Poe and Leo Marquez, saw its potential value in helping them fix problems they themselves recognized. Spinney began giving briefings to anyone who would listen within the security-clear community. And the rank of those listening grew with each briefing, from captains and majors all the way up to Tactical Air Commander General Creech. At this level, within the walls of secrecy, Spinney's study could have been ignored by the Air Force. But before long, President Carter's secretary of defense Harold Brown allowed a summary of Spinney's findings to be included in an official communication known as the Consolidated Guidance for the years 1978–80. Brown's decision to include the summary angered those who saw Spinney's findings as an attack. The media coverage that followed set off a firestorm across Washington.

In October 1979, investigative journalist James Fallows popularized Spinney's message and the reformers' broader cause in a groundbreaking article in the *Atlantic Monthly* entitled "The Muscle-Bound Superpower," which questioned whether America, for all its technology, could actually prevail in a wartime situation. World events would soon underscore this question. On April 24, 1980, an operation that should have been easily accomplished by the world's largest military went awry.

Five months earlier, Iranian revolutionaries had taken sixty-six U.S. diplomats hostage inside the U.S. Embassy in Tehran—an expression of anti-American sentiment that had arisen in the long wake of the CIA's 1953 overthrow of Iran's President Mossadegh. Facing an international crisis and a challenge to American power, Carter authorized a helicopter operation to free the hostages. The mission failed miserably due to a sequence of technical equipment failures. Three helicopters were lost in the desert during the earliest stages of the operation, at which point Carter ordered the mission abandoned. To make matters worse, one of the retreating helicopters then crashed into another, causing a massive fire that took the lives of eight U.S. servicemen and destroyed almost as many helicopters. Though pilot error was in part to blame for the failed operation, the debacle became a symbol of the Pentagon's readiness crisis. The U.S. military did indeed seem to be destroying itself from within.

Carter's loss of face in the hostage crisis helped his Republican challenger Ronald Reagan win the 1980 presidential election, and the interval of transition between the two administrations proved a moment of vulnerability for the Complex, during which Spinney's ideas gained a foothold. At the time, Democratic senator Sam Nunn of Georgia was a rising star in the defense establishment and chairman of the Readiness Subcommittee of the Senate Armed Services Committee. In November 1980, during the lame-duck period between Reagan's election and the inauguration, Nunn received a briefing by Spinney on his findings and asked Spinney to produce an unclassified report for inclusion in the *Congressional Record*. But Nunn went further, working through the bureaucracy to ensure that Spinney's concerns would carry over into the next administration.

In February 1981, just weeks after Reagan's inauguration, the issues in Spinney's report were raised at the confirmation hearings for Caspar Weinberger as secretary of defense. Things were going smoothly for Weinberger until Nunn expressed his concern that voices of reform within the Pentagon were being "squelched." Nunn asked Weinberger if he had read Spinney's report. Weinberger was unprepared for the question and confessed he hadn't. The exchange thrust the concerns raised by *Defense Facts of Life* onto the congressional defense agenda just as the new secretary of defense was taking office. It also brought yet more public attention to Spinney and the reformers. In an effort to control the damage, David Chu, a Republican political appointee and head of the directorate at which Spinney worked, ordered that he stop working on *Defense Facts of Life* and shift his energies elsewhere.

Spinney complied with respect to the specific report but continued his larger crusade. Over the next eighteen months, he developed a second report, entitled *The Plans/Reality Mismatch*, which proved even more incendiary. The new report took no prisoners in revealing the disconnect between what the defense sector had promised at the time it sought congressional appropriations for certain programs and what was actually delivered under those programs. It cited embarrassing figures, revealing that even when quantities went down, costs went up, and fingered specific programs.

Once again, Spinney was ordered by Chu to stop publicizing his findings until an "independent study" could be conducted, which took a year. When the results confirmed Spinney's conclusions, he was told by Chu that, despite his report's accuracy, it was now too late to act on it. In response, the reformers did something clever. They leaked the independent study (rather than Spinney's report, which was classified) to the media. Before long, all of Washington was abuzz about Spinney's mysterious report.

When Iowa Republican senator Chuck Grassley sought a copy of the independent study from the Pentagon, he was rebuffed by Secretary Weinberger, who downplayed it as outdated and irrelevant. According to Spinney, "Grassley got into his car and drove over to the Pentagon and demanded to see me." After their meeting, Grassley used his own turf war skills to compel a joint committee hearing on March 4, 1983, at which Spinney would give his briefing. In the end, thanks to Grassley's persistence, a battle the Military Reform Movement's adversaries had hoped would either be squelched or take place in a nondescript hearing room somewhere deep in the Capitol instead took place in the huge Senate Caucus Room, site of the McCarthy Hearings, as well as those on Watergate and the Iran/Contra affair. Attendance was standing-room only. For Weinberger and his allies, the hearing was a disaster.

Armed with meticulous rear-projection slides and graphs, the young Spinney earnestly and methodically reported his findings. His analysis looked at the annual projections going back seven years to show that for each year in that period, no matter who was president or which party controlled Congress, the gulf between the amount requested for the defense budget and the actual amount spent that year was vast. Particularly striking was his finding that Reagan's actual defense spending was $500 billion more than the five-year total the president had projected in making his request for the 1984 budget. Spinney's report was an impenetrable fortress of interlocking data. In the years since, no part of it has been contradicted, as Spinney used the Pentagon's own computer tapes to generate his analysis. The GAO was asked on several occasions to evaluate the methodology, and when the office eventually issued a report, it found no fault.

The week after Spinney's appearance at the hearing, *Time* magazine put him on its cover, devoting eleven pages to a comprehensive article on Boyd, the Military Reform Movement, and Spinney's terrifying conclusions. Information is like water—it wants to flow around every obstacle. In their efforts to dam the free flow of Spinney's ideas, those opposing reform had created explosive pressure for the information's release. Once the dam broke, it erupted into a full-blown national scandal.

Spinney's findings would be used to kick-start a process of increasing scrutiny and criticism of defense spending that would culminate in the most concerted and effective effort in the post–World War II period to rein in its growth. Buoyed by congressional reaction to Spinney's testimony, Senator Grassley was able to build a consensus among the Republican-controlled Senate to freeze Reagan's defense budget in constant dollars after 1985—a huge achievement for the reformers. Even so, the defense budget's overall growth bounced back in later years, resuming its upward trajectory under Clinton and exploding under the administration of George W. Bush.

SPINNEY LOOKS SOBERLY AT THE REFORMERS' ACHIEVEMENTS

Reflecting on the impact of his reform efforts, Spinney has mixed feelings: "A retired British field marshal wrote that the work we did helped defeat the Soviet Union," he laughs incredulously. "I was involved in the struggle. But in many ways, you could say we failed. Things are worse today than they've ever been. They correctly recognized that we were a threat and rolled over us. But, honestly, if we failed, you can say that Eisenhower failed, too. But at least he warned people."

Though his efforts would never recapture front-page visibility, Spinney remained a vigilant watchdog inside the Pentagon for two more decades until his retirement in May 2003. During these years, he became a kind of tenured professor deep inside the DoD, constantly scrutinizing defense corruption. He continued to resist becoming a whistle-blower, yet increasingly came to see himself not only as an internal watchdog but as a vital source of responsible public information in a democracy.

"In my capacity as an analyst in the Office of the Secretary of Defense," he explains, "I knew we had some very serious problems. And the only way we could get these problems addressed by Congress and the American people was to have people better informed about the pathologies that infected the decision-making processes in the Pentagon."

The pathologies to which Spinney refers are central to understanding how his thinking has evolved over the decades since the first battles between Boyd and the bureaucracy. Having watched so many clashes over particular weapons or systems come and go, Spinney has developed a broader understanding of the patterns of behavior at work. Like his predecessor Boyd, he has become more philosophic in his thinking, coming to see himself and others like him as a vital bulwark for the Constitution itself.

UNNATURAL SELECTION: FRONTLOADING AND POLITICAL ENGINEERING

"Follow the money" is typically a good starting point for tracing the flows of power and influence in any large institution. But as Spinney explains it, "the military-industrial-congressional complex is so Byzantine in its complexity that even the simple effort to depict it in an organizational chart crashes into the limits of two-dimensional space. It requires something closer to a hologram."

As Spinney describes the inner workings and interrelation of the various components of the Complex, a hologram of dizzying intricacy indeed takes shape. The first complication lies in understanding the components of the Complex themselves. Though the term "military-industrial-congressional complex" suggests a convergence of three institutions with coherent and uniform agendas, the actual inner workings of each component reveal the opposite to be true. In fact, each one—military, industrial, and congressional—is internally textured by competing interests: interservice, corporate, and congressional rivalries respectively.

The military, for example, may from the outside seem monolithic in its crew-cut uniformity. But it's actually an array of disparate service branches vying against each other for federal funding and other benefits. Whether the Navy wants a new attack submarine, the Air Force a new fighter, the Army a new ground combat system, or the Marines a new transport, their development is the basis of fierce rivalry between the services. Similarly, industry is by no means monolithic, since within this sector are literally hundreds of corporations competing for government contracts. For its part, Congress is notoriously riven by inner conflict—from its broadest party lines to the smallest district level, with individual representatives competing to bring jobs and money to their districts.

The three also interact in a fashion more complex than simple co-conspiracy. Picture a many-headed hydra, each of whose heads has a mind of its own. At times they may collaborate; at others, compete. But whether the individual heads are snapping at each other or feasting together on the same hunt, the beast to which they belong grows larger and more powerful. As Spinney explains it, as in a natural system in which only the fittest survive, the components of the Complex evolve through their competition and collaboration toward a state of heightened voracity whose cumulative effect accrues to the benefit of the system as a whole.

"Let's use the example of buying a weapon—like a new fighter plane for the Air Force," Spinney explains, "'cause that's the easiest and most concrete to understand. Essentially, the sponsors of any particular weapons program are a diffuse alliance of people in Congress, in the Pentagon, and in the defense industry. Each has his own agenda. The defense contractor wants the program to sell for obvious reasons. The program manager within the Pentagon bureaucracy wants it to happen for career reasons. And the congressman wants it because it will increase his political clout or bring him some other kind of benefit."

According to Spinney, in the simplest terms, most new weapons systems are born out of a close dialogue between defense companies and their associates in the military. Through this collaboration with the procurement personnel of a given service branch, the company learns about the needs of that branch and develops products to meet them.

Colonel Wallace "Wally" Saeger, for example, is the director of munitions at the Air Logistics Center at Hill Air Force Base in Ogden, Utah. His "portfolio," as he calls it, is a $22 billion Air Force inventory of everything from the ammunition that goes into the guns on aircraft to the bombs that are loaded underneath the wings, to ejection and guidance systems for the bombs. There's an almost eerie matter-of-factness in the way he describes buying billion-dollar tools of destruction as though they were curtain rods or pieces of plumbing hardware.

"Say you have the same car year after year," he says. "If industry didn't change the car at all, would you buy a different car? No. But when they come out with something that's got extra bells and whistles on it that suits what you need it to do, then you'll buy more. Industry does the same thing with the government."[4]

One key phrase in this description offers a window into how the procurement process is tilted by its participants toward increased procurement: *that suits what you need it to do.* Though this suggests that the bells and whistles added by the seller are useful to the buyer, it also reflects how the buyer and seller work together in developing the product to ensure that it represents a happy marriage of their interests. It's a defensible process in that the taxpayer would certainly rather have a defense contractor spend his money designing products that meet the needs of the services than work in isolation. But the collaboration also increases the risk that the public interest represented by the service arm becomes blurred with the private interest of the contractor.

When Fuji and Tooms' commander Colonel Treadway describes his squadron's relationship to defense contractor Lockheed-Martin, his tendency to use matrimonial language evokes the pros and cons of military-industrial collaboration. "Whenever we find a new way to improve the processes, Lockheed is involved," he declares proudly. "We are wedded to the factory and the company. They are our prime source of parts and expertise. And they are a part of all we do. It is a wonderful marriage of industry with military."

Out of this marriage, according to Spinney, the defense company and its service branch fashion a proposal for a weapons system. Representatives of the company and the branch must then work to win the support of those in the Pentagon and Congress who control the purse strings. To do this, the military-industrial collaborators engage in two key patterns of behavior, which Spinney calls "frontloading" and "political engineering."

" 'Frontloading' and 'political engineering,' " Spinney explains, "are terms of art we use in the Pentagon to describe our bureaucratic gaming strategies. You want Congress to fund your new system. So the name of the game is to turn on the money spigot and lock it open. The way you do that is by first *frontloading* the decision. You *overpromise* what it's going to do. And you *underestimate* the kind of burdens (economic and other) it's going to impose. Overestimate the benefits. Underestimate the burdens. When those benefits don't materialize, and when the burdens are higher than predicted, you have to set up some sort of safety net, making it impossible to shut off the money flow. That’s where political engineering comes in.”

Political engineering, according to Spinney, is a common practice by which a defense contractor intentionally spreads contracts and subcontracts for a particular system to a wide range of congressional districts in order to build a constituency within Congress that provides strong and lasting support for that system.

To illustrate how frontloading and political engineering undermine the wisdom of congressional decision making, Spinney uses Lockheed-Martin/Boeing’s F-22 Raptor fighter as a case study. The F-22 is a highly advanced stealth aircraft program whose nearly twenty-year design and development process has been shadowed by controversy over its spiraling costs and diminished usefulness in the wake of the Cold War, for which it was originally intended. “When a contractor builds a major system like the F-22, the first thing they do is to lowball the initial estimate,” he explains. “With the F-22, they said it was going to cost $30 million and weigh 50,000 pounds. The plane is now up well over $300 million a copy and climbing. And it’s got all sorts of technical problems. Worst of all,” Spinney exclaims, “it’s an air-to-air combat aircraft originally conceived to fight the Soviet Union, and today we don’t even have an enemy with an air force!”

This, according to Spinney, is where political engineering comes in. “Frontloading enables you to get the program going. But to keep it going, you start flooding money and jobs to as many congressional districts as possible as quickly as possible. So when the program’s true costs become apparent, or its performance problems become apparent—when it doesn’t do what you said it was going to do and it costs far more than you said it was going to cost and it requires more people to operate than you said would be required to operate it—by the time that all becomes apparent, the system is locked up and you can’t do anything about it.”

In the case of the F-22, its construction was contracted and subcontracted in forty-four states. This means a majority of the Senators on Capitol Hill have been given a vested interest in perpetuating the program.

As a watchdog over Pentagon waste, Spinney saw frontloading and political engineering firsthand as strategies to thwart his efforts to challenge the continued legitimacy of systems like the F-22. "Let's say, hypothetically, that Chuck Spinney in the Pentagon wants to kill the F-22," he explains. "So I do a study that says the Cold War's over and we don't need the F-22 anymore. While I am doing this, word will get out, and I become a threat to the welfare of people working on the F-22—the contractor's employees, the Air Force sponsors, and the people on the Hill who benefit from jobs and money flowing to their districts."

So what do they do?

"It just takes one phone call from the program manager in the Pentagon to the president of the company to unleash a torrent. Now in this case it's Lockheed-Martin. So the president of Lockheed makes a few calls, turns on his lobbyists. Makes a couple more calls to his subcontractors, who in turn call their subs. Now they're all going to turn on their lobbyists. And that's when the fax attacks start. They start lobbying Congress, and Congress gets inundated with studies showing why the F-22 is absolutely vital to the survival of Western society. The studies will say, 'Yes, the F-22 might have had some problems in the past, but we've overcome them.' And meanwhile in the newspapers there'll be op-eds singing the F-22's praises written by people in think tanks funded by the defense industry."

According to Spinney, when the lobbyists make their case to Congress in support of the F-22, they find a sympathetic ear. And this is where political engineering takes its most ominous form. "They'll have some congressional hearings," he continues. "And mounds of paper will be produced not only showing why it's absolutely essential to continue the F-22 but also saying 'By the way, Mr. Congressman, here are maps showing you the money and jobs you will lose in your district if this program is slowed or canceled.' "

Spinney's former colleague Tom Christie confirms this, recounting a particularly egregious episode that took place in the Reagan administration between Secretary of Defense Weinberger and proponents of the B-1 bomber.

"During the Reagan years," he recalls, "a B-1 manager was briefing Weinberger, and he had a chart showing where all the contracts to build it were spread all over the country. Weinberger became furious. 'That's not how we do business,' he said. 'I don't want to see that kind of chart again!' Well, today, that kind of thing is standard, it's expected."

To Spinney, the district-targeting maps used in political engineering represent the most voracious state to which bureaucratic gaming strategies have evolved. "The beauty of all this," he emphasizes, "is that it just takes a few phone calls and all hell breaks loose. Everyone's interests are at stake. So it doesn't take a whole lot of close control. It takes only the loosest form of control in the form of an alert mechanism. If I can come up with a way of threatening your income, it will move you to action, right? Well, that's what happens. Now multiply that example of one weapons system by hundreds of examples going on in hundreds of congressional districts every day."

When one imagines the explosion of so many such initiatives through the arteries of the Complex, one begins to understand why Spinney tends to describe it in terms usually reserved for a vast natural system. For part of what makes the MICC so difficult to reform or restrain is the diversity of counterintuitive and multi-directional ways in which its components interact with one another. When one component's interest conflicts with that of another, either competition or compromise results. Let's say the Air Force and the Navy find themselves at loggerheads over their respective desire for control of a certain weapons program. If an internal compromise can be reached, it will be, making the task of congressional or Pentagon oversight more complicated. If no compromise can be reached, one side prevails. If, for example, the Air Force outmaneuvers the Navy in winning a specific program, the Air Force will be strengthened, the Complex will grow and prosper from this victory, and the Navy will go back to the drawing board, examine the lessons learned from its loss, and live to fight more effectively another day. Too often, though, everyone wins, resulting in explosive overall budgets.

To make matters more complicated, Spinney notes that his example of a single weapons system developed jointly by military and industrial actors and then promoted in Congress by way of frontloading and political engineering is misleadingly simplistic. The drive behind a given system, he argues, rarely comes from just one traceable source. At times, a member of Congress may push for a weapon to be developed in his or her district. At others, a military program procurement officer or defense manufacturer may be the driver. Or more typically, as was the case in Spinney's story about the F-22, all three arms of the Complex may be maneuvering both alone and in tandem to preserve their individual and collective interests. Once their program is under way, these members of the triangle increasingly move in a seamless lockstep with one another that insulates their program from reduction or cancellation. With such an intricate collusion of individual parts, addressing any one component by, say, investigating a single transaction, congressional decision, or acquisitions procedure leaves the other components free to find ways to continue to press the collective interest forward.

Over time, as in any adaptive system, these actors grow increasingly adept at ensuring their own growth and prosperity. Along the way, Spinney argues, "behaviors and qualities that have proven most effective for members of the Complex are reinforced while less effective ones fall away." Like a species whose survival skills are honed by natural selection, the Complex has evolved to a heightened level of sophistication for pushing forward ever more expensive programs.

MORE THAN MONEY

The system of corruption Spinney describes explains profligacy from $800 Pentagon toilet seats to the $70 billion spent on an air-to-air combat aircraft—like the F-22—despite America no longer having an enemy with an air force. The system unquestionably leads to waste and abuse. But does it lead to war?

Spinney's answer is yes, and the process by which it does so relies on two discrete but related underlying forces in public policy: the evolution of Congress into what Madison once called a "majority faction" and the systematic overshadowing of the legislative branch by the executive. Understanding these forces and the way they combine to misguide public policy helps explain how it was, for example, that America entered as ill-considered a war as that in Iraq.

Manufacturing Consent: The Rise of the Majority Faction

Essential to understanding how corruption in the Complex leads to war is to appreciate that the U.S. Congress has become what Madison in *The Federalist Papers* fearfully called a "majority faction." *Federalist* No. 10 is often cited as proof that, although political parties had not in a formal sense taken shape at the time the Constitution was drafted, the framers—Madison in particular—saw the danger of partisanship in the country's future. Though both the words "party" and "partisan" appear in *Federalist* No. 10, Madison's fear of partisanship has been more commonly traced to his frequent use of the term "faction."

"By a faction," Madison wrote, "I understand a number of citizens, whether amounting to a majority or a minority of the whole, who are united and actuated by some common impulse of passion . . . adversed to the rights of other citizens, or to the permanent and aggregate interests of the community."

Madison feared any faction within a society imposing its will on others, yet he recognized that, in a democracy, the "sinister views" of a minority could be easily overruled and kept in check by the "regular vote" of the majority. Conversely, though, if a faction within a society itself constituted a majority, Madison feared that "both the public good and the rights of other citizens" could be imperiled. "The superior force of an interested and overbearing majority," he argued, could create conditions contrary to "the rules of justice and the rights of the minor party." In essence, Madison saw the principle of majority rule as inadequate to protect individual rights and the common good. Still, while he feared that majoritanism could devolve into mob rule, he also recognized that a certain measure of factionalism—the tendency to form opposing parties, classes, and groupings—is "sown into the nature of man" and cannot be controlled out of existence. What could be controlled, he reasoned, were the effects of such factionalism.

"To secure the public good and private rights against the danger of such a faction and at the same time to preserve the spirit and the form of popular government," he wrote, "is then the great object to which our inquiries are directed." To this end, he felt that a "pure democracy" (i.e., a system in which the public participates directly in its own governance without the intermediary involvement of representatives) "can admit of no cure for the mischiefs of faction." Instead, he believed that a representative republic "promises the cure for which we are seeking."

Through what Madison called "the delegation of the government . . . to a small number of citizens elected by the rest," the republic avoids the danger that the infectious passions of a convened multitude may run roughshod over the interests of the few. A republic can "refine and enlarge the public views, by passing them through the medium of a chosen body of citizens, whose wisdom may best discern the true interest of their country, and whose patriotism and love of justice will be least likely to sacrifice it to temporary or partial considerations." Expressing a faith in the elite that might seem naive today, Madison asserted that "it may well happen that the public voice, pronounced by the representatives of the people, will be more consonant to the public good than if pronounced by the people themselves, convened for the purpose."

While Madison is to be credited for his early sensitivity to the dangers posed by partisanship, his prescription against it—namely, to form a representative republic—has backfired. It is impossible to know whether Madison's reasons for fearing majority faction were principally altruistic or self-serving. Was he earnestly concerned about the need to protect minorities from majorities—a driving theme of American twentieth-century liberalism? Or did he selfishly see himself and his fellow framers as a minority ruling class of wealthy property owners vulnerable to being overrun by the growing majority around them? Either way, and assuming a bit of both, the assumption that a distinguished body of legislators could prove a "cure for the mischiefs of faction" has been disproved by the evolution of America's political economy over the two centuries since.

The league of gentlemen in whom Madison put such faith as a measure against majority faction has proven more conducive to such factionalism than the "people themselves" might ever have. Madison's assumption that a small group of representatives would make more considered decisions than the masses may be understandable for its day. But in fact, a centralized 535-member body (435 representatives and 100 senators) has simply made for a far easier group in which to cultivate a majority than a nation of 300 million people. Essentially, rather than canvassing an entire country, one only need find a way to either persuade or incentivize a majority of those 535 people to foster the illusion that a national majority has been achieved.

The example of the F-22 is again illustrative. As Spinney explains, the F-22 has been politically engineered to the point that its individual components are produced in 44 states, employing some 25,000 people nationwide. The production of the F-22 thus affects an average of about 500 people and their families in any given state—a tiny minority of the country. Yet when one hears that the F-22 is produced in 44 states and supported by representatives in those states, the impression is that a true majority of the public has been heard in its support.

Spinney feels compelled to defend Madison's efforts against critical twenty-twenty hindsight. "It's easy today to look back and point out the flaws," he cautions, "but it was an important conception in its time. Then time marches on and systems adapt. And people learn how to game restraints that are put on them. The founders built something with cracks in it and people gaming the system have learned to work those cracks."

Recalling that the Industrial Revolution was just dawning as the U.S. Constitution and *The Federalist Papers* were being written, it's perhaps not surprising that Madison's design against majority faction failed to anticipate just how the power of concentrated wealth resulting from industrialization would come to affect public policy. More specifically, Madison could not have predicted the degree to which a congressperson's survival and prosperity today is defined by his capacity to bring jobs and money to his district. That these have come to assume such significance in a congressmen's calculus of personal interest makes them exploitable currency through which to win his support for any given program. Of course, that's just one representative. But when one recalls the technique of political engineering, one sees how a majority faction can be achieved by exploiting each individual's need to bring jobs and money to his district. When I ask Spinney to explain, in specific terms, how this exploitation takes place, he returns to the case of the F-22.

What he delivers is an eye-opening account of how a congressperson in whose district some part of the F-22 is produced, in order to keep jobs and money flowing into his district, becomes effectively a representative of the F-22's producers and advocates both to his colleagues on Capitol Hill and, ultimately, to the executive. In this way, for his own survival and prosperity, the congressperson makes himself vulnerable both to the executive's wishes and to a tangled network of horse trades with his congressional colleagues. When one imagines that each of these representatives, in turn, is likewise representing his corporate benefactors to the legislative and executive branches, the system takes on the holographic complexity Spinney describes.

A chessboard has sixty-four squares. There are two players. Each has sixteen pieces that can only move in preset ways. And there is in chess a finite set of rules that each player must follow. Yet the number of possible variations in the game of chess (approximately 10^{120})[5] exceeds the number of atoms in the universe. By comparison, the complex has 435 districts, in which thousands of corporations and dozens of government agencies all interact under far less clearly defined rules than the players at a chessboard.

When one multiplies the number of states and districts by the number of corporations and agencies, and then accounts for all the interactions among them, a system of infinite permutations emerges. Within this, a majority faction may be established for any number of goals from a weapons system to any other commercial product, public program, or private cause whose advocates have been able to secure support from a majority of those in Congress. Thus, Madison's backfired effort to prevent majority faction accounts for the funding and support of countless programs every day. As Spinney explains, war is just one such program. But who is its advocate? Who has the power to make Congress into a majority faction for war?

Unleashing the Dog of War: The Primacy of the Executive

To understand Spinney's explanation of the mechanics by which corruption in the MICC actually leads to warmaking, one must recall both Madison's view "that the Executive is the branch of power most interested in war, and most prone to it," and Jefferson's corollary belief that the separation of powers provide an "effectual check to the Dog of war." Yet, the rise of the executive branch over time to become the most powerful branch of government, Spinney explains, has given it the leverage to pressure Congress into supporting its warmaking goals.

When the framers spoke of executive power, they drew from their firsthand experience under the British Crown. This was a monarchy subjecting colonies to its rule and taxation through the threat of force. As *The Federalist Papers* attest, the framers were also no strangers to the fact that parliamentarianism produces its own brand of mischief. In designing the checks and balances, they assumed that no man was an angel, and they hoped that by pitting the competing interests of men against one another and requiring cooperation between them, the self-interest of each would act as a check on the other. Madison described this brilliant conception of power sharing thus: "ambition must be made to counteract ambition."[6]

Yet the framers did not anticipate the mechanisms by which the executive branch has become so powerful relative to the other branches. "We're talking about eighteenth-century philosophers who had no way of seeing how things would change," Spinney comments. "They wanted to prevent the rise of a tyrant. Everything was about that. Congress raises the Army and Navy. A congressperson can't spend money for more than two years. And up until the late 1800s, the biggest form of patronage the president had control over was jobs in the Post Office. In that situation, the president had no economic leverage over Congress. What's happened, starting with the progressive reforms of Theodore Roosevelt up through Woodrow Wilson, FDR's New Deal, and the permanent military mobilization after World War II, is that the president has gained more and more power, which has given him that much more patronage."

A list of the agencies and departments of government housed under the executive branch speaks volumes about this explosion of executive power. Take the Departments of State, Justice, Treasury, Commerce, Labor, Agriculture, Energy, Transportation, Homeland Security, Health and Human Services, Education, and add agencies like the CIA, NSA, FBI, DIA, EPA, FDA, SEC, and FCC, as well as the National Security Council, not to mention many other instruments of decision-making power not provided for in the Constitution. Add to this the fact that the military is entirely housed under the executive branch, and the total number of executive branch employees exceeds a staggering five million. By comparison, the number of people employed by Congress including staffers, aides, legal and operational assistants totals about 30,000. And the total number under the judicial branch is approximately 34,000.[7]

"The executive branch," says Spinney, "has become the go-to branch for so many parts of our national life. It can now control money going to different congressional districts either directly—by supporting weapons systems, for example—or indirectly, through incentives like the oil depletion allowance. The executive can also use his power punitively, and just the threat of that can compel whatever behavior he desires from Congress. The balance of power has shifted, because the president controls so much of the nation's resources."

The problem of congressional dependence on patronage has been exacerbated by the realities of modern campaigns. "The problem," explains Charles Lewis, founder of the Center for Public Integrity, "is the nature of our electoral system and, in particular, the cost of elections. A total of $150 million was spent on political ads in 1980; in 2002, it was $1 billion. Substantive campaign coverage dwindles every cycle. So, if you're a politician, the primary way to get your message out is through ads. If a politician doesn't have money, they don't have ads. They don't have ads, they don't get elected. It's a very simple equation. So the most powerful and most relevant forces today for any politician are their contributors. And for the most part those are not ordinary citizens. Most Americans don't meet their politicians. Half the country doesn't vote. Ninety-six percent don't write [contribution] checks."[8]

Spinney concurs, explaining in concrete terms how this economic reality of congressional life requires the congressperson "to become a pleader on behalf of his corporate benefactor to both the executive and his fellows in congress." What follows is a distillate of his analysis, oversimplified to illustrate the mechanics by which the congressperson is subordinated to the will of the executive.

BEGINNER CLASS: THE RISE OF THE PROFESSIONAL PLEADER

Using a simplified scenario, imagine that on a Monday, a member of Congress contacts the executive branch to argue against the cancellation of the F-22. Inside the executive branch, his call is most appropriately directed to the Department of Defense. So the member advises the DoD that the citizens of his district—so many of whose lives are touched by the largesse of contracts related to the F-22—are proud to be involved in its production, and that they see it as a vital part of America's defense. Yes, the congressman recognizes, there are voices that have questioned its continued relevance in a post–Cold War world, but those are just naysayers who don't realize how effective the F-22 can be in the war on terror. The Defense Department responds that they, too, value the F-22, that they are examining hundreds of such systems in connection with an upcoming budget review and will take his call on advisement, and that they thank the people of his district for their continued dedication to America's defense. That's on a Monday.

On Tuesday, the congressman's phone rings and on the other end is a different member of the executive branch. This time it's the president, who says, "Hi, Congressman. I have reason to believe there are WMDs in Iraq. And I'm hoping I can count on your support if I feel the need to take military action." Now, for a congressperson politically aligned with the president or sympathetic to his view of the threat posed by Saddam Hussein, this is a no-brainer. He would likely offer his unqualified support. But for a congressperson who is not politically aligned with the president or who might be disinclined to see Saddam as a significant threat to America, is that person going to boldly fulfill his Jeffersonian duty to assert himself as a "check to the Dog of war"? Is he going to demand that the president show him the evidence of such WMDs? Remember that just the day before, he was the one calling the president's own executive branch to curry favor for his benefactor. How vocal is he really going to be?

This does not, of course, mean that the congressperson will necessarily be the most ardent supporter of the president's war plans. But it may account for why he falls noticeably silent when crucial votes arise.

In February 2003, as the Iraq War inexorably approached, Democratic West Virginia senator Robert Byrd reflected on this critical silence of his colleagues on Capitol Hill. "On this February day," he lamented, "as this nation stands at the brink of battle, every American on some level must be contemplating the horrors of war. And yet this chamber is for the most part ominously, ominously, dreadfully silent. You can hear a pin drop. Listen. There is no debate. There's no attempt to lay out for the nation the pros and cons of this particular war."

Byrd's haunting remarks touched on a crucial question: as the executive marched to war in Iraq, why did Congress acquiesce? Why did members of Congress—even some whose constituencies might have expected them to oppose the administration's plans—prove so accommodating?

"Where is the outrage?" was the recurring question among Democratic voters during the Bush years confronted by the apparent compliance of their representatives. Even after the Iraq War became widely unpopular and the president's ostensible political opponents retook control of Congress, they expressed only sporadic and half-hearted restraint, voting in a fashion reflective of their conflicts of interest.

Joe Cirincione asks, with specific reference to the Democratic party, what made even the president's political opponents defer to his desires, "What happened here? Was it just the experience of September eleventh that made being seen as opposing strong defense policies a liability? Did the scandals of the Clinton years damage the Democrats and thus give license to a radical Republican agenda? Was it the fact that the legislative and judicial branches were all aligned to the same party as the executive? Was it genuine fear of another attack? Or is there something else going on here?"

Surely, all these factors in part contributed to Congress's unflinching support of Bush's policies in the months after 9/11. But Congress's continued support—despite occasional episodes of dissent once power changed hands in 2006 and the Iraq War surpassed its critics' worst predictions—suggests deeper forces at work.

Just as the missing "C" in Eisenhower's farewell has proved a glaring omission given Congress' obvious role in military-industrial corruption, so too—and for reasons that turn out to be related—Congress checking power over the executive was woefully lacking during the lead-up to the Iraq War.

"Over time," Spinney explains, "there has been a natural selection where it has been the best pleaders, rather than the best statesmen, who have risen to the top. The result is that we don't have a Congress of statesmen, we have a Congress of professional pleaders."

ADVANCED CLASS: THE CORPORATE-CONGRESSIONAL-MILITARY-EXECUTIVE COMPLEX

After Spinney's explanation of the F-22 example, I repeat back to him what I've understood to make sure I've got it right.

"If only it were that simple!" He laughs. "You've got all the action coming from the congressperson. And you've got it happening in response to an emergency, like a weapons system being up for review. But it doesn't work like that. All the players are involved, pushing their interests not just when they're under fire, but all the time. The name of the game is to keep the money and the jobs flowing. There are exceptions, of course, where the president is not so intent on war. But those exceptions prove the rule. If he wants war, he can get it. Because, with so much agency under him, Congress has come to need the executive for so many things."

Also misleading in the example, says Spinney, is the focus on the F-22 as a case study. This could be understood to suggest a conventional vision of the military-industrial complex—one in which defense contractors are singled out more than other members of the corporate sector for their capacity to put the legislative branch in a position of vulnerability to the executive.

Spinney's analysis, though, is not limited to currying favor within the defense sector. As he points out, senators and representatives who did not have an F-22 or other major defense program in their district also voted to support the war in Iraq. So, if not to keep defense jobs and money flowing, then why?

New York senator Hillary Clinton, for example, voted for the war in Iraq although hers is not dominantly a military-industrial state. Mrs. Clinton needs the executive's blessing for other more immediate purposes. It is not just military-industrial interests that can cause her to be subordinated to her president, but industrial and economic interests per se. Any entity that represents a source of jobs and money to any representative in any state or district is, by definition, able to put that representative in the position of pleading to the executive branch.

It could be a military base in a district facing closure, the loss of which would affect jobs. It could be a pharmaceutical company that needs the congressperson's help in appealing to the executive branch's Food and Drug Administration. It could be a media company seeking help in lobbying the FCC. It could be a Wall Street securities firm seeking friendly policies from the SEC. It could be an industrial giant seeking leniency from the EPA for its polluting practices. And it's not limited to the corporate sector. It could be a nonindustrial special interest group that wants to press for a certain social, political, religious, or philosophic agenda, such as antiprofanity legislation by the FCC, or executive activism with regard to abortion, church and state, or gay marriage. The executive has simply become, over time, so much the go-to branch for guiding national expenditures that every senator and representative, no matter what their party affiliation, is likely to have some agenda for which the president's blessing is needed.

Warning that his next comments might offend some who believe in certain progressive reforms of the twentieth century, particularly those that provide government subsidies to people in need, Spinney notes that these programs, too, lead to a concentration of power in the executive and, in turn, the subordination of Congress.

Though public assistance programs are often argued against by their detractors with a regrettable lack of sensitivity, the point is valid that with so many agencies of public assistance concentrated under the executive branch, even when the executive is acting magnanimously, these programs contribute to a situation wherein congresspeople, intent to deliver these benefits to their constituents, become vulnerable to the executive's will. Here, Spinney echoes Eisenhower's own critique of public assistance, delivered at his inauguration as president of Columbia University in 1948:

> The concentration of too much power in centralized government need not be the result of violent revolution or great upheaval. A paternalistic government can gradually destroy, by suffocation in the immediate advantage of subsidy, the will of a people to maintain a high degree of individual responsibility. And the abdication of individual responsibility is inevitably followed by further concentration of power in the state.

Even where Federal assistance is concerned, a congressperson's need to curry favor with the executive is yet another part of the interlocking tapestry of the Complex. Between one member of Congress and another, this need becomes a commodity in the tangled network of horse trades at work every day. Congressman A, for example, may support the executive's desire to go to war while Congressman B may not. Yet, if Congressman B wants Congressman A's support on an agriculture bill B is sponsoring, winning A's support for it may require B to vote favorably for the war. This way, Congressman A gives his help to B while B enables A to earn the executive's recognition that he delivered B's support for war.

Just as the term "military-industrial-congressional complex" should come to replace the somewhat antiquated "military-industrial complex," so too it could be argued that what is in evidence today can best be described as a "corporate-congressional-military-executive complex" in which the word "military" indicates less the involvement of the military than the way in which the intersection of economic and political interests gives license to the militarist tendencies of the executive.

One can get lost in a sea of hyphenated tongue-twisters and acronyms, none of them as catchy as Eisenhower's MIC. Yet in order to mount any kind of meaningful reform, it's necessary to understand more precisely how the arrangements of shared interest between industry, Congress, and the executive lead to militarism. It is also vital to recognize, beneath all of this complexity, the basic human tendencies at work.

Episodes of insecurity, such as those that followed the attacks of 9/11, foster conditions that grant the executive greater license than the people might otherwise afford him. When a crisis hits, there is a natural human tendency to say, "There's no time to deliberate. Just do something!" And, indeed, it stands to reason that the pageantry of congressional debate is incompatible with the need for rapid response. Yet this implicitly shifts responsibility from the legislative branch, which must deliberate, to the executive, who can simply act at his own discretion. This is why, whatever its relative merit, each episode of war in American history has slowly and steadily increased the powers available to the executive. The effect of this has been magnified by the rising influence of the corporate sector over the public's representatives into a vicious, self-reinforcing cycle of increasing executive and decreasing legislative power. To extend Spinney's use of metaphors from the natural world, conditions have emerged over time in which competition and collaboration among the various actors in the system has not only rendered the larger system more voracious but, within it, empowered one actor above all others. Those below end up occupying parasitic positions in a symbiotic balance not of the kind desired by the framers, but of imbalance, in a system inherently tilted toward war.

7

Shock and Awe at Home

Because I do it with a tiny craft, I am called a pirate; you have a mighty navy, you're called an emperor.

A pirate from Augustine of Hippo's
Concerning the City of God Against the Pagans

In the previous chapters, the American way of war has been examined as an emergent phenomenon—the product of an evolutionary rather than revolutionary process. Yet, while it is vital to understand how increasing militarism and corporatism in American history have in many ways produced today's constitutional crises, it must also be said that the Bush years may well have been the straw that broke the republic's back.

A survey of the individual scars the republic has suffered on George W. Bush's watch reads like an accident report from a terrible car crash. So much of the republic's intricate skeleton has been shattered, so many of its tendons and ligaments torn, its arteries broken, its vital organs weakened, its lifeblood dissipating, its outward appearance mangled beyond recognition, and even its inner memory of its own past distorted by the trauma of concussion—that one who sets about seeking reform is hardpressed to know where to begin.

Yet, by assembling several examples of overarching executive power into a kind of laundry list of crimes against the republic and its Constitution, one can begin to make an advised set of choices on a possible course of treatment and rehabilitation.

THE CONCENTRATION OF POWERS: THE EXECUTIVE

An Unpatriotic Act

The principal legislative tool introduced by the Bush administration to fight terror, the USA Patriot Act, was drafted by the executive branch and passed by Congress in an infectious spirit of post-9/11 unity. Were it not for this fervor, the name of the act itself might have been fair game for a legal challenge. Since the extreme opposite of "patriotism" is "treason," the administration's choice of wording implied that for anyone to oppose the act was inherently treasonous. The Patriot Act in fact violated several parts of the Constitution. Based on the premise that the freedom of American society made the nation vulnerable to attack in a new age of global terror, the act overtly challenged long-cherished constitutional protections outlined in the First, Fourth, Fifth, Sixth, Eighth, and Fourteenth amendments in the name of defending the country. Simply put, hidden behind the Orwellian doublespeak of an act that claimed to set the standard for a nation's patriotism was a group of measures highly contradictory to basic principles of that nation's Constitution.

First Amendment. In contravention of the First Amendment's protection of free speech, Section 215 decreases judicial oversight of government telephone and Internet surveillance, and grants the FBI almost unlimited access to business records without requiring that it meet customary standards for criminal evidence. Sections 215 and 805(a)(2)(B) also authorize the investigation of American citizens who exercise their freedom of speech and assembly by sharing views with social or political groups of their choice. Further, recipients of federal search orders are legally gagged from telling others about those orders.

Fourth Amendment. Section 215 also undermines Fourth Amendment freedoms by allowing state and federal enforcement officials of almost any rank or security clearance to tap phones, read e-mails, secretly bug, and clandestinely search the premises or homes of U.S. citizens without first obtaining a warrant.

Fifth Amendment. Section 415 contravenes the Fifth Amendment's provisions for due process and equal protection under law by permitting, without judicial review, the indefinite incarceration and deportation of persons associated with groups the government may later declare to be terrorist organizations.

Sixth Amendment. Section 412 violates Sixth Amendment protections by allowing detained persons to be held by the government without a declaration of the charges against them.

Eighth Amendment. Section 412, from which the U.S. government assumed the prerogative to engage in the practice of torture on persons detained domestically and abroad, also infringes on the Eighth Amendment's unmistakable protection against "cruel and unusual punishments."

Fourteenth Amendment. Section 412 additionally violates the Fourteenth Amendment's due process and equal protection clauses, authorizing the attorney general to certify that a noncitizen endangers national security, and in such an event, to detain such persons indefinitely in anticipation that they may be deported. While immigration and/or criminal charges must be filed within seven days of such detention, the charges can be based on evidence that would never have otherwise resulted in such detention.

Despite passionate opposition and a Democratic filibuster in the Senate, the most controversial provisions of the Patriot Act were signed into law once again by President Bush on March 9, 2006, less than five years after their original enactment. Fourteen of the sixteen sections that were set to expire were made permanent and the bill added "sunset" expiry provisions to a few of these. With only these limited changes, the act was preserved.

The Patriot Act is a direct assault on constitutional liberties reserved to the people and thus an assertion of increased power for the federal government over the people and the states. But within the Federal government itself, the act also undermines the separation of powers between the branches. By authorizing the executive to operate in new ways at its own discretion in the domestic policing of terror, the act tilts the balance of power away from the legislative and judicial branches.

The Preemption Problem

Though the Patriot Act's principal impact was domestic, the Bush Doctrine would prove to be the most radical expansion of American foreign policy since the Truman Doctrine. Calling al Qaeda "a new kind of enemy," President Bush argued that, after 9/11, America could no longer wait for a foreign threat to fully reveal itself. Instead, it would act preemptively to "confront the worst threats before they emerge."[1] This new commitment was contradictory to America's tradition of resorting to military action only as a last resort in response to a clear and present danger and represented the most radical departure yet in U.S. history from the framers' reluctance toward foreign entanglement. By committing the country to the principle of preemptive action, the Bush Doctrine runs the risk that, without the due process of coming to a national decision that war is necessary, preemptive action against a potential enemy can make war a self-fulfilling prophecy, gravely undermining Congress' constitutional authority to declare war.

When one recalls Richard Perle's rhetorical query, "What's the big fuss about preemption?" one sees how brazenly the advocates of such preemption flew in the face of a previously held tenet of U.S. foreign policy. Though many of Bush's policies can indeed be traced back to previous administrations, a resistance to preemptive military force has remained a significant strand of America's foreign policy tradition. Certainly, covert actions have long been undertaken in which America fired the first shot. But the very fact that these were covert underscored that they were an exception to the rule that America was not prepared to embrace military preemption as an official part of U.S. policy.

That the Bush Doctrine departed from this tradition so brazenly makes yesterday's aberration today's standard operating procedure and, in turn, raises the bar for aberrations to come.

The Iraq "Fix": A War of Lies

In the October 27, 2003, issue of *The New Yorker*, Seymour Hersh described the mechanics of "stovepiping," a process by which Bush administration officials provided raw intelligence from the field directly to high-level officials, bypassing vital filters that are intended to refine intelligence, determine its accuracy, and separate legitimate information from meaningless or misleading chatter. Hersh claimed that members of the administration had provided their superiors with information of unverifiable quality on which to base foreign policy decisions. The executive branch then provided this information to Congress, the media, and UN member states, characterizing it as "slam-dunk" evidence of a case for war against Iraq.

Though administration officials sought to dismiss Hersh's claims, two years later, on May 1, 2005, a top-secret memorandum recording the minutes of a July 23, 2002, meeting between British prime minister Tony Blair and his senior ministers confirmed them. The so-called Downing Street Memo revealed that, following 9/11, members of the Bush administration "wanted to remove Saddam, through military action, justified by the conjunction of terrorism and WMD." The memo goes on to recount that "the intelligence and facts were being fixed around the policy."[2]

By "fixing" the intelligence, the Bush administration skirted vital checks on its conduct of office. It also undermined the authority of the legislature by presenting as facts to members of Congress manufactured claims on which to base their vote on *House Joint Resolution 114*, the Authorization for the Use of Military Force Against Iraq. This authorization gave the executive branch unprecedented license to declare war against Iraq at its sole discretion. The administration deceived not only Congress but the public as well. On June 5, 2008, the Senate Intelligence Committee published its "Phase II Prewar Intelligence Report" detailing its findings on the administration's handling of prewar intelligence. The report confirms what many already suspected—that the Bush White House exaggerated evidence against Saddam Hussein and Iraq's possession of weapons of mass destruction. "In making the case for war," declared Intelligence Committee Chairman Senator Jay Rockefeller upon the report's release, "the administration repeatedly presented intelligence as fact when in reality it was unsubstantiated, contradicted, or even nonexistent. As a result, the American people were led to believe that the threat from Iraq was much greater than actually existed."[3]

Though the Senate Intelligence Report underscores the gravity of the administration's wrongdoing in how it misguided the nation to war, only time would reveal the extent to which, buoyed by the public and congressional support his administration had manufactured, the president undertook to bypass further checks and balances at home (such as the writ of habeas corpus and the Fourth, Sixth, Eighth, and Fourteenth amendments) and to exempt America abroad from conventions (such as Geneva) to which it was a signatory. With time, this brazen disregard for domestic and international laws would produce the administration's first and most lasting public scandal.

Looking into the Abyss

When, six months after revealing the dynamics of intelligence stovepiping in launching the Iraq War, Seymour Hersh brought to light in May 2004 that members of the U.S. military had abused detainees at Abu Ghraib Prison in Iraq, the revelation represented a milestone in the perception of the war by the American people. The young Americans depicted in photograph after deplorable photograph were showcased in the throes of depraved activities of abuse and denigration of the Iraqis in their custody. Yet, again, as with so many scandals whose inner mechanics would require deep national introspection, in its media coverage and in the public mind, the most salacious facts about Abu Ghraib came to eclipse its substantive legal, constitutional, and moral implications.

As anthropologist Laura Nader pointed out in her groundbreaking 1969 essay, "Up the Anthropologist," the study of social systems is too often directed downward, "at the colonized instead of the colonizers, at those less powerful rather than those in power."[4] Consistent with Nader's premise, the American people were robbed of a deeper understanding of what Abu Ghraib meant by the disproportionate way in which the mass media focused on the personal identities and actions of those at the lowest level of the command chain. A great deal was learned about the soldiers and MPs involved—from Army Colonel Janis Karpinski to specialists Lynndie England and her colleague (and lover) Charles Graner. Yet all were portrayed as bad apples who had gone off-script and commited abuses of their own accord, without official sanction.

"An exceptional, isolated case," Defense Secretary Rumsfeld said of the revelations.

"The night shift," echoed chairman of the Joint Chiefs, Richard Meyers.

Though time would reveal these arguments to be dishonest, they worked to shelter those in positions of power from accountability and, more broad, to save face for the American military.

This highly spun impression might have prevailed were it not for the publication of a June 8, 2004, article in *The Washington Post* documenting the existence of the so-called Torture Memo, a secret document drafted for the president by his Office of Legal Counsel.[5] Written in August 2002, the memo reassessed the executive's prerogatives and responsibilities under U.S. law and under the Geneva Convention Against Torture and Other Cruel, Inhuman and Degrading Treatment or Punishment. The memo reinterpreted the meaning of the word "torture" to give the executive broader license than that traditionally interpreted from the Geneva Conventions and U.S. law. It argued that the administration could engage in "cruel, inhuman, or degrading treatment or punishment" so long as it did not cause a level of pain "equivalent in intensity to the pain accompanying serious physical injury, such as organ failure, impairment of bodily function, or even death."[6]

The Torture Memo suggested a widespread and premeditated program authorized by the executive branch to interpret the Geneva Conventions and U.S. law more liberally than had any previous administration. Still, accountability for the memo, even in the court of public opinion, was largely limited to those credited with drafting it, as opposed to the superiors for whom they did so, in particular, two White House legal advisers, Jay S. Bybee and John Yoo, and the vice president's legal counsel, David Addington.

The Torture Memo represented a major assertion of executive power to arbitrate—and to circumvent Congress and the courts in doing so—the laws and conventions America would adhere to in prosecuting the war. An article in *The Washington Post* documented the existence of a "hidden global internment network" administered by the executive branch as part of the war on terror.[7] This hidden universe of "black sites" had secretly engaged in the kind of interrogation practices foreseen by the Torture Memo in an unknowable number of episodes around the world. Given the controversy that had surrounded the Abu Ghraib scandal and the release of the Torture Memo, the exposure of this secret network revealed that the executive had simply circumvented congressional opposition it deemed inconvenient. As such, it catapulted the ever-complicating torture scandal into a far-reaching crisis of executive contempt for the Constitution, a precedent that will haunt future executives, legislatures, and judiciaries.

According to Colonel Wilkerson, Rumsfeld engaged in a time-proven technique with respect to torture activities, by which authorization for underlings to commit controversial acts is not directly communicated from above but indirectly implied. This achieves the desired outcome while minimizing the accountability of those in command. A prime example of this, according to Wilkerson, is the now infamous Defense Department "Action Memo," in which the DoD's general counsel, William J. Haynes II, recommended that Rumsfeld give his approval for certain limited "counter-resistance techniques to aid in the interrogation of detainees at Guantánamo Bay." Rumsfeld signed his name by the "approved" box, but then, in an act of unofficial whimsy, scrawled a handwritten side note: "However, I stand for 8–10 hours a day. Why is standing limited to 4 hours?"

To Wilkerson, this glib remark holds deep implications. In effect, it is a command framed as a hypothetical question. "It's almost like Henry II saying, 'Won't someone rid me of this troublesome priest?' " Wilkerson explains, "and then someone goes and murders Thomas à Becket." In other words, for all those to whom Rumsfeld's Action Memo filtered downstream, was his query understood to imply official sanction? Since it was just a query, it was something he could defend as not constituting an official command. Yet in reality, when a hypothetical notion is expressed in so public a fashion by a figure of Rumsfeld's authority, the implication of his preference is clear and of great force. Those below him do not need to have it spelled out for them. If they understand anything, his wish becomes their command.

On April 1, 2008, nearly four years after *The Washington Post* first revealed the existence of the Torture Memo, the Pentagon released a

March 2003 memo that went further than the original 2002 memo in arguing that the wartime powers of the executive as commander in chief of the armed forces are not subject to limitation by UN treaties against torture.

In the memo, then–deputy assistant attorney general John Yoo argued "that customary international law is not federal law and that the president is free to override it at his discretion." In a revealing sign that the administration recognized the possible legal vulnerability of its interrogation practices, the memo went on to provide the basis for a legal defense: "Even if the criminal prohibitions outlined above applied and an interrogation method might violate those prohibitions," wrote Yoo, "necessity or self-defense could provide justifications for any criminal liability." The release of this memo thrust midlevel administration operatives like Yoo, Bybee, and Addington into the spotlight. Eight days later, ABC News would break the more far-reaching story that, contrary to previous administration efforts to assign blame for these activities to a small group of rogue actors, "in dozens of top-secret talks and meetings in the White House, the most senior Bush administration officials discussed and approved specific details of how high-value al Qaeda suspects would be interrogated by the Central Intelligence Agency."

In its groundbreaking report, ABC revealed that among the select group of so-called principals from the administration who participated in "high-level discussions about these 'enhanced interrogation techniques' " were Vice President Cheney, Secretary of Defense Rumsfeld, Secretary of State Colin Powell, and national security adviser Condoleezza Rice. "Highly placed sources," ABC reported, "said a handful of top advisers signed off on how the CIA would interrogate top al Qaeda suspects—whether they would be slapped, pushed, deprived of sleep or subjected to simulated drowning, called waterboarding."[8]

These combined revelations—first of the more strident 2003 Memo and then of high-level administration involvement in meetings approving such controversial practices—gave the lie to previous claims that escalated interrogation techniques happened without high-level administration knowledge or approval. Rather, it was now apparent that members of the administration at all levels—including but not limited to the president's legal advisers—knowingly sought to bypass international and domestic law in order to give the president all means at his disposal to prosecute the wars on terror and in Iraq, including forms of conduct that violate international law and standardized wartime norms.

Ultimately, it was revealed that in the executive's reckless abuse of power and defiance of domestic and international law, the bad apples had indeed been higher up the tree than was previously suggested.

Dynamiting the Foundation: The Attack on Habeas Corpus

Just as the bombs of Operation Iraqi Freedom blasted vast fissures deep beneath Iraq, the Bush administration has fractured and undermined core constitutional premises on which the American republic itself was founded. None is more fundamental among these than the writ of habeas corpus. A cornerstone of Western political systems since the Magna Carta, habeas corpus is a catchall for a body of fundamental legal principles that protect the rights of the individual against wrongful prosecution and detention by the state. So basic is habeas corpus to American law that it is codified in Article I of the Constitution, predating even the freedoms of speech, religion, and assembly.

Following 9/11, the administration transferred hundreds of alleged Taliban and al Qaeda detainees to the U.S. Naval Base at Guantánamo Bay, Cuba. Classifying them as "enemy combatants" rather than prisoners of war, the Bush administration denied the detainees protection under the Geneva Conventions. Basing its actions on the 1942 Supreme Court decision *ex parte Quirin* (discussed in Chapter 2), the administration labeled the Guantánamo detainees "unlawful," thus denying them access to U.S. courts and forcing them instead to face military tribunals. In such tribunals, detainees do not have the privilege of the writ of habeas corpus provided for by the Constitution. Hearsay, coerced testimony, and secret evidence may also be used. No appeal of any verdict may be filed with federal courts. Rather, it is subject to final review by the president himself.

Like Lincoln and Roosevelt before him, George W. Bush determined that, at a time of "invasion or rebellion," the Constitution gave the president the right to deny detained "unlawful combatants" constitutional legal protections. While he is thus not the first American president to do this, and although he was empowered by the precedents of Lincoln and Roosevelt, no administration has ever asserted more unilateral discretion over when and to what extent the country will abide by the constitutional requirement to uphold the writ of habeas corpus.

That the sanctity of the constitutional provision protecting habeas corpus has been violated by several presidents is distressing, not only because the writ of habeas corpus is so central a philosophic tenet of the nation's founding but also because the Constitution does not expressly assign the president the power to suspend it. Whereas so many of the Constitution's provisions in its main articles and Bill of Rights articulately ascribe limits and powers to one branch or another (i.e., "Congress shall make no law," the "House of Representatives shall choose their Speaker and other Officers," etc.), the responsibility to uphold the writ of habeas corpus—and conversely to determine when the writ may be suspended—is not ascribed to any particular branch. The Constitution simply states in the passive voice that "the Privilege of the Writ of Habeas Corpus shall not be suspended, unless when in Cases of Rebellion or Invasion the Public Safety may require it." If anything, since the passage referring to habeas corpus appears in Article I, Section 9, entitled "Limits on Congress," this would seem to suggest that the authority to suspend it might rest with the legislative branch.

Five years after the fact, some restraint on the president's assertion of executive power in this area has been imposed. On June 29, 2006, after challenges from legal experts and members of Congress, the Supreme Court ruled in the landmark decision *Hamdan v. Rumsfeld* that the Bush administration's use of military tribunals "violate[s] both the Uniform Code of Military Justice and the four Geneva Conventions." By then, hundreds of detainees at Guantánamo (and an untold number elsewhere) had been denied due process under U.S. law and were subject to violations of the conventions.

To make matters worse from a constitutional perspective, despite the resounding comdemnation by the Supreme Court in *Hamdan* v. *Rumsfeld*, the administration sought not to curtail these practices but rather to codify them legally. When the judicial branch tried to fulfill its mandate to act as a check on the executive, the executive (and its allies on Capitol Hill) responded by pushing for a new law.

On October 17, 2006, President Bush signed the Military Commissions Act of 2006, providing for the continued controversial practices in its detention and treatment of "unlawful combatants." "The president can now," wrote American Civil Liberties Union executive director Anthony D. Romero, "with the approval of Congress—indefinitely hold people without charge, take away protections against horrific abuse, put people on trial based on hearsay evidence, authorize trials that can sentence people to death based on testimony literally beaten out of witnesses, and slam shut the courthouse door for habeas petitions."[9] Reducing the court's powers to check the power of the executive branch, the Military Commissions Act provides a retroactive, nine-year immunity for U.S. officials who authorized, ordered, or committed possible acts of abuse on detainees prior to its enactment. This is a historic injury to the Constitution, whose repercussions will be felt by future generations.

Contempt of Court

A recurring strategy of the Bush administration was to get a jump on its critics by tarring them with the very criticisms that might more appropriately be leveled at itself. So it was that an administration that massively increased the size and expenditure of the federal bureaucracy could accuse its opponents of seeking "big government." So it was, too, that Bush was able to question the wartime patriotism of his challenger in the 2004 election John Kerry, even though Kerry had served in Vietnam while Bush remained stateside. Repeating this clever strategy, the administration deployed the phrase "activist judges" to impugn the partisanship of judges and judicial nominees it didn't like even while engaging in activities that amounted to one of the most partisan and, above all, activist chapters in the history of the judicial system.

One need only recall Franklin D. Roosevelt's Judiciary Reorganization Bill of 1937 to recognize that George W. Bush is by no means the first U.S. president to have sought to bend the courts to his will. Indeed, the term "judicial activism" itself dates back to a 1947 *Fortune* magazine article by political historian Arthur Schlesinger, Jr., in which he analyzed the political leanings of the then-sitting Supreme Court. Yet, as was the case in many areas of its policy making, the Bush administration distinguished itself not so much by being the first to pursue a partisan agenda in the courts but by the dogmatism, audacity, and recklessness with which it did so.

In December 2006, the firing of eight U.S. attorneys by the Justice Department represented both a politically motivated purge of unwanted members of the executive branch and, in turn, a preemptive attack on the judicial system more broadly. Amid the scandal that arose over the firings, the White House argued they were driven by poor job performance. Yet it quickly became clear that they had been politically motivated. Interestingly, the firings were not partisan in any predictable pattern. Of the eight attorneys fired by the Republican administration, six were Republicans, two were Independents, and none were Democrats. All had been appointed by President Bush and had served only two of the four years of their appointments. Yet what they also had in common was that each had supported prosecution of corruption cases against Republican politicians, had refused to pursue politically motivated investigations supported by the administration, or in some other way qualified as being out of step with the White House's political goals. Carol Lam, the U.S. attorney in San Diego, for example, had prosecuted Republican Congressman Randy "Duke" Cunningham, resulting in a bargain in which he pled guilty to charges of conspiracy to commit bribery, mail fraud, wire fraud, and tax evasion and was sentenced to eight years and four months in prison.

To dismiss a U.S. attorney before at least one four-year term has been completed is highly unusual. In this brazen campaign, the administration took advantage of new provisions in the Patriot Act assigning increased discretion to the attorney general's office in the appointment of federal prosecutors. Previously, any prosecutor appointed in an "interim" capacity to the Federal bench—i.e., to fill a vacancy—was, due to his interim status, not subject to Senate approval. Such appointments were limited to terms of 120 days. The Patriot Act, however, empowered the attorney general to make interim appointments exceeding that 120-day limit, and the Bush administration sought to exploit this power in order to replace attorneys it didn't like with its own new appointees and thus circumvent the need for congressional approval.

When the scandal came to light, congressional outrage was bipartisan, as were calls for Attorney General Alberto Gonzales to resign. By late 2007, along with his deputy, chief of staff, and several other members of the Justice Department, Gonzales stepped down. Still, at the time of writing, congressional efforts at accountability for the scandal continue to mount, and the larger legal consequences of this campaign of executive abuse remain to be seen.

Beyond seeking to stack them with politically motivated prosecutors, the administration demonstrated further contempt for the independence of the federal courts by aligning itself and in some cases fostering public outrage against what the president himself called "activist" judges. This contributed to a climate of contempt toward the courts that, following her retirement, Justice Sandra Day O'Connor noted in a *Wall Street Journal* op-ed. Though "scorn for certain judges is not an altogether new phenomenon," O'Connor wrote, "the breadth and intensity of rage currently being leveled at the judiciary may be unmatched in American history." Justice O'Connor spoke from intense firsthand experience. In February 2005, she and fellow justice Ruth Bader Ginsburg had been the target of an Internet death threat for having cited foreign court decisions in their rulings from the bench.[10]

"The 'ubiquitous activist judges' who 'legislate from the bench,'" O'Connor wrote, "have become central villains on today's domestic political landscape. Elected officials routinely score cheap points by railing against the 'elitist judges,' who are purported to be of touch with ordinary citizens and their values. . . . Though these attacks generally emit more heat than light, using judges as punching bags presents a grave threat to the independent judiciary." Though O'Connor drew particular attention to the pressures being directed at judges by such activist groups as "J.A.I.L. 4 Judges," a national grassroots campaign to expose federal judges to greater legal accountability for their decisions, her words might as well have been directed at the Bush administration itself. For arguably no one had been more aggressive in attacking the independence of the judiciary.

Two Birds with One Stone: Short-Circuiting FISA

On May 10, 2006, *USA Today* revealed a further assault on the U.S. judicial system—the existence of a secret program conducted by the National Security Agency of the Department of Defense to monitor and catalog phone calls made from the four largest telephone carriers in the United States. The discovery of this program and an estimated database of 1.9 trillion phone call records generated immense national controversy.

Critics charged that the program violates the Constitution's Fourth Amendment protection against warrantless search and seizure as well as the 1978 Foreign Intelligence Surveillance Act (FISA). FISA is a federal statute that governs how and to what extent the federal government may conduct surveillance in the gathering of foreign intelligence. Since neither Congress nor the courts have their own intelligence instruments, the act implicitly regulates the conduct of the executive branch. It was passed by Congress after an investigation by the Church Committee—headed by Idaho senator Frank Church—into transgressions by the executive in its conduct of covert activity and intelligence gathering at home and abroad during the late 1960s and 1970s, notably in the Nixon years.

Among the activities the act sought to prohibit was the use of intelligence tools by the executive branch to conduct surveillance against American citizens. Nixon in particular had sanctioned domestic surveillance. By establishing elaborate procedures for the executive to follow in its covert and intelligence-gathering activities, FISA was designed to prevent this from recurring. To facilitate this, FISA established a dedicated court under the federal court system—the Foreign Intelligence Surveillance Court (FISC)—for the granting of warrants for wiretapping and other forms of surveillance. It also established strict procedures under which the executive must secure warrants for such activity.

Advocates of the vast NSA wiretapping program maintain that the collection of such information was a necessary means by which to monitor communication between possible terror actors in the United States and their accomplices abroad. When the scandal broke at the end of 2005, the president defended the program, saying, "As president and commander in chief, I have the constitutional responsibility and the constitutional authority to protect our country. Article 2 of the constitution gives me that responsibility and the authority necessary to fulfill it."[11] In response to the program's critics, Attorney General Alberto Gonzales and his deputy assistant attorney general John Yoo further argued that when Congress enacted its joint resolution vesting in the president the authority to "use all necessary and appropriate force" to prosecute those responsible for 9/11, it implicitly exempted him from FISA's restrictions. Since there is no language to this effect in Joint Resolution 114, this may in part explain why advocates of the NSA program have also offered the haphazard addendum that they sidestepped FISA because it is an unconstitutional infringement of executive power.

Wherever the truth lies, and whatever the merit of his administration's view of FISA, Bush chose not to challenge the act in a legal setting. Instead, he simply had the NSA secretly work around it. This represents a far-reaching attack not only on Congress' authority to pass but on the courts' authority to enforce laws governing the conduct of the executive.

P.S.S.

In the face of so many scandals that nipped haplessly at his administration's heels, President Bush argued with increasing vigor for what his office came to call the "unitary executive"—a phrase not found in the Constitution yet central to his administration's unique vision of the executive branch as being superior to the other branches. Nowhere did this vision manifest itself more bluntly than in the president's far-reaching use of so-called presidential signing statements to exert unprecedented executive power to reinterpret of laws passed by Congress.

Reportedly pioneered with significant contribution from Vice President Cheney's legal counsel David Addington, these statements are written proclamations by the president upon his signing of a bill into law. The use of such a technique avoids the need for the president to incur the political cost of vetoing a bill passed by Congress. Instead, he can give the appearance of going along with the bill, but then quietly add a "P.S." to the end of the document that indicates the assumptions under which he is signing it. These assumptions then influence the future way the law is applied. In this way, the president minimizes the political cost but maximizes the effectiveness of his opposition to a given measure.

Addington, who was instrumental in the administration's robust use of this procedure, had once been a legal adviser to President Reagan and had advocated at that time that signing statements be used to help exempt Reagan from responsibility for the Iran-Contra affair. Previous presidents have used signing statements, but none has done so as often as President Bush, nor, as *The New York Times* has reported, in a way so designed as "to make the president the interpreter of a law's intent, instead of Congress, and the arbiter of constitutionality, instead of the courts."[12] President Bush has used these statements to mount over 750 challenges to new and existing laws, asserting the executive's right "to construe [such laws] in a manner consistent with the constitutional authority of the President to supervise the unitary Executive Branch and as Commander in Chief."[13] In July 2006, the American Bar Association determined that the president's use of signing statements to modify the meaning of duly enacted laws "is contrary to the rule of law and our constitutional system of separation of powers."[14]

Exploiting the Troops: The Cruel Cowardice of the Stop-Loss Order

Given the deep corporate roots of so many in the Bush administration, it is ironic that the administration has come to be so notoriously associated with "stop-loss," a term most commonly associated with Wall Street. In that context, it refers to an order to buy or sell a security when its price rises above or below a set price. Used in reference to the Bush administration, though, it refers to the official U.S. military policy under which the president may elect to extend the active duty of a U.S. servicemember "who the President determines is essential to the national security of the United States."[15] Though on paper this distinction might sound flattering to an individual soldier, its purpose is to protect the military from a drawdown of personnel.

The policy was introduced after the Vietnam War in response to plummeting enlistment figures and has been used in several conflicts since. Yet, as with presidential signing statements, while previous administrations have employed stop-loss, none used it as aggressively as the Bush administration. The reason for this is that, as the Iraq War proved more costly and longer in duration than the administration anticipated, their original rosy troop strength estimates gave way to more sober assessments. Meanwhile, the post-9/11 fervor in which many young recruits had joined was giving way to public fatigue with the war, doubts about its purpose, and a significant drop in recruitment.

In May 2008, 58,000 American soldiers discovered, just when they thought their term of service was up, that they were being compelled to stay.[16] In a particularly poignant episode just prior to the fifth anniversary of President Bush's declaration that "major combat operations in Iraq have ended," Sergeant 1st Class David L. McDowell was killed in action in Afghanistan on his *seventh* consecutive overseas tour of duty.

As depicted in the 2008 feature film *Stop-Loss,* for a soldier who misses his loved ones to learn that his term of service has been forcibly extended is a rude awakening. But it may be an even ruder one for the American people to consider the implications of the stop-loss policy for the separation of powers in wartime decision making. Stop-loss has not been called a "backdoor draft" unjustly, for it enables the president to avoid the political fallout of conscription. This short-circuits the power of Congress to influence the warmaking decisions of the president, allowing him to avert a politically costly trip to Capitol Hill to admit error in his original estimates. Insofar as the policy allows him to avoid a draft, it is also a powerful buffer against the prospect of public protest. This misuse of America's servicepeople adds to their job of defending the country from "enemies foreign and domestic" the task of protecting the executive from the domestic political fallout of his own shortcomings.

The Self-Loathing Executive

In a fulfillment of Lord Acton's dictum that "absolute power corrupts absolutely," and an echo of the plot of a heist movie in which the greed of a gang of crooks ultimately leads each to turn on the other, the Bush administration not only asserted primacy over the other branches but created a hierarchy within itself in which hawks dominated doves.

Though the marginalization and ultimate firing of Colin Powell is the prime example of this, the suppression of dissent was by no means limited to the State Department. The Bush administration squelched all levels of internal resistance, as when certain high-ranking military figures like General Eric Shineki, tried to advise administration war planners that their troop strength estimates were too low.

As the war continued to unfold, unraveling ultimately into the quagmire these soldiers had feared, other high-ranking voices of concern began to emerge from within the executive branch. From the National Security Council's counterterrorism adviser Richard A. Clarke to Treasury secretary Paul O'Neill to CIA officer Valerie Plame Wilson, whose husband, Ambassador Joe Wilson, had publicly taken issue with the Bush administration's early claims about the danger posed by Saddam Hussein, the administration proved cutthroat in its willingness to punish its own.

Abuse of Executive Privilege

At other times, the Bush administration sought to protect its own at all cost, even that of damaging fundamentally the separation of powers between the branches. Nowhere was this reflected more vividly than in the vigor with which the administration repeatedly invoked or threatened to invoke executive privilege, the principle that members of the executive branch cannot be forced—even by subpoena—to disclose their confidential communications when such disclosure might damage the operations or procedures of the executive branch. Though first formally asserted (and coined) by Dwight Eisenhower in 1954, a recognition of the idea of executive privilege dates back to the 1803 case of *Marbury* v. *Madison*, in which the courts recognized that there are times when a president must retain the power to engage in candid and confidential discussions with his staff without fear that he or they may be compelled to reveal the content of these. Such a power is, of course, not enumerated in the Constitution but has been recognized under certain circumstances by the Supreme Court, particularly when national security is evoked as a concern. Still, when Richard Nixon and Bill Clinton personally found themselves under criminal investigation, claims of executive privilege were denied.

The Bush administration has actively invoked executive privilege, or the threat of it, to avoid unwanted attention amid several scandals. Though these episodes are too numerous to list, a few key examples demonstrate the far-reaching precedent set by the administration in this practice. One of the administration's earliest and most controversial decisions to invoke executive privilege began less than a month after taking office, when a task force headed by Vice President Cheney began a series of confidential meetings with representatives from the energy industry. As events unfolded over the ensuing years—from Bush's decision to withdraw America from the Kyoto Protocol to his decision to launch a war in an oil-rich region to an unseemly national scandal of skyrocketing fuel prices and historic energy-sector profits—the content of these energy meetings became a cause for concern to environmental and public policy watchdog groups as well as the administration's critics in Congress and the press. Rejecting congressional and public demands for the records of these meetings—which included meetings with disgraced Enron executive Kenneth Lay and ExxonMobil vice president James J. Rouse—the executive branch evoked its privilege. This was upheld by the U.S. Supreme Court as well as the Circuit Court of Appeals for D.C., who determined that "in making decisions on personnel and policy, and in formulating legislative proposals, the president must be free to seek confidential information from many sources, both inside the government and outside."[17]

The Supreme Court's ruling—undermined by Justice Antonin Scalia's refusal to recuse himself over his friendship with the vice president—demonstrated the administration's willingness not only to use executive privilege to defy Congress but to involve a seemingly sympathetic Court in doing so. With almost Orwellian circular reasoning, the Court ruled that, since there was no evidence energy lobbyists were involved in these meetings, there were no grounds on which to compel the disclosure of the records. But of course, since the meetings were secret, no such evidence could be gathered without access to the documents.

The Bush administration formally invoked executive privilege seven times between 2001 and 2008, yet brandished its willingness to do so many more. It did so when asked about the records of meetings that led to the decision for war in Iraq. It did so when executive branch testimony was sought during an investigation of possible White House involvement in the outing of CIA officer Valerie Plame Wilson's identity to the media. It did so when asked about the firing of U.S. attorneys by the attorney general's office. And it did so when it was revealed that a vast surveillance and wiretapping program had been secretly undertaken by the National Security Agency. In some of these cases—notably those involving domestic wiretapping and the firing of U.S. attorneys—Congress met assertions of executive privilege by asserting or threatening to assert its own power to subpoena the release of necessary documents or testimony.

At the time of writing, the Bush administration and the 110th Congress are locked in an unresolved standoff over the power of executive privilege relative to Congress's subpoena power, which the Associated Press has called "a fight of epic historical proportions." What is clear is that executive privilege—a concept not found in the Constitution—has come to represent a troubling wild card in the balance of powers, licensing the executive to claim exemption from accountability to Congress and the courts. Though past administrations have asserted the privilege from time to time, the Bush administration has done so with unprecedented vigor, bringing into focus a critical constitutional dilemma. Long before and after Eisenhower coined the term in 1954, the idea of executive privilege was already a principle of law, yet one that occupied a legally ambiguous area the courts have done little to clarify.

Thus, while the executive and legislative branches of the Bush years each claim there is historical precedent to support its position, the outcome remains to be seen. From a constitutional perspective, the stakes could not be higher. Until this standoff comes to a place of greater resolution, the administration's use of executive privilege to defy congressional subpoenas represents an attack both on Congress' authority to demand executive branch testimony and on the Court's authority to issue a binding subpoena in connection therewith.

In a surreal coda to the executive privilege saga of recent years, Vice President Cheney remarkably asserted in 2007 that his office was not part of the executive branch after all. During an investigation of possible White House involvement in the outing of CIA officer Valerie Plame Wilson, questions arose regarding the procedures inside the office of the vice president for handling information. Under Executive Order 12958, it falls to the Information Security Oversight Office of the National Archives (ISOO) to optimize such information-handling procedures and, accordingly, ISOO Director Bill Leonard asked the vice president's office to provide his staff with information about certain classified documents and to submit to a routine inspection in which ISOO would review its information security practices.

Cheney rejected this demand, however, asserting that, since his office was not part of the executive branch but rather the legislative (since he presides over the Senate), the ISOO had no jurisdiction to monitor his information security practices.[18] The episode led to a wildfire of incredulous editorials and blogs, but, more important, underscored again the administration's contempt for Congress. In this case, though, where the internal contradiction of Cheney's position was so shameless, the contempt took on an even more imperious, unaccountable quality. Still, as with so many other areas of controversy facing the administration, Cheney's absurd position prevailed.

Needle in a Haystack

Amid so many of the above-cited measures that have disrupted the balance of power, a recurring question among the Bush administration's critics has been—"Where's the outrage?"—almost a bookend to the question so many asked after 9/11, "Why do they hate us?" And yet beyond the steady decrease of the president's popularity in recent years, public protest has been scarce. That did not stop the administration from hedging its bets when, on the same day the president signed the infamous Military Commissions Act into law, he quietly signed a lesser known but equally ominous piece of legislation. This law would give the president greater power to use the military to suppress domestic public dissent and "restore public order."

Public Law 109-364 (H.R. 5122), or the John Warner National Defense Authorization Act of 2007, was enacted in a private Oval Office ceremony on October 17, 2006. Overshadowed by the controversy attending the Military Commissions Act, it went largely unnoticed. On its face, the act is designed "to authorize appropriations for fiscal year 2007 for military activities of the Department of Defense, for military construction, and for defense activities of the Department of Energy, to prescribe military personnel strengths for such fiscal year, and for other purposes." Those last four words, "and for other purposes," are deceptively innocuous. Though most of the act addresses how an additional $500 billion is to be allocated to military activities for the 2007 budget year, buried deep within its sprawling 439 pages is the Bush administration's most brazen attack on the Constitution and American legal precedent.

Prior to the John Warner Act, the power of the executive to authorize military action within the American homeland had been governed by a combination of the Insurrection Act of 1807 and the Posse Comitatus Act of 1878 (18 U.S.C. §1385). Both imposed strict limits on the executive's power to respond to insurrection or other forms of public disorder. Specifically, the Insurrection Act provided that the president could, in the event of "insurrections in any State against its government . . . call into Federal service . . . the militia of the other states . . . and such use of the armed forces" as he deemed necessary to "suppress the insurrection." Yet it required that the president only do so "upon the request of [a state's] legislature or of its governor if the legislature cannot be convened." The Posse Comitatus Act went further, making the use of the Army or armed forces by the president or anyone else as a force for controlling public disorder a crime punishable by fine and/or imprisonment, unless such use was authorized by "the Constitution or Act of Congress."

With the stroke of a pen, President Bush's enactment of the John Warner Act sought to overturn both the Insurrection and the Posse Comitatus acts. It gave him expanded discretion to determine that a "major public emergency" exists and to deploy the military in response. Whereas under the Insurrection Act such action needed to be in response to "insurrection, domestic violence, unlawful combination, or conspiracy," these conditions were amended by the John Warner Act to additionally include "natural disaster, epidemic, or other serious public health emergency, terrorist attack or incident, or other condition." This broader definition—particularly the widely interpretable phrase "or other condition"—gives the executive unprecedented latitude.

The act also authorizes the president to determine, at his sole discretion, that the authorities of a given state or possession are "unable, fail, or refuse" to address a public emergency. In that event, he is authorized to "employ the Armed Forces, including the National Guard in Federal Service," to "restore public order." This latter clause empowers the president to take command of state National Guard units without the consent of the governors.

After the act was passed, Senate Judiciary chairman Patrick Leahy (D–VT) announced publicly that it contained "a provision to allow the President more control over the National Guard . . . to restore domestic order without the consent of the Nation's governors."[19] Leahy went further in the *Congressional Record* a few weeks later, noting that the tiny but far-reaching provision "subverts solid, longstanding posse comitatus statutes that limit the military's involvement in law enforcement, thereby making it easier for the President to declare martial law." As a procedural matter, Leahy also noted that the provision had been "slipped in . . . as a rider with little study" and that "other congressional committees with jurisdiction over these matters had no chance to comment, let alone hold hearings on, these proposals."[20]

Leahy's reference to "little study" calls to mind Michael Moore's 2003 film *Farenheit 9/11*, in which Congressman John Conyers responds to Michael Moore's incredulous realization that many members of Congress had never read the Patriot Act. "Sit down, my son," Conyers sighs. "We don't read most of the bills. Do you really know what that would entail if we were to read every bill that we passed?" The tangled complexity of the vast array of bills and measures moving through a contemporary Congress affords the executive the latitude to shape policy in ways that are often a fait accompli by the time they are discovered.

Playing catch-up to undo the damage done by the John Warner Act, Leahy was joined over the subsequent two years by other members of Congress who sought to pass laws repealing the portion of the act that amended the Insurrection Act. Their resistance, though, ultimately just underscored the Bush administration's determination to retain unchecked power. In 2008, a new national defense authorization act, H.R. 1585, was passed, repealing the changes implemented by the John Warner Act. Yet, consistent with his general contempt for measures of restraint by Congress, the president allowed the law to expire, due to a technicality of procedure during a congressional recess, exercising what's called a pocket veto.

Following this veto, the National Defense Authorization Act for Fiscal Year 2008 (H.R. 4986) was ultimately passed, restoring the Insurrection Act to its original 1807 wording. Bush signed this new act into law on January 28, 2008. But after signing the act, Bush employed one of his many presidential signing statements to declare that certain "provisions of the Act . . . purport to impose requirements that could inhibit the President's ability to carry out his constitutional obligations to take care that the laws be faithfully executed, to protect national security, to supervise the executive branch, and to execute his authority as Commander in Chief. The executive branch shall construe such provisions in a manner consistent with the constitutional authority of the President."

Perhaps more than any other episode of the Bush years, the stealthy insertion of martial law provisions into the John Warner Act, and the subversion of congressional efforts to counter those provisions, is a clear-cut attack on the separation of powers. For, should the public wish to protest any of the administration's other assertions of unchecked executive power—the dubious path to war, the torture, the spying, the stop-loss abuses, and the invoking of executive privilege—the very act of protest could be deemed a public emergency and, as such, the president would be authorized, under the executive power asserted in his signing statement, to deploy domestic military force to suppress it.

Of all Bush's actions, the administration's efforts to accrete expanded domestic security powers are perhaps the most haunting in their fulfillment of the framers' fears of executive tyranny.

THE ABDICATION OF POWERS: THE LEGISLATIVE

While the Bush years are a case study in the excesses of executive power, many of these efforts were made possible by the active acquiescence of those in the legislative branch. Applying the framers' words to contemporary situations risks a kind of constitutional fundamentalism that fails to recognize that there is much about today's complex and shrinking world the framers could not have anticipated. Having lived nearly two centuries before air travel, they could not have dreamt, for example, that foreign agents could fly airliners into skyscrapers. It could thus be argued that their worldview did not account for the kind of mass destructive, nonstate terror that revealed itself on 9/11. By extension, their idealism about the need for balance between security and liberty and the importance of avoiding foreign entanglements could, on some level, be seen as a naive luxury unavailable to modern Americans, who live on an increasingly interconnected planet where minding one's business as an isolationist power is impracticable.

Yet it is equally remarkable just how applicable the founding concepts in the Declaration of Independence, *The Federalist Papers*, and the Constitution remain. "If men were angels," Madison famously argued, "no government would be necessary." The framers forged the separation of powers precisely because they recognized that an ideal form of government would pit the self-interest and powerlust of each branch against that of the others. They disapproved of the executive seeking to gain disproportionate power, but they expected it and were nonetheless confident that his effort to do so would be mitigated by the equal and opposite ambitions of the other branches.

Thus, no matter how excessively George W. Bush asserted executive power, he was in many ways doing exactly what the framers expected of him. What they could not have anticipated was that the other branches would acquiesce, abdicating so much of the authority vested in them by the Constitution. Nowhere was the abdication of congressional authority and responsibility to act as "a check to the Dog of war" more costly than in the days immediately following 9/11.

On September 18, 2001, the House and Senate approved Joint House Resolution 23, authorizing the president to use all "necessary and appropriate force" against those whom he determined "planned, authorized, committed, or aided" the attacks. In so doing, Congress effectively abdicated its war-declaring powers and conferred them on the president. Since it is now clear that members of the administration had wished for the overthrow of Saddam Hussein long before 9/11, when empowered by Congress to use "any force necessary," these officials were predisposed to launch a military campaign to unseat Saddam Hussein. But beyond empowering the executive to undertake this campaign, Joint Resolution 23 had larger implications in arming the Bush administration with a view of itself as unaccountable to the other branches in arenas far from the battlefield.

Overnight, Bush had become a wartime president. And just as children learn from their first days on the school bus not to talk to the driver while the bus is in motion, it was understood that while Bush was prosecuting the war on terror, he should not be questioned on the motives or merit of his decisions. Throughout the course of the administration's power grab, members of Congress—Republican and Democrat alike—have been remarkably supportive.

When the Abu Ghraib scandal broke, gasps of horror were heard among members of Congress on both sides of the aisle at a Capitol Hill slideshow of 1,800 harrowing images.[21] Yet the subsequent inquiry was short-lived. As Susan Milligan revealed in stark contrast in a 2005 *Boston Globe* article, while a Republican-controlled House in the 1990s "logged 140 hours of sworn testimony into whether former president

Bill Clinton had used the White House Christmas card list to identify potential Democratic donors . . . in the past two years, a House committee has managed to take only 12 hours of sworn testimony about the abuse of prisoners at Iraq's Abu Ghraib prison." Though scandals over international and domestic executive mischief have gone largely unscrutinized on Capitol Hill, Milligan recalls, congressional committees have exhaustively covered such topics as steroid abuse in professional sports and the tendency of universities to become "diploma mills."[22] The long-term consequences of this remain to be seen, but Congress' abdication of responsibility sets a precedent on which future executives will rely when seeking increased presidential authority and weakened congressional oversight thereof.

THE AMBIGUITY OF POWERS: THE COURTS

The record of the judicial branch during the Bush years has been a more textured one than the executive's extreme assertion of power on the one hand and Congress's unsettling abdication on the other. The American court system is also a multitiered institution comprised of the Supreme Court at the highest level but with many inferior courts as well. Across this judicial landscape, there is a variety of focus, political alignment, and inclination that makes generalization difficult. Yet, to understand the most fundamental questions facing the judicial branch, an analysis of the Supreme Court during the Bush years is instructive. Here, what one sees is consistent with the way past Courts have attempted a delicate balancing act between the reality of partisanship on the Court and the academic impulse to play a fair, nonpartisan, constitutionally determined role. Yet, despite the Court's efforts at such balance, it does not operate in a vacuum and, given the influence exerted upon it by the executive branch, the Supreme Court under Bush may have ultimately helped to foster a condition of legal ambiguity, which, by not actively obstructing the administration's pursuits, produced a condition conducive to them.

It bears recalling that the Bush presidency was itself born in an episode of partisanship on the Supreme Court. In *Supreme Injustice: How the High Court Hijacked Election 2000*, Harvard law scholar Alan

Dershowitz argues that "the decision in the Florida election case may be ranked as the single most corrupt decision in Supreme Court history, because it is the only one that I know of where the majority justices decided as they did because of the personal identity and political affiliation of the litigants. This was cheating, and a violation of the judicial oath."[23] Dershowitz's analysis reflects the sentiment of many who saw in the 2000 election a candidate awarded an electoral victory despite a loss in the popular vote by a Supreme Court seen as politically aligned in its majority with that candidate.

Over the next eight years, two justices—William Rehnquist and Sandra Day O'Connor—would retire and, in their stead, the president would appoint conservative Republican justices John G. Roberts and Samuel Alito, amid considerable congressional controversy. Critics of these appointments saw them as ensuring that, for an indefinite period, the Court will be firmly tilted conservative Republican. Writing for *The New Yorker*, legal analyst Jeffrey Toobin argues that Roberts and Alito "have joined Antonin Scalia and Clarence Thomas in a phalanx that is more radical than any that the Court has seen since F.D.R.'s appointments." Toobin cites several measures by the Roberts Court, including efforts to cripple school desegregation (amid hints that affirmative action may be next), the Court's decision to uphold a controversial 2003 federal law banning so-called "partial-birth" abortions (a similar law had been struck down by the Court in 2000), as well as its efforts to limit the reach of job-discrimination laws and the latitude for challenging the mixing of church and state. When the Court ruled 5–4 in June 2007 to allow certain forms of discrimination in high school choice programs in Louisville, Kentucky, and Seattle, Washington, Toobin notes that even Justice Stephen Breyer was compelled to declare from the bench, "It is not often in the law that so few have so quickly changed so much."[24]

Not mentioned by Toobin but no less noteworthy are two other decisions taken by the Court in June 2007. The first diluted part of a U.S. campaign finance law upheld in 2003 that prevented labor unions and corporations from endorsing candidates prior to elections. The second partially rolled back the effect of *Tinker* v. *Des Moines*, a 1969 case protecting a student's "constitutional rights to freedom of speech or expression" inside "the schoolhouse gate." In *Morse* v. *Frederick*, the Court concluded that when Juneau, Alaska, high school principal Deborah

Morse confiscated a banner fashioned by eighteen-year-old student Joseph Frederick that read "BONG HiTS 4 JESUS" and suspended Frederick, she had not violated his "constitutional rights to freedom of speech or expression" as defined in *Tinker*. Concurring with Toobin, Supreme Court reporter Joan Biskupic wrote in a June 29, 2007, *USA Today* story titled "Roberts Steers Court Right Back to Reagan" that "in a remarkable first full term of the remade Supreme Court, a narrow majority of justices changed the law on race, abortion, free speech and a swath of other issues affecting American life."[25]

These and other developments are clearly steering the Supreme Court in a rightward direction. Yet, though this may be disconcerting to those who disagree and certainly ironic given the Bush administration's indignant rhetoric about "activist judges," it is well within a long-standing partisan tradition of presidents using their appointment power to sway the Court.

As Toobin himself recognizes, the justices appointed by FDR "allowed the New Deal to proceed, and set the stage for the noblest era in the Court's history, under Chief Justice Earl Warren, when the civil and individual rights of all citizens finally received their constitutional due." Certainly, for those who do not share Toobin's enthusiasm for the New Deal or, perhaps, for many legal developments of the civil rights era, the "judicial activism" of the Bush years may not seem so unprecedented. And it isn't. Until FDR, the Court of the first half of the twentieth century was considered highly conservative, even striking down a law limiting the number of hours one could work in a bakery, since it would impose on "freedom of contract."

It must also be noted that the record of the Supreme Court, in particular, in recent years has been a mixed one that did not always concur neatly with the administration's wishes. With particular respect to the president's assumed wartime powers, the Court has heard four major cases, and in only one of which—*Padilla* v. *Rumsfeld*—it voted in favor of the administration (and that on a technicality). In the three other decisions, the Court rejected and restrained the administration's broad assertion that the president may detain anyone, anywhere, without following the Geneva Conventions or even obtaining congressional authorization. Still, in a worrisome demonstration that doing nothing can be as significant as doing something, the Court refused in October 2007 to hear the appeal of Khaled El-Masri, a German citizen of Lebanese descent who claimed to have been tortured by the CIA in connection with the war on terror. Naturally, the Court's decision to let the ruling of a lower court stand in this matter may have had any number of motivations, and this decision when weighed alongside several other decisions that have restrained executive power should in no way be interpreted as a signal of the Court's support for the administration's radical policies in the handling of detainees. Yet for those who believe that the administration's decisions in the treatment of detainees represent a legal and moral crisis in the conduct of U.S. foreign policy, the Court's reluctance to hear such an appeal may seem inadequate to the situation at hand.

Thus, while the Court's partisan activities are consistent with past patterns of Court behavior, it has also made decisions that restrain some measure of executive power. It must be remembered that under America's system of justice the Supreme Court chooses only a certain number of cases from among those brought before it. And a small handful of cases about presidential warpowers can in no way cover the vast range of issues raised by the administration's sweeping assertions of executive power. Worse still from this perspective, whatever reluctance the Court may have to hearing any given case, the number of cases that even reach the Court is already prelimited by several factors, chief among them executive privilege and the way it obstructs Congress and the courts from holding the executive accountable.

When the House Judiciary Committee subpoenaed the executive in connection with the firing of U.S. attorneys, administration lawyers called the situation unprecedented and argued that "never in American history has a federal court ordered an executive branch official to testify before Congress."[26] Citing George Washington, Grover Cleveland, Richard Nixon, and Bill Clinton, they maintain that clashes between the legislative and executive branches tend to be resolved without going to court.

Reporting on this confrontation, the title alone of a May 2008 Associated Press article speaks volumes: "Bush Wants Court Out of Subpoena Fight."[27] "For over two hundred years," the article cites the arguments written by administration lawyers, "when disputes have arisen between the political branches concerning the testimony of executive branch witnesses before Congress, or the production of executive branch documents to Congress, the branches have engaged in negotiation and compromise." The lawyers went further to urge U.S. District Judge John D. Bates not to "tidy this process up" by enforcing the Judiciary Committee's subpoena. The ambiguity, the attorneys argued, leads to the kind of political compromises and give-and-take the framers intended, whereas setting the record straight on executive privilege "would forever alter the accommodation process that has served the Nation so well for over two centuries."

The Administration's desire to settle its dispute with Congress on its own informal terms, without the involvement of the courts, is a shadowy tactic that implicitly undermines the power of the judiciary to enforce Congress' oversight authority. This poses a compound problem for the judicial branch. On the one hand, executive privilege is used by executives to undermine the Court's power to interpret the laws that apply to any number of areas of dispute between the executive and the legislative branches. On the other, executive privilege is inherently a matter that requires the Court's consideration—a principle whose legal validity has not been fully determined and over which the judicial branch has expressed itself too haltingly. Despite his critics' dismay that he has invoked executive privilege so brazenly, it may just be that, by forcing the issue, Bush has invited a debate on its constitutionality, one that could establish either that such privilege is an overreach by the executive or that Congress's subpoena authority—one of its most powerful oversight tools—shall henceforth be formally abridged.

Of course, for the Supreme Court to weigh in on the matter of executive privilege, a case involving it must find its way through the legal system. At present, there is a heartening glimmer that such a case may be doing just that. On May 10, 2008, general counsel for the House Judiciary Committee filed "a civil suit seeking declaratory and injunctive relief to enforce the subpoenas" issued by it in connection with the U.S. attorney firing scandal.[28] The case, *Committee on the Judiciary, United States House of Representatives* v. *Harriet Miers, et al.*, has been filed in the D.C. Circuit Court against President Bush's former counsel Harriet Miers and Chief of Staff Josh Bolten. The action seeks a declaration by the Court that Miers is not immune from the obligation to appear before the Committee in accord with its subpoena, that she and Bolten are required to produce logs of all documents withheld on grounds of executive privilege, and that such claims of executive privilege are, in any event, outweighed by the Committee's demonstrated, specific need for the subpoenaed testimony and documents.

At the time of writing, this case is only in its nascent phases, and one can predict neither the outcome in D.C. Circuit Court nor the possibility that the case may ever advance to the Supreme Court. Given its past reluctance to settle this matter definitively, whether the Supreme Court would adjudicate this issue also remains unknowable. Nonetheless, since the present action in D.C. Circuit Court so centrally challenges the power of executive privilege in relation to Congress' subpoena power, it raises the prospect that the courts may yet be compelled to go some distance in addressing what is clearly an obvious threat to the separation of powers so fundamental to the republic.

THE DISASTROUS RISE OF MISPLACED POWER: THE CORPORATE SECTOR

No summary of the Bush administration's trespasses can fail to address the problem of corporate-political collusion. So much has been written on the scandals of cronyism during the Bush years—from Jack Abramoff to Duke Cunningham to the unaccountable misconduct of Blackwater, among others—that it is fruitless to cover them in detail here. A troubling feature of the majority of media coverage of these scandals, though, has been to characterize them as exceptional rather than part of a pattern. They are better understood as the expression of a deeply problematic blurring of the lines in America between government responsibility to the public good and private business interests. Thus, although frontloading and political engineering have thus far been discussed as activities that produce congressional corruption, the constitutional implications of such activities require further exploration. An increasingly worrisome side effect of rising corporate power on the checks and balances has been to reduce the transparency of public policy by transferring its implementation to the private sector.

No company is more closely associated with this problem during the Bush years than the Texas oil services giant Halliburton, and its subsidiary Kellogg Brown & Root (KBR). An examination of the company's historic ties to the executive branch speaks volumes about the dangerous blurring of private and public interests. These ties are bipartisan and long predate the Bush administration. As early as 1937, a symbolic relationship developed between Brown & Root and Lyndon B. Johnson. During Johnson's first run for Congress, the company provided him with vast campaign support, and he delivered for his benefactor, securing President Roosevelt's approval for federal funding for a dam project the company sought to build.[29]

In 1941, contributions by the company to Johnson's Senate campaign led to an IRS investigation of alleged criminal campaign finance violations and earned Johnson the moniker "the senator from Brown & Root." The case was quietly settled, allowing the relationship between the company and Johnson to continue into his presidency, when controversy again arose over the awarding of several contracts to build military bases during the Vietnam War. As one of four companies contracted to build 85 percent of the Army's infrastructure during the war, Brown & Root earned the dubious nickname "Burn and Loot" among the war's critics.

When, during the Bush years, KBR's parent company Halliburton emerged as a key beneficiary of American warmaking, becoming the leading recipient of contracts servicing U.S. operations in both Afghanistan and Iraq, the problem of cronyism was taken to a new level by the history of close ties between the company and Vice President Dick Cheney. Yet Cheney bears a deeper distinction in the legacy of military privatization. For it was he who, as secretary of defense in 1991, was instrumental in encouraging a shift in policy toward the increased privatization of activities previously performed by the U.S. military.

Charles Lewis, who founded Washington's Center for Public Integrity, has intensively studied the effect of Cheney's Halliburton ties on the company's fortunes during the Bush years. He recounts that "in 1992, a $9 million contract was given out by the Pentagon to study the efficacy of using the private sector more aggressively to do some heretofore support-type functions like food service, latrine duty, but even some military activities as well. The secretary of defense at the time was Dick Cheney. The company was Brown & Root. So, Cheney awards the contract. Brown & Root comes back and says, 'We think this is a terrific idea.' And the next ten years they get seven or eight hundred contracts to do just that."[30]

Cheney left office in 1993. Two years later, he became CEO of the company—a post he held until being elected vice president in 2000. According to Lewis, Cheney's personal income rose between 1995 and 2000 "from a million dollars or less to $60 or $70 million in the span of five years." Though not all of Cheney's tax returns from this period have been made public, what is available appears to confirm Lewis's claim, reflecting an adjusted gross income of $36 million in the year 2000 alone.[31] During this same period, according to Lewis, the company's fortunes also rose, doubling the number of federal government contracts they received. Under Cheney's leadership, the company also doubled its lobbying expenditures and campaign contributions.

It was therefore perhaps not surprising that when Cheney took office, the awarding of so many contracts to Halliburton—more than twice the amount awarded to any other contractor—drew fire from critics. Just weeks into Cheney's first term in office and six months before 9/11, Halliburton was granted a contract by the U.S. Navy. Awarded over the protests of the General Accounting Office, which questioned the methods for evaluating competing bidders, the contract would span five years and be worth up to $300 million.[32] Yet this was only a modest beginning. Over the next seven years, Halliburton was awarded more than $20 billion in contracts in connection with logistics, oil, and reconstruction services for Iraq and Afghanistan. To make matters worse, during the same period, a litany of scandals arose regarding the no-bid conditions under which these contracts were awarded, and over Halliburton's practices in charging the federal government.

In February 2004, an investigation by the Pentagon's inspector general was launched to examine whether KBR had overcharged the government for importing fuel from Kuwait to Iraq. Later that year, the Defense Contract Audit Agency withheld $186 million in payments following two audit reports in which deficiencies in KBR's billing system were documented. Then, on August 3, 2004, the Securities and Exchange Commission fined Halliburton $7.5 million for failure to disclose a change in its accounting practice that resulted in misleading filings for 1998 and 1999.

During the early years of the Bush administration, Halliburton released a revealing television ad in which its CEO, Dave Lesar, spoke directly to the camera, addressing head-on the rising wave of negative publicity enveloping the company and, in particular, its link to the vice president. "We're serving the troops," Lesar declared indignantly, "because of *what* we know, not *who* we know."

It's remarkable to think that the public controversy surrounding Halliburton had heated to such a boiling point that its CEO felt compelled to spend precious advertising time addressing charges of cronyism when he could have spent that time boasting about the number of employees the company had all over the world, its decades of experience, or its advanced proprietary technologies. The company's most noted strength—its connection to the vice president—had become its greatest liability. And yet, for all the public controversy, legal and economic accountability for Halliburton has been minimal compared to the benefits it has reaped from no-bid contracts and questionable billing practices. But even more important, what Halliburton represents from a constitutional perspective is not just the rising political influence of corporations as rogue actors in the American political landscape, but a new and highly advanced dynamic in which the corporate sector and the public sector have become dangerously blurred in American life.

Part of the reason that accountability has been so scarce for Halliburton is that its activities—despite being conducted at the behest of the federal government—are relatively invulnerable to public or congressional scrutiny. As Congressman Henry Waxman (D–CA) incredulously noted in 2004, "we can't even find out how much Halliburton charges to do the laundry. It's inexcusable that they should keep this information from the Congress, and the people."[33]

It may be inexcusable, but it is consistent with America's free market tradition, in which the activities of a corporation are seen as the province of that corporation, and neither the public nor Congress has a fundamental right to access information about them, other than such basic financial reporting as is required in tax filings and sent to shareholders. As Jane Mayer writes in *The New Yorker*, "unlike government agencies, private contractors can resist Freedom of Information Act requests and are insulated from direct congressional oversight. Jan Schakowsky, a Democratic representative from Illinois, told me, 'It's almost as if these private military contractors are involved in a secret war.' Private companies, she noted, can conceal details of their missions from public scrutiny in the name of protecting trade secrets. They are also largely exempt from salary caps and government ethics rules designed to protect policy from being polluted by politics."[34]

By allocating so much of the work that had previously been the province of the public sector to the corporate sector, the Bush administration has created a condition in which the nature and practice of government activities may be hidden under the thick camouflage of corporate privacy.

The framers' design for the separation of powers did not account for outside agents like Halliburton. This concerns Charles Lewis on a level far beyond one company, and not just on the theoretical ground that it undermines the separation of powers but because, in practical terms, it has vast implications on the world stage. "We keep learning more and more," he says. "Now it turns out we're using private security contractors to interrogate prisoners. That's the most sensitive thing in the world you would ever do—interrogate prisoners. And what's the danger? Accountability. Is a private military company obligated, under any kind of international law that governs nations, to worry about human rights abuses? Torture? Is anyone liable for those things, or can they say *we were hired by the U.S. government* and then the government says *we don't know anything about it? We hired them to do a job, and, gosh, something must have gone wrong.*"

In the event that such abuses should take place at the hands of private military contractors, Lewis echoes the point that the Freedom of Information Act doesn't apply to companies. "We can't even find out how many private contractors the U.S. has employed on the ground in Iraq, let alone details about anything taking place. This could be Indonesia; it sounds like Russia, Nigeria. No, it's the United States of America. And everything that I just said is entirely legal. And it is our system of legal corruption where it looks like hell. It is laughed at and held in great disdain around the world. And in Washington, D.C., it's become standard operating procedure."

According to KBR's corporate literature and the signage that hangs over its defense industry trade show booths, the company is "the Army's Contractor on the Battlefield." At one such booth in 2004, KBR had remarkably chosen a magician as its corporate front man—a sleight-of-hand expert named Harrison Carroll. For a company notorious for the lack of transparency in its accounting and contracting practices, the decision to employ a prestidigitator as its corporate face seems more like brazen self-irony than utter cluenessness.

"Literally, I'm a magician," Carroll laughs as he sets up his magic table, "but I specialize in the corporate market. My degree is in marketing, so it's easy for me to understand what the company wants to accomplish. And it's more than doing just tricks for people. It's almost like a tool to get them into the booth so I can communicate their message."

As Carroll performs truly mind-boggling tricks for passersby—asking them to name certain cards and then finding those very cards hidden in previously sealed envelopes distributed among other members of his growing audience—KBR's corporate message is peppered shamelessly into his banter. "Name any playing card that would come into your mind," Carroll declares to his enrapt group of onlookers. "Now, we've never met before. No collusion, which is really odd, because collusion is our business."

"Yes." Carroll smiles deliciously. "Collusion with the military."

Taking a break between shows, Carroll shares some thoughts on his approach to delivering KBR's message. "In the last show," he laughs, "the lady thought of a queen of diamonds. I said, 'Think of a card,' she thought of a queen. I said, 'It's funny you thought of royalty, even our competition thinks of royalty when they think of—boom—KBR, or whatever.' And then I go into a blurb about 'the Army's contractor on the battlefield.' "[35]

The message Carroll delivers to those passing KBR's booth is the same message that KBR has leveraged to become America's largest recipient of contracts in Afghanistan and Iraq. It's the same message its advocates have used to argue in its defense amid so many scandals. It's the same message that undergirded Dick Cheney's original recommendation to transfer so many public functions to Halliburton, and seventeen years later, the same message that, as vice president, he communicated to the late Tim Russert on NBC's *Meet the Press*, six months after the start of the Iraq War.

"One of the things to keep in mind," Cheney told Russert, "is that Halliburton is a unique kind of company. There are very few companies out there that have the combination of the very large engineering construction capability and significant oil field services, the first- or second-largest oil field service company in the world, and they've traditionally done a lot of work for the U.S. government and the U.S. military. That expertise has stood the military in good stead over the years, but it's a great company. There are fine people working for it."[36]

To hear a sitting vice president give so unabashed an on-air plug to a major defense contractor, let alone one that is his former employer and one that is the country's largest recipient of wartime contracts under his administration, speaks volumes about what Eisenhower called "the disastrous rise of misplaced power."

Implicit in Halliburton's message, whether delivered by a hired traveling conjurer or a polished sitting vice president, is a Faustian bargain that pits the public good against the private interest. It essentially says: *We at KBR can do all these remarkable things on the battlefield and in the nation's petroleum interest, because through the largesse of successive administrations over nearly a century and our own hard work we have developed a level of capital and expertise that even outstrips what today's governments themselves can boast. But if you want us to do these remarkable things, you have to accept a level of corporate mischief and a lack of transparency.*

Remarkably, in the latter part of Eisenhower's Farewell Address, he articulated in quite specific terms how such far-reaching corporate influence could tighten its grip on American policy making. Having warned the nation about the dangers of the military-industrial complex, he turned his attention to a separate but equally dangerous by-product of military-industrial growth. "Akin to, and largely responsible for the sweeping changes in our industrial-military posture," Eisenhower declared, "has been the technological revolution during recent decades." This revolution, Eisenhower argued, had led to an explosion in the cost of research that brought great risk both to the freedom of scholarship in America and to the freedom of choice among policy makers.

"Today, the solitary inventor, tinkering in his shop, has been overshadowed by task forces of scientists in laboratories and testing fields," he warned. "The prospect of domination of the nation's scholars by Federal employment, project allocations, and the power of money is ever present—and is gravely to be regarded."

As though these words were not radical enough, Eisenhower completed his thought by revealing an extraordinarily prescient aspect of his thinking and coining a term as significant as "military-industrial complex," yet less well remembered. "In holding scientific research and discovery in respect, as we should," he said, "we must also be alert to the equal and opposite danger that public policy could itself become the captive of a *scientific-technological elite.*"

When the vice president responds to Tim Russert's questions about cronyism involving Halliburton by underscoring how indispensable the firm is to America's prosperity, it might appear that public policy has indeed become captive to a scientific-technological elite.

YOO AND ME: A CONVERSATION ON THE FATE OF THE REPUBLIC

Having enumerated several instances of the Bush administration's power grab, the pressing question is: Will the country redress these trespasses once Bush leaves office? Will the president's excessive accretion of power do permanent damage to the constitutional separation of powers and the health of the republic? A leading architect of the administration's justification of these excesses argues not, and his argument warrants consideration.

At the time of writing, John Yoo's fate as a figure of the Bush years is as unclear as that of the republic he helped undermine. Having become very much the public face most closely identified with the legal underpinnings of the Administration's controversial interrogation practices, Yoo has become another casualty of the administration's practice of making low- to midlevel functionaries the scapegoats for far-reaching activities that later prove to have been sanctioned at higher levels. At Abu Ghraib, it was the soldiers and MPs who went off-book, only for the public to learn definitively in April 2008 that in fact conduct violative of the laws of war had been condoned and organized with great specificity by a group of high-level administration officials, including Dick Cheney, Donald Rumsfeld, and Condoleezza Rice. In the matter of the outing of Valerie Plame's identity to the media, a previously little-known operative in the vice president's office named Scooter Libby was the only person to face any measure of accountability. And in this far broader campaign to exempt the executive branch from domestic and international laws regarding torture, a few lawyers would be fingered—David Addington, the vice president's legal counsel; Jay Bybee, then assistant attorney general under John Ashcroft; and, most pointed, John Yoo, whose signature alone appears at the bottom of some of the most notorious legal documents from this enterprise.

"In wartime," Mr. Yoo sweepingly declared in the 2003 follow-up to the Torture Memo, "it is for the President alone to decide what methods to use to best prevail against the enemy." The fact that the president of the United States, on matters as significant as torture, the Geneva Conventions, and his own vulnerability to war crimes charges, took his legal cues from a thirty-four-year-old "deputy assistant attorney general for the Office of Legal Counsel" would be funny if its consequences were not so globally tragic and constitutionally troubling. Though the Justice Department in 2004 issued a legal opinion withdrawing the controversial 2002 and 2003 memos and declaring that "torture is abhorrent both to American law and values and to international norms," one cannot help but wonder at both the pain inflicted by the policies Mr. Yoo advocated on any number of America's prisoners during this period, and at the longer-term consequences.[37]

In a November 2005 Canadian television program entitled *A Few Bad Apples,* interviewer Gillian Findlay questioned Yoo about what he and those in the administration had done. Ever loyal to those who have since scapegoated him, Yoo was unflappable in his defense both of his own actions and those of the president, defiantly telling her that the president "doesn't have to justify" his actions "to the people of Canada."[38]

Findlay then asked Yoo the most pointed question on many people's minds: "As you know, there are some people in your country who believe that, based on the evidence that they have seen, that war crimes have been committed here. They go further and say that war crimes have been committed by people within the administration. And I think I would be remiss if I didn't point out that some of them implicate you. And I'm wondering what you think of that?"

Yoo responded defensively. "I'm not denying that there were criminal actions that occurred in Iraq. But people are just speculating if they think President Bush or Secretary Rumsfeld or certainly even me ordered people or are in any way responsible for what happened in

Iraq when the policy of the government was very clear that the Geneva Conventions applied." Since Yoo, along with other members of the Justice Department and the White House legal team, had advocated precisely the position that the Geneva Conventions did *not* apply to the executive, it would be difficult to characterize this statement as anything short of a lie.

Unable to contain her antipathy at Yoo's rather glib poise on a matter of such significance, Findlay went on to ask a biting personal question, resulting in an awkward but telling exchange.

"Have you lost any sleep over this?" she asked.

"I sleep quite well," Mr. Yoo bristled. "Thanks."

"You do . . ." she pressed, incredulous.

"M-hmm. You could ask my wife."

Confrontations like these are becoming increasingly common for Yoo. He has come to be seen as a kind of mild-mannered ghoul with a law degree, who did the administration's dirty work. "In the past few months alone," noted *The Washington Post* in January 2006, "international lawyers have called for his [Yoo's] criminal indictment, students have broken into his classroom at Berkeley (where the former deputy assistant attorney general now teaches law) to stage a mock detainee hearing, and lecture halls where he is scheduled to speak have been boycotted."[39]

"Is John Yoo a Monster?" reads the headline of a May 2008 *Esquire* magazine feature article. "He's been accused of war crimes and compared to the Nazi lawyers who justified Hitler," writes John H. Richardson. "Many good Americans would like to see him fired, shamed, even imprisoned. But in his classroom at Berkeley School of Law, John Yoo is a charming and patient teacher, popular with students and cordial to all."

Perhaps underestimating the gravity of the charges against him (or overestimating the old saw that any press is good press), there is a sense that behind his placid smile, Yoo almost seems to enjoy the rising controversy around him. And yet, with each new discovery about the activities in which he was involved, Yoo's legal exposure seems to increase in seriousness. On May 6, 2008, attorneys from the National Lawyers Guild testified before the House Judiciary Committee that certain Justice Department lawyers were "part of a common plan to violate U.S. and international laws outlawing torture." That same day, the House Judiciary Committee issued a subpoena to the vice president's counsel

David Addington to compel him to testify before them. Under the threat of a similar subpoena, Yoo agreed voluntarily to testify.

On May 12, the National Lawyers Guild called on Congress to appoint a Special Prosecutor, "Independent of the Department of Justice, to investigate and prosecute high Bush officials and lawyers including John Yoo for their role in the torture of prisoners in U.S. custody." These developments continue to unfold. But given the administration's track record in insulating its highest ranking officials from accountability, Yoo's likelihood of being held accountable may be as high as are his superiors' chances of avoiding the same.

Whatever becomes of John Yoo, he has made a lasting and important contribution to any understanding of the American way of war: where it has come from and where it is headed. In many ways, Yoo's most strident opinions are the ones that have most attracted attention and now, perhaps, some measure of accountability. Yet behind these lies a more textured vision expressed in a handful of editorials he has written, and in his 2006 book *War by Other Means*. Taken together, and contrasted with the sweeping legal arguments he provided the Bush administration, these offer a deeper and more considered rationale for the assertion of executive power per se. In contrast to the secrecy of so many in the Bush administration, Yoo is to be commended for embracing public exposure and discussion of his views and the policies to which he contributed. In *War by Other Means*, Yoo writes that these policies were "the result of reasonable decisions, made by thoughtful people in good faith, under one of the most dire challenges our nation has ever faced,"[40] and he is unashamed to defend them.

"John Yoo deserves much credit," wrote Georgetown law scholar Neal Katyal in *The Washington Post*, "for helping open up a secretive subject for public discussion, even when it has meant unpleasantness for himself . . . [he] should be commended for not hiding behind the standard Washington cliché of saying, 'That's classified. I can't talk about it.' "[41]

As Yoo himself notes in *War by Other Means*, "much of the attention on me is due to the fact that there are few Bush administration veterans who will defend their decisions in the war on terrorism in public." In contrast to his colleagues, whom he criticizes for a tendency "to run and hide," Yoo is unabashed in standing by the decisions taken—even those that have been traced ultimately to embarassing national controversies like the NSA scandal and Abu Ghraib.

Since leaving the administration, Yoo says he has taken his cue from Alexander Hamilton in encouraging public discourse—as Hamilton did in *The Federalist Papers*—by vigorously defending policies to which he subscribes in an effort to provoke an equally vocal expression of countervailing views. "These questions still confront us and they are not going to go away," he argues. "They do not have easy answers, despite the claims of critics."[42]

For those who strongly disagree with Yoo's views (and those who might wish he had not given such "easy" answers in his infamous legal memos), his passion for continuing to justify them even in the face of so much failure by the administration may simply inspire increased animosity. Yet, whatever one thinks of John Yoo and the policies he continues so vocally to advocate, a discussion of his most considered views is vital for understanding the impact of the Bush administration on the American way of war.

"To his critics," Yoo wrote in a September 2006 *New York Times* editorial, "Mr. Bush is a 'King George' bent on an 'imperial presidency.' " However, Yoo argues, "the inescapable fact is that war shifts power to the branch most responsible for its waging: the executive."[43] Though this assertion may simply seem a convenient justification for the extremism with which the Bush administration asserted limitless authority over the other branches in the name of security, it demands our consideration. For war has, throughout American history, provided a pretext for the assertion of executive power over the other branches. From Lincoln's suspension of habeas corpus in the imprisonment of his political rivals during the Civil War to Roosevelt's internment of Germans and Japanese-Americans during World War II to Nixon and Reagan's concealment of their activities from the oversight of Congress, the history of expanding executive power in wartime is a bipartisan one.

Under the Bush administration, these episodes of executive expansion have been invariably accompanied by significant rollbacks of America's constitutional liberties. Writing in *Federalist* No. 8 in 1787, Yoo's hero Alexander Hamilton predicted this, putting a fine point on the underlying tension between war and liberty:

> The violent destruction of life and property incident to war; the continual effort and alarm attendant on a state of continual danger will compel nations the most attached to liberty, to resort for repose and security to institutions which have a tendency to destroy their civil and political rights. To be more safe, they at length become willing to run the risk of being less free.

While characterizing critics of the Patriot Act and other security measures with civil liberty implications as "absolutists," who have "exaggerated the threat to civil liberties," John Yoo recognizes that during the war on terror, "the government's powers have been expanded" and certain constitutional protections have been abridged. "Scandals du jour," he concedes rather glibly, "do sometimes cause unwise legislation." Still, he does not share his critics' concern about the suspension of certain liberties. "Fighting a network like al Qaeda will require more information gathering at home than in previous wars," he maintains. "Reducing the chances of a future 9/11 justifies some loss of privacy."

The threats of today, Yoo argues, were unimaginable not only to the framers, but even to policy makers a generation ago, such as those who drafted FISA. "If there were an emergency that Congress could not prepare for, it was the war brought upon us on 9/11," he writes. "FISA was a law written with Soviet spies working out of their embassy in Washington D.C. in mind. No one then anticipated a war with an international terrorist organization wielding the destructive power of a nation."[44]

Yoo believes that Hamilton and the other framers, while fashioning the separation of powers, assigned significant war powers to the executive "because of his ability to act with unity, speed, and secrecy."[45] In this context, 9/11's revelation of what Yoo calls "a terrorist enemy intent on carrying out the catastrophic destruction of our nation" demands unprecedented levels of covertness and that alacrity belong only to the executive. "While everyone would like the certainty and openness of a congressional act," Yoo argues, "the success of the NSA surveillance program depends on secrecy and agility, two characteristics Congress as an institution lacks."

This argument in favor of expanded executive power relies on the very dynamic that so concerned Madison when he wrote that war "favors" the executive. For essentially, if, as Yoo argues, the president is to be seen as uniquely capable to respond to the needs of wartime, then it follows that it is during wartime that he accretes powers not naturally available to him during peace.

Yoo acknowledges that "historical precedents provide some support" for the argument that "the government consistently overreacts to crises by oppressing dissenters and infringing on individual rights."[46] As he sees it, though, the historical tension between security and liberty moves on a pendulum, which during wartime swings toward security and then toward a restoration of liberties when peace returns.

"History does not show," he writes in *War by Other Means*, "that wars have reduced American civil liberties, either before or after the war. The Union reduced civil liberties during the Civil War, but it also liberated the slaves and expanded individual rights against the states afterward. FDR interned Japanese-Americans during World War II, but civil liberties surged in the decades after."[47]

While this point is well taken, Yoo goes on to assert a more debatable one. He argues that, though certain historical intervals of compromised liberty have definitely occurred, America has in the macro only become more free. "Despite a succession of wars and emergencies since the Civil War, civil liberties in our country have expanded steadily," he writes. "Recurring wars and foreign threats have not produced a permanent national security state."[48]

His argument is a pragmatic one, bordering on cynical. For it assumes that there are times when, in order to fulfill her first principles in the long term, the nation must suspend these in the short term.

If Yoo is wrong in his view that America has over time become more free, then it may be that, despite certain social advances, her episodes of reduced liberty have in fact built upon one another in a continuum of increasing erosion for the republic's vital freedoms. To extend the pendulum metaphor, imagine that the pendulum rests on a slanted surface. Though each rightward swing may appear to be counterbalanced by an equal and opposite leftward return, the pendulum, being on a slant, is being drawn gravitationally ever rightward with each repetition of the pattern. Considering the laundry list of anti-republican activities during the Bush years, one can certainly see how the administration was emboldened by past precedents, how yesterday's extremism becomes the justification for today's further encroachments.

In December 2003, in his first and only interview after retiring from his post as commander in chief of U.S. Central Command during the Iraq War, General Tommy Franks made a startling confession to *Cigar Aficiando* magazine.

"The worst thing that can happen," cautioned the general, "[is] a terrorist, massive casualty-producing event somewhere in the western world . . . that causes our population to question our own Constitution and to begin to militarize our country . . . which, in fact, then begins to potentially unravel the fabric of our Constitution."[49] His concern that a single episode of terror could "potentially unravel the fabric of our Constitution" would seem an indication, at the highest levels of command, that the republic is far more vulnerable than most Americans might have imagined.

Four years after Franks' comments, in an extreme illustration not only of how quickly a contemporary government can suspend its constitution but of how much past American precedents can provide the justification for such suspension, America's ally in the war on terror, President Pervez Musharraf of Pakistan, imposed martial law overnight on November 3, 2007. Declaring a state of emergency, suspending the country's constitution, and firing the supreme court, Musharraf appeared on television, citing the precedent of Abraham Lincoln's conduct during the American Civil War as a justification for his actions.[50]

"As an idealist, Abraham Lincoln had one consuming passion during that time of crisis, and this was to preserve the Union," Musharraf declared in his emergency address. "Towards that end, he broke laws, he violated the Constitution, he usurped arbitrary power, he trampled individual liberties."[51]

When the president of Pakistan is citing Lincoln as his precedent in suspending his country's constitution, and when the highest commander of U.S. forces in the Iraq War is warning cigar smokers that the American Constitution is itself one terrorist attack away from suspension, one might need to question Yoo's argument that historic episodes of abridged civil liberties have not had lasting consequences.

Has America, in fact, become more free? Or is Yoo wrong? And if he is wrong, then is it just that the country appears to be more free?

Certainly, at a time when the 2008 presidential candidacies of Senators Hillary Clinton and Barack Obama illustrate that a woman and an African-American can legitimately vie for the highest office in the land, it would be difficult to argue that America has not made significant social progress over the past two centuries. Yet it may still be the case that wartime episodes of reduced civil liberties have weakened the nation's constitutional foundations such that, broadly speaking, the republic is today more precariously built than ever before. Though people may be socially more liberated, the framework of their constitutional protections has been dangerously eroded. If this is the case, then Yoo's argument—and the far-reaching architecture of legal precedents it has produced—are of grave future concern from a constitutional and a republican point of view.

If Yoo, is right, however, that the pendulum swings inevitably back toward the protection and even the extension of liberties once war has ended, his argument is then gravely undermined by the nature of the war on terror. In the past, war gave way to peace when victory was achieved. This meant that the enemy capitulated and the threat to the nation was gone. To register this, any of a number of significant and telling events had to take place. A capital needed to be conquered, a leader deposed, a military defeated, a fleet sunk, or a territory overrun.

This is where Yoo's own argument—made to justify the administration's radical policies in the war on terror—is undermined by the reality of that very war. For it was the president himself who called the war on terror "a war unlike any we have fought before"—a fight "much broader than the battlefields and beachheads of the past."[52] Since 9/11, the public has repeatedly been told that the rules of engagement have changed—that the war on terror involves "non-state actors" who "know no borders" and have "no capital or nation-state to defend."[53]

In *War by Other Means*, John Yoo asks: "Is the Bush administration using public fear to consolidate political power? If it is, it has only another two years to go, and new security policies generally last only as long as the emergency."[54] This optimistic reflection ignores the defining quality of the war on terror and, in so doing, overlooks the gravity of the threat it poses to the health of the republic.

Since in the war on terror there is no capital to conquer, no nation-state to defeat, no fleet to sink, and since the adversary has multiple leaders divided into cells of influence such that the death of any one would not end the conflict, there is simply no natural rollback moment at which the war is likely to be seen as a success, the threat eliminated. Because the war on terror can have no defined endpoint, there is no clear occasion for the pendulum to swing back from its wartime extremity to peacetime regard for the republic's first principles.

In this context, there is a poetic linguistic irony in the recurring emergence of the word "sunset" in connection with so many of the most controversial legislative acts of the Bush years. Once upon a time it was said that the sun never set on the British Empire. In the war on terror, the word "sunset" has taken on its own meaning, relating not to geography but to time. Several of the most controversial aspects of the Patriot Act were drafted with what are called "sunset" provisions. The idea of these is that they are just the kind of fleeting emergency measures to which Yoo refers, and that there will come a moment when the sun sets on their necessity and they will then expire, unless renewed dialogue gives them extended life. In the context of the war on terror and its particular quality of endlessness, however, it would seem that, as was the case with Great Britain's projection of global power, the sun never sets on America's either.

Conclusion: If I Ran the Zoo

Because, therefore, we are defending a way of life, we must be respectful of that way of life as we proceed to the solution of our problem. We must not violate its principles and precepts, and we must not destroy from within what we are trying to defend from without.

Dwight D. Eisenhower

This book began with a confession and it ends with one. The preceding pages reflect an education that required me to reconsider many prejudices. I am a second-generation American—my mother's parents came to America as children fleeing Russia's czarist pogroms of the early twentieth century and my father came to America as a boy fleeing Nazi Germany in 1939. In the shadow of this legacy, my siblings and I were all taught growing up that we were children of flight who owed America our very existence. Franklin Delano Roosevelt was a hero. Yet with our admiration came an awareness that, for all her strengths, America was a work in progress, made better by the tough love of those who cared for her. As FDR himself noted when announcing his New Deal, "I do not look upon these United States as a finished product. We are still in the making."

Among other challenges, my analysis required that I disabuse myself of my unqualified adoration of Roosevelt himself. I had to see him, too, as less than a finished product. This is not to detract from his accomplishments, but rather to acknowledge a crucial lesson—that even a necessary war can, in its unfolding, challenge the very foundations of the nation for which it is fought.

I also had to acknowledge that, whatever the framers' intentions, their ultimate impact has likewise been mixed. Despite the enduring vitality of their words, America's founding documents are as imperfect as the men who crafted them, men of complex and varying motives no more able to see the future than you or I.

It's intimidating to try to offer any kind of concluding prescription to repair a system that is so complex, and one whose devolution has taken place over such a long period with so many forces at work. Yet it would seem remiss, even cowardly, to offer no thoughts by way of solution.

The problems we face are far from simple, and serious, concerted effort from a wide range of disciplines will be needed to address them. As the Bush years give way to those of a new administration, the silver lining of his presidency may just be that by having radicalized U.S. policy with so little resistance from either party in Congress, George W. Bush has produced a far-reaching collapse of public trust in government and the status quo. This invites and requires serious dialogue on America's course. What follows is an effort to contribute to that dialogue.

TWO FORMATIVE EXPERIENCES

Though any number of voices have contributed to my thinking about America's future, two issues, raised by Chuck Spinney and Colonel Wilkerson respectively, have impressed me as most urgent and very much at the root of all the others. The first is Spinney's concern that something must be done to address the fact that Madison's solution to the dangers of a majority faction, namely, the formation of a representative republic, has backfired, producing in Congress a class of professional politicians who can be corrupted by strategies like frontloading and political engineering. The second is Wilkerson's concern that the National Security Act of 1947 has outlived its usefulness and needs to be replaced, both because it ill-equips America to meet today's security challenges and because it upset the balance of power between the branches so dangerously toward the executive. Of course, to institute such fundamental changes as reducing the influence of money in politics and rebalancing power between the branches by way of a new national security act, one must overcome inevitable resistance among those who benefit from how things presently work. To this end, particularly given the extreme abuses of the Bush years, any effort at meaningful reform must begin with serious efforts to hold those who committed such abuses accountable. Without accountability, there is insufficent motivation for reform.

While I am indebted to Spinny, Wilkerson, and others for drawing my attention to these two areas of needed reform, each was given greater depth and urgency by two personal experiences during the course of my research.

A Rough Ride in Washington

In November 2005, as the national release of my documentary *Why We Fight* approached, I visited Washington for a follow-up visit with Arizona senator John McCain, who appears in the film. When the film premiered at the Sundance Film Festival earlier that year, and in subsequent test screenings, McCain had wowed audiences with his outspoken words onscreen. Referring to the evolution of U.S. foreign policy, he had said, "Where the debate and controversy begins is, how far does the United States go? And when does it go from a force for good to a force of imperialism?" On the subject of defense industry corruption, the senator declared: "President Eisenhower's concern about the military-industrial complex—his words have unfortunately come true. He was worried that priorities are set by what benefits corporations as opposed to what benefits the country."

As a courtesy, and in the hope that he might make an appearance at the film's theatrical premiere, I arranged a visit with Senator McCain. That morning, security at the Russell Office Building was lighter than I'd expected, and I found myself searching the halls with time to kill.

Drifting through those corridors of power as flurries of lobbyists and news crews scurried to grab the attention of this senator or that, I wondered whether I was more awed by the sheer power concentrated inside the building or by the task facing anyone hoping to make a dent in its corruption. Each time I visit Washington, I feel like Frank Capra's Mr. Smith, part of an age-old American dream of taking my cause to Capitol Hill.

When I entered Senator McCain's office that day, twenty minutes before my scheduled appointment, his receptionist was busy fielding a torrent of calls. *"Senator McCain's office, please hold,"* she said repeatedly. *"The office of Senator McCain, please hold . . ."* She pointed me to a seat on the couch. On a TV flickering silently in the reception area, I saw that that morning Nevada senator Harry Reid had forced a closed Senate session to discuss the administration's handling of prewar intelligence on Iraq. The Senate was in a frenzy of partisan posturing. Outside the Beltway, I wondered if Americans even cared at all.

The calls coming in to the receptionist seemed to suggest they did. From her responses, the callers were concerned with an array of subjects facing the senator. *"The Senator is unavailable at the moment,"* she would say. *"May I pass on a message? Yes, he is familiar with that issue. You say you support it? Yes? I will pass that on to the Senator. Thank you for calling."* Some version of this conversation (some expressing support, others dissent on various issues) was repeated ten times in the first fifteen minutes I spent waiting.

During a lull, I approached the receptionist and asked her how many such calls she fields each day. "Oh, hundreds," she said, smiling, adding that what comes to her is just a small fraction of all the calls. "Is there a system for passing all this on to the senator?" I asked. "Oh yes," she replied, brandishing a steno pad with an immaculate handwritten tally of the views expressed. "I share this with him at the end of the day." Impressed and inspired, I returned to the visitor's couch. For a moment, Washington seemed to be working for America.

As I waited, though, I overheard a conversation on the opposite side of the room among a group of businessmen seated at a conference table with what appeared to be two of the senator's staffers. I hid behind a sailing magazine and pretended not to listen. From what I could gather, the businessmen represented a defense interest seeking the senator's support for some sort of guidance system produced by their firm.

Since my film examines the influence of military-industrial-congressional collusion, the situation could not have been more ironic. I'd been in Washington for barely an hour and was already witnessing in microcosm the tension of forces acting upon policy making. On my right, the voices of Eisenhower's "alert and knowledgeable citizenry," seeking their senator's ear through his receptionist's headset. On my left, representatives of the military-industrial sector, seeking with quiet confidence to influence the senator on a matter of mutual interest.

A balanced picture? How could it be, really? As Charles Lewis so bluntly put it, "given the enormous costs of elections and the need for members of Congress to bring home jobs, the most important people for any politician, Republican or Democrat, are those whose companies write big checks and create jobs."

Sitting in that waiting room, with the hopes of representative democracy on my right and the dangers of corrupt capitalism on my left, the problem was laid bare. I wondered: *What if I could build a wall right here, to separate these two? Why were the founding fathers so aware of the need to build what Jefferson called a "wall of separation" between church and state and to keep the branches of government separate from one another, and yet unaware of the potential for industrial capitalism to undermine the very framework they so meticulously built?*

It's noteworthy that 1776, the year the Declaration of Independence was signed, was also the year that Adam Smith published his influential work *The Wealth of Nations*, widely seen as the Bible of the modern "free market" system. By 1791, Smith's ideas were influential enough to have been contested by the first secretary of the Treasury, Alexander Hamilton, in his "Report on Manufactures." Yet, in drafting the Constitution, the framers failed to provide any real structural defense against the future capacity of industrial corporations and other actors in the free market system to exert influence over policy making.

Two centuries later, the question must now be asked: *What defenses can we construct to counteract the corrosive influence of money?* John McCain himself co-sponsored the 2002 McCain-Feingold Act, a bipartisan piece of legislation intended to better regulate the financing of political campaigns. The bill especially targeted soft money—corporate and union contributions that bypass federal limits by being donated not to the candidate but to independent pressure groups.

Yet beyond the addition of the now hackneyed tagline in political ads, "I'm Senator So-and-So and I approve this message," the act has done more to reroute the flow of campaign finance corruption than to arrest it. Such techniques as "bundling," for example, enable a contributor to gather donations from several different donors and curry favor by presenting the sum of these to a campaign, thus skirting the soft money limits of McCain-Feingold.

As Chuck Spinney so clearly explained, actors in any system work to bypass the limits placed on them. Somewhere between McCain-Feingold's intent and implementation, deeply vested interests with uncompromising patterns of corruption have played an interfering role. And yet even McCain-Feingold, at its best, would only have regulated a few small arteries of corruption in the larger campaign finance system. To prevent such systemwide techniques as political engineering, an entire "wall of separation" is needed.

So, what hope is there for deeper reform of the campaign finance system? For many Americans, the idea of converting our electoral system to one wholly driven by public financing seems an absurd abandonment of the free market. As in so many other cases, the public increasingly not only accepts but assumes that areas of public life—including the financing of elections—will be dominated by private forces. This viewpoint reflects what philanthropist and political scientist George Soros calls "market fundamentalism," an overzealous reliance on the forces of the marketplace to meet society's needs. Like so many "isms," market fundamentalism takes some elements of truth—e.g., that profit-seeking enterprises can be efficient, that governments can be inefficient, that some level of competition is inherent in the human spirit, and that government regulation can be as problematic as that which it seeks to regulate—and spins these into an overzealous ideology.

Elections driven dominantly by public financing are commonplace in such Western industrialized democracies as Britain, Germany, and France. So there is no reason that America cannot seriously consider such an option. At a time when the evidence is clear that the transfer of public functions to private corporations has yielded disastrous results—from Enron's speculation on California's deregulated power grid to Halliburton's overcharging of U.S. taxpayers—questioning market fundamentalism in public policy should be not only acceptable but required.

To be fair, beyond the predictable resistance from those who profit from the way the system currently works, such a radical conversion would pose its own challenges. First, one would have to determine where the government should get the money to pay for campaigns. A quick answer might be from the savings in the reduction of corporate overcharges to the federal government. As a crude example, in 2005, the Pentagon's Defense Contract Audit Agency confirmed over $213 million in overcharges by Halliburton between 2003 and 2004, enough to fund a presidential candidacy even at today's level of expenditure. Combined with the overcharges of so many other companies, there would no doubt be sufficient savings to support a robust public election system. A second, more considered answer is that without the capacity to draw on such massive resources from the corporate sector, politicians would be forced to spend a good deal less, finding cheaper ways to reach the public than expensive television commercials and print ads.

Today in America, public campaign finance is an option that a candidate may exercise if it is in his or her interest to do so, accepting that it imposes certain overall spending limits. The exercise of this option can also be strategically threatened by candidates receiving significant private support but seeking to appear more populist than their opponents, as demonstrated by the 2008 presidential candidacies of Senators John McCain and Barack Obama—each of whom at one time or another obliquely hinted at accepting public financing. But this is a far cry from a system in which public financing is truly the rule and private the exception.

Of course, there's no guarantee that a shift to publicly financed elections would not produce its own forms of mischief, shifting the source of corruption from the private sector to the public. A quick glance at the corrupt practice of redistricting reveals that public control in no way guarantees ethical standards. Spinney supports the need for public financing of elections, but warns that it "only solves half the problem. You can stop the flow of money that way. But the corporate interests can still use political engineering to bring or withhold jobs to districts to incentivize desired congressional behavior."

Still, half the battle is a start.

To deal with the other half, political engineering must be tackled. Both the government and the public have strong incentives for doing so. Clearly, it is in the government's interest not to be overcharged for the goods and services it purchases. And no matter how many people in a given district benefit from the extra jobs a fat corporate contract brings, those benefits cannot possibly outweigh the excess tax burden imposed on the wider public as a consequence of such noncompetition.

Of course, the impetus for reform is unlikely to come from those already part of a corrupt venture. No matter how much public influence over Congress is outweighed by that of corporations, those citizens calling McCain's office are a vital—likely *the* vital—factor in making meaningful change. As consumer activist and political lightning rod Ralph Nader has noted, "Think of how many people in this country belong to *bird-watching* clubs. Now imagine that many people belonged to local *congress-watch* groups. You'd have a different country."

We hear arguments against this kind of idealism every day. Yet, despite the too oft-noted apathy among large cross sections of the public toward the Iraq War and other crises, a measure of political awakening has taken place in recent years, particularly among young Americans. The presidential candidacy of Howard Dean in 2004 and more recently the candidacy of Barack Obama have been the primary staging grounds for this development—with the Internet and individual contributions taking on particular new relevance. Still, the full implications remain to be seen. Is this new spirit of engagement simply a reflection of spiraling antipathy toward George W. Bush? Will it abate upon the election of his successor? Or will it persist?

Phrases like "where is the outrage?" are misguided in that they blame the American people—so many of whom already find themselves struggling to make ends meet—for not making the time to inform themselves more fully and mount resistance. The very idea of seeking change from "the American people" is deceptive, since the public is an impossibly complex grouping: countless subsets of the population with varying degrees of inclination, understanding, and ability to seek reform. So, no one prescription for what everyday people can do can possibly be applied across the board. Yet it's clear that reforming the way money influences the American system is unlikely to be driven by those in Congress. Only everyday people in organized groups—some already in existence, others still to come—will be instrumental in bringing about reform. As Margaret Mead once said, "Never doubt that a small group of thoughtful, committed people can change the world. Indeed, it's the only thing that ever has."

I would submit that if we have come to a point as a society where it seems naive to suggest that such a process of citizen-driven reform is possible, then our founding principles of government "with the consent of the governed" are themselves naive, the public's voice already drowned out by that of a corporate-political elite. And yet, given the egregious failures of the American system during the Bush years, it may be equally naive to imagine that America can continue on its current path. To turn on the evening news today is to watch a cavalcade of crises—economic, political, and spiritual. They are global problems, and America is far from the only involved party. But increasingly, from Katrina to Baghdad to the housing crisis to the oil crisis to corporate scandals to a broken health care system and a seeming epidemic of violence across American society, the nation's systemic shortcomings are starting to form a disconcerting pattern that reveals the enormous cost of maintaining the status quo.

In the fall of 2008, ABC Television plans to broadcast *Earth 2100*, a special report on global crises. When a major network like ABC devotes a primetime slot usually reserved for *Desperate Housewives* and *Dancing with the Stars* to examining the question, "Are we living in the last century of our civilization?" it may just be that fears about sustainability itself have become the catalyst needed to compel the public to engage in a deeper re-evaluation of the American system.

Which returns me to John McCain's office, where the plot began to thicken. I didn't get to see the senator, but met instead with his chief of staff, Mark Salter. I explained to him my hopes for the film and the fact that Senator McCain's outspoken remarks in it were proving popular with audiences weary of Washington. I indicated my desire that we arrange events to inspire public discourse at which the senator might appear. Slater seemed mildly disinterested and thanked me perfunctorily for my visit.

Before the film was released nationally in January 2006, I sent a finished copy to Mr. Salter as a matter of protocol, but did not hear from him again until after the release. When I did, he was agitated. Over several days, I received repeated phone calls from Salter and other members of McCain's staff. They had heard of the film and wondered what it was about. It became clear in talking to Salter that he had neither seen the film nor recalled meeting me the previous November. I reminded him of our meeting and pointed out that a copy of the film was actually sitting in his office. He asked me to hold, presumably confirmed this, then returned awkwardly to say he would get back to me.

When next I heard from Mr. Salter, it wasn't pretty. He clearly didn't share my enthusiasm (or that of audiences) for McCain's role in the film. He felt the senator's critical comments about the dangers of preemption and of American imperialism gave the impression that McCain was opposed to the Iraq War, which Salter assured me he wasn't. But one moment in the film in particular seemed to be the source of his greatest concern. About forty-five minutes into the film, in response to a question about the controversial awarding of no-bid contracts to Vice President Cheney's former employer Halliburton, McCain concedes: "It looks bad. It looks bad. And apparently, Halliburton more than once has overcharged the federal government. That's wrong." When pressed on how he would tackle this problem, McCain bluntly declares onscreen: "I would have a public investigation of what they've done."

At that moment a phone rings and Senator McCain is advised by an offscreen staffer that Vice President Cheney is calling. With an apologetic laugh, McCain excuses himself. "The vice president's on the phone," he stammers, disappearing offscreen, leaving the camera rolling on his empty chair.

For audiences, this moment tends to generate a laugh of recognition. Having heard from countless viewers, I've found that different people see the scene differently. Some see McCain's sudden departure as perfectly normal. He's a high-ranking Republican senator. The vice president, who is after all the president of the Senate, is calling. It's a time of war. An interview is simply a lower priority. Others see McCain's departure as evidence of too close a relationship with the vice president. They note a certain anxiety and even subservience in McCain's body language. To those who see the scene as standard procedure, this is nothing more than his awkwardness at leaving an interview in midstream. To a third small group of conspiracy theorists, McCain's reaction is further evidence of Dick Cheney's omnipotence in Washington. One viewer laughingly told me that, given the administration's penchant for wiretapping, "perhaps Mr. Cheney had decided the interview had gone on long enough."

Jokes aside, most viewers do sense a special awkwardness in

McCain's body language when he gets a call from Cheney while answering a question about the appearance of improprieties by Halliburton. It is akin to the awkwardness that arises when one talks badly about a person who then suddenly enters the room.

When McCain's office expressed their concern, I was initially confused. If anything, I thought they might be worried that the scene could be interpreted as suggesting close ties between McCain and Cheney. When Salter instead told me that I was "making it look like John McCain was critical of the vice president," and that "Vice President Cheney has nothing to do with Halliburton," I began to realize that what he was objecting to was not that McCain might seem too close to Cheney, but rather not close enough. Salter then demanded I send him a transcript of the senator's entire interview, not just the parts that appear in the film. Since out of the more than twenty interviewees who appear in the film no one else had seen any such thing, and since I valued the film's independence from political pressure, I told Salter I did not feel comfortable doing that but would seek advice from others on how to proceed.

Salter next resorted to threats, including that, unless I complied, he would exert pressure on the film's principal funder, the British Broadcasting Corporation, to never work with me again. I responded that I thought the BBC would be unlikely to welcome such pressure from an irate chief of staff to a senator. I wasn't trying to be snide. I recognized that he was genuinely outraged. And in many ways his job requires him to be one step ahead of news stories involving the senator. Having just threatened me, Salter now changed gears, appealing to my better instincts. "When Senator McCain sat down to talk to you, he thought he was talking to a television crew from the BBC," he explained. I said I understood that, and indeed, the film was originally produced for broadcast by the BBC, but as luck would have it, I was later able to secure a U.S. theatrical release. Then something troubling dawned on me.

"If you don't mind my asking," I submitted, "are you saying that there are things Senator McCain will say to a British audience that he isn't comfortable saying to the American people?"

Needless to say, this didn't help the situation.

Salter reiterated his threats to punish me by contacting the BBC and telling the media I had manipulated the senator's words. I countered that the senator speaks in complete sentences in the film and that the words are his own. I also knew that, far from having included McCain's most controversial comments in the film, I had left certain remarks that were more dangerous to his presidential chances on the cutting-room floor. In an explanation of the roots of neoconservatism, for example, McCain had counted himself among the neocons, saying, "in some ways, I am one, in some ways." Given the unraveling of public confidence in the neoconservatives that took place between the time Senator McCain was interviewed and the film's completion, his remark would certainly have drawn fire. Had I intended to tarnish him, I would have included it. But it was simply not material to my inquiry. I was also surprised that Salter had offered explanations of Vice President Cheney's relationship (or lack thereof) to Halliburton. At one point, hearing how focused he was on defending Cheney's record, I intimated that, if I didn't know better, I would have thought he worked for the vice president.

I now recognize that it was surely not lost on Salter that Senator McCain might be running for president in 2008, and that, already facing a struggle to appeal to the Republican base, the last thing he needed was to be portrayed as out of sync with the White House. This may be why Salter's efforts didn't end when the phone call was over.

On February 8, 2006, Mark Salter made good on his promise to smear my name in the media. In an article in *Roll Call* entitled "An Angry Star Is Born," Mary Ann Akers wrote: "Attention, Sen. Barack Obama (D–Ill.): You're not the only punching bag for Sen. John McCain (R–Ariz.). The 2008 presidential hopeful is also really mad at the producer of the Sundance Film Festival award-winning film 'Why We Fight'. . . . McCain—and especially his chief of staff—think the movie producer intentionally twisted McCain's few lines in the film so that he comes off as critical of Vice President Cheney." The article goes on specifically to quote Salter as calling me a "slippery son of a gun" and accusing me of " 'doing manipulative editing' to make it look like McCain is questioning Cheney's involvement in the awarding of contracts to Halliburton. . . ."

Salter is then quoted as offering *Roll Call* the same confusing argument he gave me about British television: " 'McCain thought he was doing an interview on Iraq with the BBC . . . turns out to be a theatrically released film in the United States.' " Salter also offered the same disclaimer on McCain's fondness for Cheney as he had to me over the phone. The senator, the article quoted Salter as saying, has "complete respect for Mr. Cheney's integrity."

Salter was also true to his promise that my bosses at the BBC would hear from him about my alleged misconduct. He contacted them, after which they called me, a bit nonplussed. Predictably, they were more thrown by the forcefulness of his approach than by any concern about the film's content.

Ultimately, this episode came and went without further ado, and Salter's activities subsided. My assumption looking back is that it was all about damage control to ensure that the senator's presidential ambitions were not imperiled by a film in which he could be seen as critical of the Bush administration or the Iraq War. They hoped to distance McCain from his own words, which was particularly disheartening for me, as I had seen so many audiences be so moved by them.

In this eye-opening experience, while trying simply to study the forces corrupting public policy, I became for one brief moment their target, a perceived obstacle to the unimpeded flow of business as usual. Of course, Mark Salter was not trying to sell me a product or service but was simply doing his job, guarding an invisible security barrier behind which the elite machinery of corporate-political power in America proceeds with contempt for public scrutiny. The episode was also a blatant demonstration of the executive's power over Congress. Salter and McCain's concern about offending Cheney was rooted in this troubling dynamic. More troubling were the passionate lengths to which they would go to pressure a filmmaker who had chosen to include Mr. McCain's comments in a discussion among several voices on the controversial subject of Halliburton.

The threats, the smears, the effort to impact my career—all of it gave me a firsthand glimpse of the forces everyday people would face in any effort to seek reform. Most pointed, it bears remembering that what was at stake, after all, was McCain's statement that the controversy surrounding Halliburton "looks bad."

Looking back on the incident, I would have to echo Senator McCain in saying, "It looks bad."

You're on Your Way to Where?!

During the same period in which I found myself the target of Mark Salter's full-court-press in Washington, I had the privilege to be invited to show my film and speak at the U.S. Military Academy at West Point. Taking place on the forty-fifth anniversary of Eisenhower's Farewell Address, this visit to Ike's alma mater would prove to be the first of many during which an invigorating and far-reaching dialogue developed between myself, members of West Point's faculty, and their cadets. In stark contrast to the abrasiveness and backhanded activities of Senator McCain's staff, the soldiers, scholars, and cadets I met at West Point embraced me and my line of inquiry, doing a great deal to inform the pages of this book and, in particular, to give clearer shape to my thoughts about the problematic impact of the National Security Act of 1947.

Located in wooded isolation some fifty miles north of New York City, West Point very much occupies its own intellectual orbit, not entirely removed from the workings of the American defense establishment, yet not entirely in sync with them either. On my first drive there, I recall the incredulity with which friends and family reacted when I called from the road to tell them where I was going. They were surprised that a military academy would even show a film like *Why We Fight*, let alone invite a self-acknowledged critic of U.S. defense policy to address its best and brightest.

As it turns out, this incredulity reflects a prejudice that sweepingly and mistakenly equates bad foreign policy with those entrusted to implement it. While soldiers come in all types and no single generalization can be made, one finds an inspiring abundance on West Point's faculty of serious thinkers who feel a responsibility not only to train their cadets in the military arts but to educate them more broadly about the strengths and weaknesses of the nation's foreign policy system.

When *The New Yorker*'s Ben McGrath accompanied me on my second visit to the Academy two months later, he noted this remarkable phenomenon. Colonel Michael Meese, head of the Social Sciences Department and the son of Ronald Reagan's attorney general Edwin Meese, told McGrath that by having me visit and show my film, he hoped to show the cadets that "critical thinking is not insubordination."

In the months that followed, I made several more visits to the Academy, each time showing the film and speaking to ever larger groups of cadets. On my third appearance, which was attended by more than eight hundred uniformed young future officers, I had the honor to be accompanied by Colonel Lawrence Wilkerson. I was already at work on this book, and the ensuing dialogue greatly informed my understanding of the importance of civilian-military relations per se and, in particular, of Wilkerson's goal of "a new national security act."

In his opening remarks, Wilkerson underscored the film's theme that the military-industrial complex has become the very force that Eisenhower feared, exercising disfiguring influence on the policies that members of the armed forces are asked to carry out. "It has come to a point," he warned, "where the military-industrial complex is so influential on the fateful decisions a president makes that it's dangerous for your republic."

A cadet stood to ask a courageous question. "After watching the film and seeing the evidence presented," he began, cautiously, "I'm just wondering how you think we should feel as future officers who are going to be in the ranks of the military? How can we feel just and good about being part of a system that seems so corrupt?"

It was clearly not lost on the cadet that Wilkerson was a soldier of conscience—one who had, when push came to shove, gone toe-to-toe with Vice President Cheney on the issue of torture. Without alluding to his own stance, Wilkerson cited several former West Point graduates as examples of men who, when necessary, exerted resistance to the plans of the civilians under whom they served. General Shinseki was one of those he mentioned as a military officer who spoke truth to power in his sober assessments of the troop strength America would need to succeed in Iraq.

In the discussion that followed, Wilkerson and other high-ranking members of West Point's faculty emphasized that, though U.S. military policy requires obedience from those in uniform, that obedience is not supposed to be blind. Like Shinseki and Eisenhower before him, a thinking officer can, under extreme circumstances, feel compelled to exert a measure of resistance to policies that have drifted out of control or come to threaten fundamental laws or belief systems. As a civilian, I added that the cadet's very question—about his own role in the larger scheme of a corruptible system—was an inspiring one. All nations have militaries, and a certain element of warmaking is a basic fact of life. Yet the cadet who has the courage to ask such a precise and probing question before his peers, teachers, and commanding officers is one who promises to bring the qualities of restraint and conscience to the military he serves.

French Prime Minister Clemenceau's famous remark that "War is too important to be left to the generals" has become a tenet of contemporary civilian-military relations. In considering foreign policy, the idea is that military personnel are somehow too trigger-happy to make sound decisions, and instead require the steady hand of civilians, who will make the use of military force a last resort.

Yet, if the Iraq War has taught us anything, it is that it may be just as dangerous (or even more so) to put warmaking exclusively in the hands of civilians like Cheney, Rumsfeld, and their neoconservative underlings, whose life-and-death decisions are made in air-conditioned rooms thousands of miles from their real-life consequences. When Donald Rumsfeld signaled from his rarefied height at the Pentagon his tacit approval of forms of abusive treatment of detainees, one has to think, even allowing for certain soldiers who are prone to violence, that carrying out such a policy in the field must be far harder to stomach than checking a box to initial a general policy order from halfway around the globe.

Recalling that the military is situated in the executive branch, further invitations to West Point following the discussion with Wilkerson reflected heartening efforts at reforming runaway executive power from within. According to Wilkerson, who has served the executive branch both in and out of uniform, such reform is desperately needed, and for it to take place, the combined efforts of civilian and military leaders will be required. They must arrive at a new paradigm for America's foreign policy, one that can address the external threats the nation faces as well as the internal fractures wrought by past efforts to do so.

"What I'm asking people to think about," Wilkerson declares, "is a new national security act, a new structure to address the world that we now confront. Because it's been over a half century since we did the last National Security Act. And the world's changed a lot. And part of the reason President Bush and Vice President Cheney have done what they've done is that the bureaucracy that's grown up around the '47 act has become sclerotic. It's become difficult to get to move. And so, what presidents do is, they go around it."

However effective the 1947 National Security Act may have been in its day, it has over time become problematic in two ways. First, in foreign affairs, it is ill-suited to serve the nation's contemporary security needs. Second, its domestic impact has been to disturb the vital balance of power between the branches. At the time the act was implemented, it was designed to help America defend itself from the threat posed by the Soviet Union. By contrast, the threats America faces today are of a far more intricate and counterintuitive nature than a single rival state.

Traditional military threats have been in many ways overshadowed today by nontraditional ones: climate change, infectious diseases, overpopulation, resource scarcity, nonstate terror, and international economic disorder. These and other sources of international instability are of increasing concern on an ever more interconnected planet, requiring radical solutions and unprecedented levels of international coordination.

Yet efforts at reform to date have been too confined by outmoded Cold War thinking.

The recent establishment of several new foreign policy and defense instruments, such as the Office of Homeland Security, for example, attests to a perception in Washington that America's current system is inadequate to meet these emerging security challenges. Yet such new instruments have only been introduced on an ad hoc basis; they are thus limited both in their potential effectiveness to defend the country and in their inability to better distribute power between the various branches and agencies. The National Intelligence Program was introduced in 2004 to replace what the 1947 act, as amended, had called the National Foreign Intelligence Program. The renaming of this program was accompanied by the creation of an executive branch post—"Director of National Intelligence"—to oversee the entire U.S. intelligence community. The goal was to ensure better cooperation between its various agencies in the wake of 9/11. And yet, by adding still another high-level official with directing reporting responsibilities to the president, the program serves only to further strengthen the executive.

What is needed is something far more comprehensive, both from a foreign and a domestic policy perspective. Thankfully, the two goals are closely linked. In a world of traditional threats, there's always an argument for the executive's capacity to move more quickly and cogently than a body of parliamentarians. By contrast, in a world of nontraditional threats, where an environmental disaster can set off a chain reaction of infectious diseases, refugee migration, market downturns, and even armed conflict, the response must be more textured and interdisciplinary. A new national security act must therefore swing the pendulum of power back from an executive's capacity to command swift military action to the complex and delicate balance in which the legislative branch's capacity to deliberate the full complexity of any given situation acts as a check. Likewise, given the multinational nature of the threats and the multilateral coordination required to meet global challenges (from policing international terror to addressing climate crises), a new act must redistribute power inside the executive branch from "the overgrown military establishment" that the Department of Defense has become back to the seat of international cooperation: the State Department.

Wilkerson, for one, does not believe all administrations are destined to conduct themselves like the Bush administration. Rather, he sees his experience as a worst-case test of the system's vulnerability. "In G. W. Bush," he says, "we see a president who has been able to concentrate power unlike any president in our history, in his vice president, in his secretary of defense, and therefore in the military instrument. Good leaders, like Truman, Eisenhower, and others, have tried to balance our founding republican values with keeping us as safe as is reasonably possible. And they managed reasonably well for almost half a century. But in the aftermath of the Cold War, and in an accelerated and stunning fashion during the Bush presidency, you see these things combine with bad leadership to produce disastrous consequences."

Whereas reducing the corrupting influence of money on public policy making is an avenue of reform that must be driven by the public, the task of conceiving, drafting, and introducing a new national security act is one that must be spearheaded by people with an intimate knowledge of our existing foreign policy system.

Given the nature of military hierarchy, the politics of patriotism, and the rarity of men like Shinseki willing to put principle before job security, the task would most likely be best met by retired high-ranking military and civilian officials like Wilkerson. Having served the machine faithfully for long enough to discover its shortcomings, they are the people best qualified to understand how to fix the problems within the bureaucratic and political realities of Washington.

This would require, of course, bringing civilian-military relations to a place of improved effort and understanding, and rejecting the pattern in recent years of repressing voices of dissent. In trying to imagine such an ideal of civilian-military cooperation, my ongoing visits to West Point have become a source of great inspiration.

During a question-and-answer session on my second visit, a mild-mannered young cadet rose to ask a question. "What do you hope to accomplish, sir?"

Unaccustomed to being called sir, I smiled for a moment before answering.

"I hope by showing my film, and talking and writing, to encourage people to understand that it is not just possible but necessary for us all to address these fundamental issues the republic faces as we contemplate an uncertain future."

Apparently satisfied with my answer, he said "thank you" and sat back down.

But I wasn't really finished.

"Wait a minute," I said, turning the tables, "I want to ask you a question."

He rose.

"How do you think I am going to do?" I asked.

He answered instantly and matter-of-factly before sitting back down: "I hope well, sir."

Notes

INTRODUCTION

1 Webster's New Millennium Dictionary of English, Preview Edition. Lexico Publishing Group, http://dictionary.reference.com/browse/mission%20creep. 8/6/08.
2 George Bush and Brent Scrowcroft, *A World Transformed* (New York: Knopf, 1998) p. 489.

CHAPTER 1

1 Interview with Major Mark "Fuji" Hoehn. December 2003. Interview by author.
2 Interview with Col. Dave "Tooms" Toomey. December 2003. Interview by author.
3 See David S. Cloud, "Former Top General in Iraq Faults Bush Administration," *New York Times*, October 12, 2007.
4 Patrick E. Tyler, "U.S. Strategy Plan Calls for Insuring No Rivals Develop: A One-Superpower World," *New York Times*, March 8, 1992.
5 Robert Kagan and William Kristol, "Toward a Neo-Reaganite Foreign Policy," *Foreign Affairs*, July/August 2006.
6 William Jefferson Clinton, "Executive Order: Prohibiting Transactions with Terrorists Who Threaten to Disrupt the Middle East Peace Process," PNAC, August 22, 1998.
7 Interview with Bill Kristol from the documentary *Why We Fight*, Eugene Jarecki, Sony Pictures, 2005.
8 Project for the New American Century (PNAC. 71), *Rebuilding America's Defenses*, 2000.
9 George W. Bush, Second Gore-Bush Presidential Debate, October 11, 2000.
10 Interview with Richard Perle. March 2004. Interview by Mary Jane Robinson.
11 Interview with Eliot Cohen. July 2003. Interview byMary Jane Robinson.
12 Seymour Hersh, "Selective Intelligence," *New Yorker*, May 12, 2003.
13 Francis Fukuyama, *America at the Crossroads* (Princeton: Yale University Press, 2006), p. 14.
14 Irwin M. Stelzer, *The Neocon Reader* (New York: Grove Press, 2004). Front cover.

15 Robert Kagan, "Neocon Nation: Neoconservatism c. 1776," *World Affairs* (Spring 2008).
16 Shadia B. Drury, *Leo Strauss and the American Right* (New York: Palgrave Macmillan, 1999), pp. 12, 58.
17 "Deputy Secretary Wolfowitz Interview with Sam Tannenhaus." *Vanity Fair*, May 9, 2003.
18 Albert Wohlstetter, "The Delicate Balance of Terror," P-1472, November 6, 1958; www.search.rand.org/search/?input-form=rand=simple&query=The+Delicate+Balance+of+Terror].
19 Ibid.
20 Francis Fukuyama, "After Neoconservatism," *New York Times Magazine*, February 19, 2006; www.nytimes.com/2006/02/19/magazine/neo.html.
21 Michael Novak, "Neocons: Some Memories," *National Review* online, May 20, 2003.
22 Ronald Reagan, "Remarks at a Luncheon Hosted by the New Jersey Chamber of Commerce in Somerset," October 13, 1987.
23 Interview with John McCain. February 11, 2005. Interview by Mary Jane Robinson.
24 Interview with William Kristol. July 24, 2003. Interview by author.
25 Robert Kagan, *Dangerous Nation: America's Place in the World, from Its Earliest Days to the Dawn of the 20th Century* (New York: Alfred A. Knopf, 2006), p. 37.
26 Robert Kagan, "Cowboy Nation: Against the Myth of American innocence," *The New Republic*, October 23, 2006.
27 Bernard Bailyn, ed. *Pamphlets of the American Revolution 1750–1776* (Cambridge, MA.: Belknap Press of Harvard University Press, 1965), p. 22.
28 "Political Observations" (1795-04-20); also in *Letters and Other Writings of James Madison* (1865), Vol. IV, p. 491.
29 James Madison, *Letters and Other Writings of James Madison* (Philadelphia: J.B. Lippincott & Co., 1865), pp. 131, 491.
30 Ibid., p. 131.
31 Alexander Hamilton, John Jay, and James Madison, *The Federalist on the New Constitution* (Glazier, Masters & Co., 1831), p. 480.
32 Jennifer K. Elsea and Richard F. Grimmett, "Declarations of War and Authorization for the Use of Military Force: Historical Background and Legal Implications." Congressional Research Service Report RL31133, August 11, 2006.
33 Richard F. Grimmett, "Instances of Use of United States Armed Forces Abroad 1798–2004." Congressional Research Service Report TL30172, October 5, 2004.
34 John O'Sullivan, "Annexation," *United States Magazine and Democratic Review*, vol. *17*, no. 1 (July–August 1845), pp. 5–10.
35 Robert Dallek, *Franklin D. Roosevelt and American Foreign Policy, 1932–1945* (Oxford: Oxford University Press, 1979), p. 165.
36 Fukuyama, *America at the Crossroads*, p. xi.
37 Stephen B. Smith, *Reading Leo Strauss: Politics, Philosophy, Judaism* (Chicago: University of Chicago Press, 2006), p. 188.
38 Fukuyama, *America at the Crossroads*, p. 49.

39 Ibid., p. 115.
40 Project for the New American Century, Letter to George W. Bush. September 20, 2001; www.newamericancentury.org/Bushletter.htm (viewed 1/29/08).

CHAPTER 2

1 Robert Dallek, *Franklin D. Roosevelt and American Foreign Policy, 1932–1945* (Oxford: Oxford University Press, 1979), p. 75.
2 Gallup Poll #171, September 22, 1939.
3 Dallek, *Franklin D. Roosevelt and American Foreign Policy,* p. 202.
4 Dallek, *Franklin D. Roosevelt and American Foreign Policy,* p. 101.
5 "Political Observations" (1795-04-20); also in *Letters and Other Writings of James Madison* (1865), Vol. IV, p. 491.
6 Dallek, *Franklin D. Roosevelt and American Foreign Policy,* p. 109.
7 Ibid., p. 201.
8 Ibid., p. 200.
9 Ibid., p. 140.
10 Stinnett, *Day of Deceit*, p. 275.
11 Gordon Prange, *At Dawn We Slept: The Untold Story of Pearl Harbor* (New York: Penguin, 1991), p. xi.
12 Robert Stinnett, *Day of Deceit: The Truth About FDR and Pearl Harbor* (New York: Free Press, 1999), p. 7.
13 John Costello, *The Pacific War* (New York: HarperCollins, 1982), pp. 125–26.
14 Admiral James Richardson, commander of the Pacific Fleet, who protested on more than one occasion to FDR that the U.S. fleet at Pearl Harbor was vulnerable to attack, later quoted Roosevelt as having said: "Sooner or later the Japanese would commit an overt act against the United States and the nation would be willing to enter the war"—Stinnet, *Day of Deceit*, p. 11.
15 George Morgenstern, *Pearl Harbor: The Story of the Secret War* (New York: Devin-Adair Company, 1947), p. 342.
16 Stinnett, *Day of Deceit*, p. 179.
17 Stinnett, *Day of Deceit,* p. xiv.
18 Husband E. Kimmel, *Admiral Kimmel's Story* (Chicago: H. Regnery Company, 1955), pp. 2–4.
19 Ibid., pp. 84–88.
20 Stinnett, *Day of Deceit*, p. 255.
21 Ibid.
22 David Kahn, "Did Roosevelt Know?," *The New York Review of Books*, November 2, 2000, Volume 47, Number 17.
23 Lawrence Wright, *The Looming Tower: Al Qaeda and the Road to 9/11* (New York: Alfred A. Knopf, 2006).
24 D. W. Brogan, *American Character* (New York: Alfred A. Knopf, 1994), pp. 163–64 cited in Michael S. Sherry, *In the Shadow of War* (New Haven: Yale University Press, 1995) chap. 2, note 13.
25 Susan B. Carter, et al., eds., *Historical Statistics of the United States.* Vol. 5 (Cambridge: Cambridge University Press, 2006).

26 Ibid.
27 Sherry, *In the Shadow of War*, p. 69.
28 Dwight D. Eisenhower, Letter to Milton Eisenhower, September 1, 1939, Eisenhower Presidential Library.
29 Eugenia Kaledin, *Daily Life in the United States, 1940–1959: Shifting Worlds* (Westport, CT: Greenwood Press, 2000).
30 Michael Sherry, *In the Shadow of War: The United States Since the 1930s* (Hartford: Yale University Press, 1995), p. 102.
31 Harriet Sigerman, "Oral History of Fanny Christina Hill," Columbia Documentary History of American Women Since 1941.
32 David Wyatt, *Five Fires: Race, Catastrophe, and the Shaping of California* (New York: Oxford University Press, 1999), p. 158.
33 Gerald D. Nash, *The American West Transformed: The Impact of the Second World War* (Bloomington: Indiana University Press, 1985).
34 Katharine Q. Seelye, "When Hollywood's Big Guns Come Right from the Source," *New York Times*, June 10, 2002.
35 Frank Capra, *The Name Above the Title* (New York: Da Capo Press, 1997), pp. 326–27.
36 Franklin Delano Roosevelt speaking at Ogelthorpe University, Atlanta, Georgia, May 22, 1932.
37 Franklin Delano Roosevelt, "A Date with Destiny," Speech before Democratic National Convention, Philadelphia, Pennsylvania, June 27, 1936.
38 Roland Marchand, *Creating the Corporate Soul* (Berkeley: University of California Press, 1998), p. 302.
39 Sherry, *In the Shadow of War*, p. 74.
40 "Fascismo," *Enciclopedia Italiana* edizione 1949, Vol. XI5 (Rome: Instituto della Enciclopedia Italiana, 1951), p. 847.
41 Franklin Delano Roosevelt, "Message to Congress on Curbing Monopolies," April 29, 1938.
42 Sherry, *In the Shadow of War*, p. 73.
43 Dallek, *Franklin D. Roosevelt and American Foreign Policy*, p. 109.
44 Michael Nelson, "The President and the Court: Reinterpreting the Court-packing Episode of 1937," *Political Science Quarterly*, vol. 103, no. 2 (1988).
45 Harry S. Truman, *Memoirs*, vol. 1 (Garden City: Doubleday, 1955), p. 10.
46 David McCullough, *Truman* (New York: Simon & Schuster, 1992), p. 291.
47 Kai Bird and Lawrence Lifschulzt, eds. *Hiroshima's Shadow* (Branford, CT: Pamphleteer's Press, 1998), p. 131.
48 Gar Alperowitz, *The Decision to Use the Atomic Bomb* (New York: Vintage Books, 1996), p. 23.
49 Martin Sherwin, *A World Destroyed: Hiroshima and Its Legacies* (Stanford, CA: Stanford University Press, 1973), p. 225.
50 Bird and Lifschultz, eds., *Hiroshima's Shadow*, p. 7; Alperovitz, *The Decision to Use the Atomic Bomb*, pp. 34–35, 65, 300.
51 Alperovitz, *The Decision to Use the Atom Bomb*, pp. 75–77.
52 Harry S. Truman, Broadcast to the American People Announcing the Surrender of Germany, May 8, 1945.
53 Admiral William Leahy, *I Was There* (New York: McGraw-Hill, 1950), pp. 440–42.

54 Alperowitz, *The Decision to Use the Atomic Bomb*, p. 300.
55 Ibid., p. 327.
56 Ibid., pp. 326–30. Leahy, *I Was There*, p. 441.
57 Dwight D. Eisenhower, *Mandate for Change, 1953–1956* (New York: Doubleday, 1963), pp. 312–13.
58 Harry S. Truman, Statement announcing the boming of Hiroshima, August 6, 1945.
59 Leahy, *I Was There*, p. 441.
60 Alperovitz, *The Decision to Use the Atom Bomb*, p. 114.
61 Brian L. Villa, "The U.S. Army, Unconditional Surrender, and the Potsdam Proclamation," *Journal of American History*, vol. 63, no. 1 (June 1976), p. 78.
62 Statement by President Harry Truman, May 8, 1945, White House Central Files, Harry S. Truman Library.
63 "Now Japan," *The Washington Post*, May 9, 1945, p. A6.
64 Alperovitz, *The Decision to Use the Atom Bomb*, p. 65.
65 Draft ultimatum presented by the Secretary of War to the President, in U.S. Department of State. FRUS: Potsdam, 1945, Vol. I, pp. 893–94. See also Dale M. Hellegers, *We, the Japanese People: World War II and the Origins of the Japanese Constitution* (Stanford: Stanford University Press, 2001), p. 339.
66 Bird and Lifschulzt, eds., *Hiroshima's Shadow*, pp. 15–17.
67 www.trumanlibrary.org/whistlestop/study_collections/bomb/large/documents/index.php?pagenumber=2&documentid=63&documentdate=1945-07-17&studycollectionid=abomb&groupid.
68 Harry S. Truman, July 1945; www.mbe.doe.gov/me70/manhattan/potsdam_animation.htm.
69 "Einstein Deplores Use of Atom Bomb," *New York Times*, August 19, 1946, p. A1.

CHAPTER 3

1 Harry S. Truman, Speech on the Signing of the UN Charter, San Francisco, June 26, 1945.
2 George Washington, Farewell Address to the Nation, 1796.
3 Martin K. Sorge, *The Other Price of Hitler's War: German Military and Civilian Losses Resulting from World War* (Greenwood Publishing Group, 1986), p. 127.
4 Joseph Stalin, Interview on Pravda Radio, March 14, 1946.
5 A. M. Meerloo, "Atomic War of Nerves: Fear Said to Have Paralyzing or Aggressive Effect," *New York Times*, Letter to the Times, June 2, 1947.
6 Army Signals Corps, "The Armed Forces Screen," No. 91. *National Defense.*
7 Alexander Hamilton, *The Federalist Papers*, No. 8, November 20, 1787.
8 John Lewis Gaddis, *The United States and the Origins of the Cold War* (New York: Columbia University Press, 1972), p. 348.
9 Ibid., pp. 204–06.
10 Walter LaFeber, *America, Russia and the Cold War: 1945–2002* (New York: McGraw-Hill, 2004), pp. 57, 161–62.

11 Ibid., p. 59.
12 Ibid.
13 Harry S. Truman, Address to Congress, March 12, 1947.
14 Interview with Colonel Lawrence Wilkerson. December 23, 2005. Interview by author.
15 John Barry, Michael Hirsh, and Michael Isikoff, "The Roots of Torture," *Newsweek*, May 24, 2004.
16 Karen DeYoung, *Soldier: The Life of Colin Powell* (New York: Alfred A. Knopf, 2006), p. 332.
17 William Kristol, "Reality Check," *Weekly Standard*, October 13, 2003, p. 9.
18 Assistant Attorney General Jay S. Bybee, "Memorandum for Alberto R. Gonzales Counsel to the President, and William J. Haynes II Counsel of the Department of Defense, RE: Application of treaties and laws to al Qaeda and Taliban Detainess," January 22, 2002, p. 2.
19 Jan Crawford Greenburg, Howard L. Berg and Ariane de Vogue, "Sources: Top Bush Advisors Approved 'Enhanced Interrogation,' " ABC News, April 9, 2003.
20 Interview with Chalmers Johnson. April 16, 2004. Interview by author.
21 Congressman Charles Price, Congressional Record—House, July 19, 1947, p. 9243.
22 Hanson W. Baldwin, "New Defense Set-Up Faces Obstacles," *New York Times*, July 27, 1947.
23 Congressman Edward Robertson, Congressional Record—Senate, May 14, 1947, p. 5427.
24 National Security Act of 1947, SEC. 2. 50 U.S.C. 401.
25 Michael J. Hogan, *A Cross of Iron: Harry S. Truman and the Origins of the National Security State, 1945–1954* (Cambridge: Cambridge University Press, 1998), p. 25.
26 "DOD 101: An Introductory Overview of the Department of Defense," *Department of Defense Official Website*, www.defense.gov/pubs/dod101/.
27 National Commission on Terrorist Attacks upon the United States, Thomas H. Kean, Lee Hamilton, *The 9/11 Commission Report* (New York: W. W. Norton, 2004), p. 95.
28 "National Defense Budget Estimates for FY 2009," Office of the Under Secretary of Defense, March 2008, p. 183.
29 Book review by Witold Rybczynski, "The Office," *New York Times*, June 10, 2007.
30 "DOD 101: An Introductory Overview of the Depatment of Defense. Our Global Infrastructure," www.defense.gov/pubs/dod101.html#infrastructure.
31 Hogan, *Cross of Iron*, 25.
32 Interview with Lieutenant Colonel Karen Kwiatkowski. December 29, 2004. Interview with author.
33 Seymour Hersh, "The Stovepipe," *New Yorker*, October 27, 2003.
34 Madeleine Albright, *Madam Secretary* (New York: Miramax Books, 2003), p. 230.
35 Harry Truman, "Limit CIA Role to Intelligence," *Washington Post*, December 22, 1963.

36 Evan Thomas, "Counter Intelligence," *New York Times*, July 22, 2007.
37 David M. Barrett, *The CIA and Congress: The Untold Story from Truman to Kennedy* (Lawrence: University Press of Kansas, 2005).
38 Dr. Donald N. Wilber, "Clandestine Service History: Overthrow of Premier Mossadeq of Iran; November 1952–August 1953," p. 22. Disclosed in: James Risen, "Secrets of History: The CIA in Iran," *New York Times*, April 16, 2000.
39 *Le Nouvel Observateur*, Paris (January 1998), pp. 15–21.
40 Robert Gates, *From the Shadows: The Ultimate Insider's Story of Five Presidents and How They Won the Cold War* (New York: Simon & Schuster, 1996), p. 145.
41 Interview with Roger Morris. Spring 2001. Interview by Wilfried Huismann.
42 www.cambodiangenocide.org.
43 Ronald Reagan, "Arms to Iran, Profits to the Contras: What the President Has Said," *New York Times*, July 16, 1987.
44 Gareth Porter, *Perils of Dominance: Imbalance of Power and the Road to War in Vietnam* (Berkeley: University of California Press, 2005), p. 5–8.
45 Ken Adelman, "Cakewalk in Iraq," *Washington Post*, Wednesday, February 13, 2002, p. A27.
46 Bob Woodward, *State of Denial: Bush at War, Part III* (New York: Simon & Schuster, 2006), p. 106.
47 Statement by the President on the Tenth Anniversary of the National Security Act, September 23, 1957.

CHAPTER 4

1 Interview with John S. D. Eisenhower. June 2004. Interview by Author.
2 Dwight D. Eisenhower, Farewell Address, January 17, 1961.
3 John Lukacs, "The Fifties: Another View. Revising the Eisenhower Era," *Harper's magazine* (January 2002), pp. 66–72.
4 Charles J. G. Griffin, "New Light on Eisenhower's Farewell Address," *Presidential Studies Quarterly* 22 (Summer 1992), pp. 469–79.
5 Ibid., p. 470.
6 Ibid., pp. 471–73.
7 Clark S. Judge, "Bearing the Burden of Writing the Speech," *Wall Street Journal*, August 24, 2005.
8 Interviews with Susan Eisenhower. September 2003 and June 2004. Interviews by author.
9 Stephen E. Ambrose, *Eisenhower: Soldier and President* (New York: Simon & Schuster, 1990, pp. 28–47.
10 Ambrose, *Eisenhower*, p. 47; Dwight D. Eisenhower, *At Ease: Stories I Tell to Friends* (Arlington, VA: American Anthropological Association, 1981), p. 213.
11 Dwight D. Eisenhower, *Crusade in Europe* (Baltimore: JHU Press, 1997), pp. 408–09. Pictures are available at: www.eisenhower.archives.gov/quick_links/military/WWII_concentration_camps.html.
12 Ambrose, *Eisenhower*, p. 208.
13 Ibid., p. 207.

14 Ibid., p. 218.
15 Dwight D. Eisenhower, *Mandate for Change 1953–1956* (New York: Doubleday, 1963), pp. 312–13.
16 Dwight D. Eisenhower, "The Speeches of Dwight D. Eisenhower," VHS Video Tape, MPI Home Video, 1990. Clip also available at: www.thoughtequity.com/video/clip/49314051_036.do.
17 Ambrose, *Eisenhower*, p. 228.
18 Ibid., pp. 225–27.
19 Dwight D. Eisenhower, "Memorandum for Directors and Chiefs of War Department, General and Special Staff Divisions and Bureaus and the Commanding Generals of the Major Commands. Subject: Scientific and Technological Resources as Military Assets," April 27, 1946.
20 Ibid.
21 Ambrose, *Eisenhower*, p. 238.
22 Ibid., p. 234.
23 Dwight D. Eisenhower, Inaugural Address, Columbia University, October 12, 1948.
24 Ambrose, *Eisenhower*, p. 251.
25 Travis Beal Jacobs, *Eisenhower at Columbia* (New Brunswick, NJ: Transaction Publishers, 2001), p. 247–48.
26 Ambrose, *Eisenhower*, p. 240.
27 Jack Raymond, " 'Military-Industrial Complex': An Analysis," *New York Times*, January 22, 1961.
28 Hogan, *A Cross of Iron*, pp. 222–25.
29 Ambrose, *Eisenhower*, pp. 241–42.
30 Ibid., pp. 247–48.
31 Ibid., p. 250.
32 Hogan, *A Cross of Iron*, pp. 325–27.
33 Harry S. Truman, "Address in San Francisco at the Closing Session of the United Nations Conference," June 26, 1945.
34 William B. Pickett, *Eisenhower Decides to Run: Presidential Politics and Cold War Strategy* (Chicago: Ivan R. Dee, 2000), p. 170.
35 "Table 3.1: Outlays by Superfunction and Function: 1940–2012," in Office of Management and Budget, Historical Tables, Budget of the United States Government, Fiscal Year 2008 (2004), Washington, DC, pp. 46–47. www.whitehouse.gov/omb/budget/fy2008/pdf/hist.pdf.
36 Ambrose, *Eisenhower*, p. 308.
37 Ibid., p. 356.
38 Ibid.
39 Ibid., p. 376.
40 Eisenhower, *Mandate for Change*, p. 452.
41 Smedley Butler, "Times of Peace," *Common Sense*, November 1935.
42 Chalmers Johnson, *The Sorrows of Empire* (New York: Metropolitan Books, 2004), p. 220. Walter LaFeber, *America, Russia and the Cold War: 1945–2002* (New York: McGraw-Hill, 2004), pp. 161–62. Peter Lyon, *Eisenhower: Portrait of the Hero* (Boston: Little, Brown, 1974), p. 488.
43 Ambrose, *Eisenhower*, p. 332.

44 Donald L. Barlett and James B. Steele, "The Oily Americans," *Time*, May 13, 2003.
45 Lyon, *Eisenhower*, pp. 489–90.
46 Stephen Kinzer, *All the Shah's Men: An American Coup and the Roots of Middle East Terror* (New York: John Wiley, 2003), p. 196.
47 Stephen Kinzer, *Overthrow* (New York: Times Books/Henry Holt & Co., 2006), p. 133.
48 Marty Jezer, *The Dark Ages: Life in the United States 1915–1960* (Boston: South End Press, 1982), p. 73.
49 Kinzer, *Overthrow*, pp. 129, 133–35. LaFeber, *America, Russia, and the Cold War*, p. 164.
50 Chalmers Johnson, Blowback (New York: Henry Holt & Co., 2004), p. 194.
51 Lyon, *Eisenhower*, p. 552.
52 Ambrose, *Eisenhower*, p. 333.
53 Gareth Porter, *Perils of Dominance: Imbalance of Power and the Road to War in Vietnam* (Berkeley and Los Angeles: University of California Press, 2005), p. 7.
54 Ibid., pp. 7–8.
55 Dwight D. Eisenhower, *The White House Years: Waging Peace, 1956–1961* (New York: Doubleday, 1965), p. 615.
56 Porter, p. 5.
57 Eisenhower, p. 208.
58 Peter Roman, *Eisenhower and the Missile Gap* (Ithaca, NY: Cornell University Press, 1996), pp. 36–37.
59 Richard Witkin, "Convair Aide Quits to Criticize Defense," *New York Times*, February 24, 1960, p. A1.
60 "Missiles to Miniatures," *Time*, August 15, 1960.
61 Ambrose, *Eisenhower*, p. 482.
62 Allan A. Metcalf, "Presidential Voices: Speaking Styles from George Washington to George W. Bush" (Boston: Houghton Mifflin, 2004), p. 292.
63 Statements of John F. Kennedy on Space Exploration, 1957 section. Lt. Col. Mark Erickson, USAF, *Into the Unknown Together* (Maxwell Air Force Base, AL: Air University Press, 2005).
64 Christopher A. Preble, "Who Ever Believed the Missile Gap?: John F. Kennedy and the Politics of National Security," *Presidential Studies Quarterly* (December 2003).
65 Roman, *Eisenhower and the Missile Gap*, p. 148.
66 Ibid., p. 140.
67 Robert Dallek, *An Unfinished Life* (New York: Little, Brown, 2003), p. 289–90.
68 Allen Dulles, "Memorandum for the President," August 3, 1960.
69 Interview with Susan Eisenhower. June 2004. Interview by author.
70 Ambrose, *Eisenhower*, p. 522.
71 Griffin, "New Light on Eisenhower's Farewell Address," p. 469.
72 Eisenhower, *At Ease*, pp. 40–41.
73 Eisenhower, *The White House Years: Waging Peace*, pp. 615–16.
74 John F. Kennedy, State of the Union Address, January 14, 1963.
75 Tim Weiner, "Kennedy Had a Plan for Early Exit in Vietnam," *New York Times*, December 23,1997. "Statistical Information About Casualties of the Vietnam

War," The National Archives. Revised February 2007, www.archives.gov/research/vietnam-war/casualty-statistics.html#year. Stanley Karnow, "The Vietnam Debacle," April 27, 2000, Salon.com, www.archive.salon.com/news/feature/2000/04/27/revisionists/index.html.

76 John Eisenhower, "Why I Will Vote for John Kerry For President," *Manchester Union Leader*, September 28, 2004.

CHAPTER 5

1 Interview with Colonel Richard Treadway. December 2003. Interview by author.

2 Interview with Peter Boyle. May 2004. Interview by author.

3 Interview with Joe Cirincione. January 2004. Interview by author.

4 *Rebuilding America's Defenses*, PNAC. 61.

5 Ibid.

6 Peter J. Boyer, "The New War Machine: How General Tommy Franks Joined Donald Rumsfeld in the Fight to Transform the Military," *The New Yorker*, June 30, 2003., pp. 55–71.

7 E. J. Dionne, "Behind the Failure," *The Washington Post*, August 22, 2003.

8 Boyer, "The New War Machine."

9 Boyer, "The New War Machine."

10 Matthew Engel, "Bush Backs Off Iraq Invasion; Military leaders recommend postponing mission after warning president of heavy casualties," *The Guardian* (London), May 25, 2002.

11 Boyer, "The New War Machine."

12 Interview with Peter Boyer. May 2004. Interview by author.

13 Robert Coram, *Boyd: The Fighter Pilot Who Changed the Art of War* (New York: Back Bay Books, 2002), p. 136.

14 Interview with Thomas Christie. April 2008. Interview by author.

15 Coram, *Boyd*, p. 245.

16 Interviews with Franklin Spinny. March 2003, March 2007, and April 2008. Interviews by author.

17 Tom Shanker, "After the War: Troops; Officials Debate Whether to Seek a Bigger Military," *New York Times*, July 21, 2003.

18 Colonel John R. Boyd, "A Discourse on Winning and Losing," 1987, unpublished briefing slide set available at Air University Library, Maxwell AFB, Alaska, cited in Colonel Edward Mann, USAF, "Desert Storm: The First Information War?" *Aerospace Power Journal* (Winter 1994).

19 Robert Coram, "John Boyd: Architect of Modern Warfare," *Georgia Tech Alumni Magazine Online*, Fall 2002; gtalumni.org/stayinformed/magazine/fall02/article3.html.

20 Donald Rumsfeld, "DoD News Briefing," March 21, 2003; www.defenselink.mil/transcripts/transcript.aspx?transcriptid=2074.

21 John R. Boyd, "Organic Design for Command and Control," May 1987. Unpublished briefing slide set available at: Defense and the National Interest; www.d-n-i.net/boyd/pdf/c&c.pdf, p. 27

22 John R. Boyd, "Patterns of Conflict," 1986. Unpublished briefing slide set available at: Defense and the National Interest; www.d-n-i.net/boyd/pdf/c&c.pdf, p. 92

23 Donald Rumsfled, "Secretary Rumsfeld Pentagon Town Hall Meeting," August 14, 2003. Department of Defense. www.defenselink.mil/transcripts/transcript.aspx?transcriptid=3226.

24 Note tk

25 James Traub, "W.'s World," *New York Times Magazine*, January 14, 2001, p. 30.

CHAPTER 6

1 George E. Condon, Jr., "Congressman's Betrayal of Troops Called Greatest Sin," *San Diego Union-Tribune*, December 1, 2005.

2 Thomas Henry Huxley, "Letter to Charles Darwin," November 23, 1859. From Leonard Huxley, *Life and Letters of Thomas Henry Huxley, Vol. 1* (New York: Appleton and Co. 1916), p. 188.

3 "Cost Overrun," *CBS Evening News*, February 25, 1983.

4 Interview with Colonel Wallace Saeger. December 2003. Interview by author.

5 Claude E. Shannon, "Programming a Computer for Playing Chess," *Philosophical Magazine*, ser. 7, vol. 41, no. 314 (March 1950), Bell Telephone Laboratories, Inc., Murray Hill, N.J.2.

6 James Madison, *The Federalist*, No. 51, February 6, 1788.

7 Federal Civilian Workforce Statistics: The Fact Book: *United States Office of Personnel Management*, 2005 edition; www.opm.gov/fedData/factbook.

8 Interview with Charles Lewis. May 2005. Interview by author.

CHAPTER 7

1 George W. Bush, Graduation speech at West Point, June 1, 2002.

2 "The Secret Downing Street Memo," *Sunday Times* (London), May 1, 2005.

3 "The Truth About the War," *New York Times*, June 6, 2008.

4 Laura Nader, "Up the Anthropologist—Perspectives Gained from Studying Up," in Dell H. Hymes, ed., *Reinventing Anthropology* (New York: Pantheon Books, 1972), pp. 284–311.

5 Dana Priest and Jeffrey R. Smith, "Memo Offered Justification for Use of Torture; Justice Dept. Gave Advice in 2002," *The Washington Post*, June 8, 2008.

6 Memorandum for Alberto R. Gonzales, Counsel to the President, U.S. Dept. of Justice, Office of Legal Counsel, at www.humanrightsfirst.org/us_law/etn/gonzales/memos_dir/memo_20020801_JD_%20Gonz_.pdf.

7 Dana Priest, "CIA Holds Terror Suspects in Secret Prisons," *The Washington Post*, November 2, 2005.

8 Jan Crawford Greenburg, Howard L. Rosenberg, and Ariane de Vogue, "Sources: Top Bush Advisors Approved 'Enhanced Interrogation'; Detailed Discussions Were Held About Techniques to Use on al Qaeda Suspects," ABC News, April 9, 2008.

9 "President Bush Signs Un-American Military Commissions Act, ACLU Says

New Law Undermines Due Process and the Rule of Law." www.aclu.org, October 17; www.aclu.org/safefree/detention/27091prs20061017.html 2006.

10 Sandra Day O'Connor, "The Threat to Judical Independence," *The Wall Street Journal*, September 27, 2006.

11 Julian Borger and Suzanne Goldenberg, "Defiant Bush Defends Wiretapping Powers," *The Guardian* (London), December 20, 2005; www.guardian.co.uk/world/2005/dec/20/usa.topstories3.

12 Editorial: "Veto? Who Needs a Veto?" *New York Times*, May 5, 2006.

13 George W. Bush, President's Statement on Signing the Department of Defense Appropriations Act, 2005, August 5, 2004, at www.whitehouse.gov/news/releases/2004/08/20040805-9.html.

14 American Bar Association, "Blue Ribbon Task Force Finds President Bush's Signing Statements Undermine Separation of Powers," July 24, 2006, at www.abanet.org/media/releases/news072406.html.

15 Title 10. U.S. Code, Section 12305(a).

16 Michelle Tan, "Stop-loss Likely to Last into Fall 2009," *Army Times*, May 5, 2008.

17 Charlie Savage, "Court Backs Cheney on Energy Meetings," *Boston Globe*, May 11, 2005.

18 Michael Duffy, "The Cheney Branch of Government," *Time*, June 22, 2007.

19 "Hill's National Guard Advocates Hold News Conference To Protest DOD Bill's Proposed Decisions On National Guard." Press Release for U.S. Senator Patrick Leahy's Office, Washington, September 19, 2006; www.leahy.senate.gov/press/200609/011906a.html.

20 Sen. Patrick Leahy, "National Defense Authorization Act For Fiscal Year 2007." Conference Report, Congressional Record, September 29, 2006; www.leahy.senate.gov/press/200609/092906b.html.

21 Kathy Jiely and William M. Welch, "Abu Ghraib Photos Cause Gasps in Congress," *USA Today*, May 12, 2004, at www.usatoday.com/news/world/iraq/2004-05-12-congress-abuse_x.htm.

22 Susan Milligan, "Congress Reduces its Oversight Role Since Clinton, a Change in Focus, *The Boston Globe*, November 20, 2005.

23 Alan M. Dershowitz, *Supreme Injustice: How the High Court Hijacked Election 2000*. USA, Oxford University Press, p. 174.

24 Jeffrey Toobin, "In McCain's Court," *The New Yorker*, May 26, 2008.

25 Joan Biskupic, "Roberts steers court right back to Reagan," USA Today, June 29, 2007.

26 "Bush wants court out of subpoena fight," *The Associated Press*, May 11, 2008.

27 Ibid.

28 Neil A. Lewis, "Panel Asks Judge to Rule in Contempt Case,: *New York Times*, March 11, 2008. This Lawsuit is Case No. 1:08-cv-00409 in the United States District Court for the District of Columia. The text of the lawsuit is available at www.online.wsj.com/public/resource/documents/pelosisuit.pdf.

29 Robert Caro, *The Years of Lyndon Johnson*. Vol. 1: *The Path to Power* (New York: Alfred A. Knopf, 1982).

30 Interview with Charles Lewis. May 6, 2004. Interview by author.

31 Office of the White House Press Secretary, press release, April 13, 2001.

32 Center for Public Integrity, *Windfalls of War.*

33 Jane Mayer, "Contract Sport; What did the Vice-president do for Halliburton?" *The New Yorker*, February 16, 2004.
34 Ibid.
35 Interview with Harrison J. Carroll. Ocober 8, 2003. Interview by author.
36 Transcript of *Meet the Press* with Tim Russert. Guest: Dick Cheney, Sunday, September 14, 2003.
37 Dan Slater, "Administration Declassifies 2003 Torture Memo," *Wall Street Journal Online*, at http://blogs.wsj.com/law/2008/04/02/administration-declassifies-2003-torture-memo/?mod=WSJBlog.
38 Interview with John Yoo from *A Few Bad Apples*, Gillian Findlay, CBC-TV, November 16, 2005; www.cbc.ca/fifth/badapples/interviews_yoo.html.
39 Neal Katyal, "Executive Decision; A key former Bush aide argues for wartime presidential clout," *The Washington Post*, January 8, 2006.
40 John Yoo, *War by Other Means: An Insider's Account of the War on Terror* (New York: Atlantic Monthly Press, 2006), p. vii.
41 Neal Katyal, "Executive Decision: A Key Former Bush Aide Argues for Wartime Presidential Clout," review of John Yoo's *The Powers of War and Peace*, in *The Washington Post*, January 8, 2006.
42 John Yoo, *War by Other Means: An Insider's Account of the War on Terror* (New York: Atlantic Monthly Press, 2006), p. xi.
43 John Yoo, "Editorial: How the Presidency Regained Its Balance," *New York Times*, September 17, 2006.
44 Yoo, *War by Other Means*, p. 120.
45 Ibid.
46 Yoo, *War By Other Means*, p. 97.
47 Ibid., p. 96.
48 Ibid., p. 97.
49 Marvin R. Shanken, "General Tommy Franks: An Exclusive Interview America's Top General in the War on Terrorism," *Cigar Aficianado* magazine, December 1, 2003.
50 David Rhode, "Pakistani Sets Emergency Rule, Defying the U.S.," *New York Times*, November 4, 2007.
51 Pervez Musharraf, "Declaration of Emergency," Broadcast on Pakistan television, November 3, 2007, at www.youtube.com/watch?v=U-cSj-V_II8&eurl=http://thelede.blogs.nytimes.com/2007/11/04/musharraf-and-lincoln-in-their-own-words/.
52 George W. Bush, Televised address on the Fifth Anniversary of 9/11, September 11, 2006.
53 George W. Bush, Radio address. September 29, 2001.
54 Yoo, *War By Other Means*, p. 97.

Acknowledgments

In the writing of this book, I was privileged to stand on the shoulders of giants who have struggled far longer and more tirelessly than I to shed light on the challenges of American power: Seymour Hersh, Charles Lewis, Chuck Spinney, Joe Cirincione, Winslow Wheeler, Colonel Lawrence Wilkerson, Ralph Nader, Chalmers Johnson, William Hartung, and George Soros, among others.

The book simply would not have been possible without my dedicated and tireless team of researchers and proofreaders—Alessandra Meyer, Kathleen Fournier, Julia Simpson, Nora Colie, and Joe Posner. I am grateful not only that they all follow through on my most hare-brained schemes but, more important, that they tell me so candidly which are more hare-brained than others. To Joe Posner's remarkable eye goes special recognition for his having produced the painted bomb that graces the book's jacket, capturing so perfectly my sense of the special poetry of the American story. Additional research and proofreading were also performed by William Davies, Patrick Falby, Christopher St. John, and Andreas Schneider.

I am greatly indebted to the Eisenhower family, particularly Susan and John S. D. Eisenhower, for their wisdom and openness in reflecting on both their own and the late president's remarkable ideas on public policy. At the Eisenhower Presidential Library in Abilene, Kansas, I am further indebted to Mack Teasley for helping guide me through Dwight D. Eisenhower's voluminous papers.

At the United States Military Academy at West Point, several soldiers and scholars have greatly contributed to the thinking reflected in these pages. Colonel Michael J. Meese, Colonel Cindy Jebb, Lieutenant

Colonel Isaiah Wilson, Major Jason Amerine, and Major Jason Dempsey have shown enormous intellectual courage in engaging with me on matters of great sensitivity, demonstrating above all the idealism that improved civilian-military discourse can go a long way to address the problems we face.

At Brown University's Watson Institute for International Studies I am indebted to Professors James Der Derian and Thomas J. Biersteker for having enlisted me in the effort to inform young people better about the complex dynamics of American foreign and defense policy. My collaboration with them in Watson's Global Security program coincided with and greatly informed my research for this book.

I am also grateful to Lieutenant Air Force Colonel (ret.) Peter H. Liotta, Ph.D., Director of the Pell Center for International Relations and Public Policy at Salve Regina University, and to Dr. Jane Goodall, with whom one conversation proved life changing.

My literary agent Laurie Liss at Sterling Lord Literistic and my friend and legal adviser Rosalind Lichter are responsible for having encouraged me to write this book and finding the best home for it. My agents at Creative Artists Agency, Maha Dakhil, Bob Bookman, and JP Evans have given me the artistic space to undertake this project while continuing to manage a complex slate of film projects.

Personally, I am indebted to my mother, Gloria, whose unshakable decency, ethics, and insistence on truth and justice fuel the idealism of my work, and to Melvin van Peebles, my godfather and mentor, for always knowing what is best for me.

Claudia Becker's unconditional love, as well as her endless intellect, inspiration, and shared commitment to the "big picture" have immeasurably shaped these pages and the many fits and starts that preceded them. Above all, she makes possible the support structure necessary for me to be me and do what I am driven to do (as long as it does some good). She is a lifelong inspiration, coconspirator, and true friend. I am at my best when I am able to be the same in return.

Nick Fraser, Commissioning Editor of BBC Storyville, is responsible for my education as a journalist. Not only did he take a chance on me when others wouldn't, he continues always to ask the right questions and—more important—to listen to the answers. Without him the line of inquiry that led to this book would not have been born.

Alexandra Johnes is in a class by herself. Her relentless heart and mind have shown me unfailing love, patience, and support during the most trying periods of the writing process. She is unerringly committed to truthfulness and empathy, and this has made me a better person and writer, redoubling my pursuit of truth and understanding. I am blessed to have her in my life.

Finally, nothing could have been more fortunate for me than to have had the opportunity to write my first book for Free Press and, in particular, to be placed in the capable and caring hands of editor Emily Loose. While Publisher Martha Levin and Editor-in-Chief Dominick Anfuso took a chance on a first-time author, Emily's unfathomable reserves of patience and intellect gave shape to her passion to do the very best for the book at all cost. No one deserves more direct credit for its ultimate quality than she. Behind the scenes, I am also greatly indebted to Danielle Kaniper, who invisibly labored to make Emily's tireless work possible.

Though this book thus clearly reflects the labors of many, any shortcomings in its conception or execution are mine and mine alone.

Index

About the Author

Eugene Jarecki is the acclaimed filmmaker of *Why We Fight*, winner of the 2005 Sundance Film Festival's Grand Jury Prize and a 2006 Peabody award, as well as the widely praised *The Trials of Henry Kissinger*. He has been a senior visiting fellow at Brown University's Watson Institute for International Studies and is the founder and director of The Eisenhower Project, an academic public policy group dedicated to studying American foreign policy. He lives in New York City.